AN INTRODUCTION
TO AUTOMATED
PROCESS PLANNING
SYSTEMS

PRENTICE-HALL INTERNATIONAL SERIES
IN INDUSTRIAL AND SYSTEMS ENGINEERING

W. J. Fabrycky and J. H. Mize, Editors

AMOS AND SARCHET *Management for Engineers*

BEIGHTLER, PHILLIPS, AND WILDE *Foundations of Optimization, 2/E*

BLANCHARD *Logistics Engineering and Management, 2/E*

BLANCHARD AND FABRYCKY *Systems Engineering and Analysis*

BROWN *Systems Analysis and Design for Safety*

BUSSEY *The Economic Analysis of Industrial Projects*

CHANG AND WYSK *An Introduction to Automated Process Planning Systems*

ELSAYED AND BOUCHER *Analysis and Control of Production Systems*

FABRYCKY, GHARE, AND TORGERSEN *Applied Operations Research and Management Science*

FRANCES AND WHITE *Facility Layout and Location: An Analytical Approach*

GOTTFRIED AND WEISMAN *Introduction to Optimization Theory*

HAMMER *Occupational Safety Management and Engineering, 3/E*

HAMMER *Product Safety Management and Engineering*

IGNIZIO *Linear Programming in Single and Multiobjective Systems*

MIZE, WHITE, AND BROOKS *Operations Planning and Control*

MUNDEL *Improving Productivity and Effectiveness*

MUNDEL *Motion and Time Study: Improving Productivity, 6/E*

OSTWALD *Cost Estimating, 2/E*

PHILLIPS AND GARCIA-DIAZ *Fundamentals of Network Analysis*

SANDQUIST *Introduction to System Science*

SMALLEY *Hospital Management Engineering*

THUESEN AND FABRYCKY *Engineering Economy, 6/E*

TURNER, MIZE, AND CASE *Introduction to Industrial and Systems Engineering*

WHITEHOUSE *Systems Analysis and Design Using Network Techniques*

AN INTRODUCTION TO AUTOMATED PROCESS PLANNING SYSTEMS

Tien-Chien Chang

Purdue University

Richard A. Wysk

Pennsylvania State University

PRENTICE-HALL, INC., *Englewood Cliffs, New Jersey 07632*

Library of Congress Cataloging in Publication Data

Chang, Tien-Chien.   **(date)**
   An introduction to automated process planning systems.

   Bibliography: p.
   Includes index.
   1. CAD/CAM systems.   I. Wysk, Richard A., 1948–
II. Title.
TS155.6.C49   1985   670.42′028′54   84-3346
   ISBN   0-13-478140-6

Editorial/production supervision and
interior design: Sylvia Schmokel
Manufacturing buyer: Tony Caruso

TO OUR WIVES

Printed in the United States of America

10   9   8   7   6   5   4   3   2   1

ISBN   0-13-478140-6   01

PRENTICE-HALL INTERNATIONAL, INC., *London*
PRENTICE-HALL OF AUSTRALIA PTY. LIMITED, *Sydney*
EDITORA PRENTICE-HALL DO BRASIL, LTDA., *Rio de Janeiro*
PRENTICE-HALL CANADA INC., *Toronto*
PRENTICE-HALL OF INDIA PRIVATE LIMITED, *New Delhi*
PRENTICE-HALL OF JAPAN, INC., *Tokyo*
PRENTICE-HALL OF SOUTHEAST ASIA PTE. LTD., *Singapore*
WHITEHALL BOOKS LIMITED, *Wellington, New Zealand*

CONTENTS

PREFACE

Much of the information presented in this book is the result of a research project supported by the National Bureau of Standards in Gaithersburg, Maryland. The research is also based on previous research supported by the National Science Foundation. The authors would like to express gratitude to both agencies for supporting these activities. The book focuses primarily on integrated computer-aided manufacturing (ICAM) and computer-aided process planning (CAPP).

The major contribution of the research represented in this text is the compilation of existing information in the manufacturing, computer science, graphics, industrial, and mechanical and electrical engineering areas into a unified structure so that *integrated* computer-aided manufacturing can be achieved. At the beginning of this integration is the development of a "generative computer-aided process planning system." The software, data base requirements, and structure for such a CAPP system are presented within this text. A demonstration system is also developed and illustrated within the text.

The organization of the text is intended to provide both "learning modules" and "integration modules" to the reader. The text begins with an overview of ICAM. This overview is followed by several "learning modules" on graphics, CAD, computer-aided graphics, process planning, and manufacturing systems modeling. The remainder of the text focuses on integration issues, where all of these topics are assembled

ix

into a common structure. A textbook-like quality is required to eliminate information voids for the professional who will be reading the book as well as for the academic audience that will use it as a textbook.

TIEN-CHIEN CHANG
RICHARD A. WYSK

AN INTRODUCTION
TO AUTOMATED
PROCESS PLANNING
SYSTEMS

INTRODUCTION TO MANUFACTURING

1.1 MANUFACTURING INDUSTRIES

A production facility may be the most complex system that confronts today's modern engineer. In spite of the fact that the production function is the primary purpose of a manufacturing industry, the production process often appears completely forgotten in the midst of marketing, accounting, or other organizational planning activities. Perhaps it is the lack of recognition, and attention, given to manufacturing systems that has led to our decline in industrial productivity.

The impact of our declining productivity is so severe that productivity improvement has probably become the most challenging problem facing the United States today. Two of the effects of our declining productivity include:

1. A reduced position in the international marketplace (the direct result of this would be a reduction in the U.S. "standard of living").
2. Manufacturing superiority usually indicates a nation's ability to produce military hardware, thereby providing tactical superiority as well as a deterrent to aggressive countries.

It is not an appealing legacy to leave the next generation of Americans with a poorer standard of living than has been experienced in the recent past. Never in the United States has this occurred. Similarly, many historians cite both tactical as well

1

as industrial deficiencies as a major cause of aggression (again, not a very appealing legacy to leave to future generations). If our ability to produce high quality products provides us with the basis for our standard of living and for our defense, then why is it that we spend the majority of our efforts (money and time) with ancillary issues such as marketing (packaging, advertising, etc.), accounting, and other administrative issues? A product's (and company's) success must begin with a well conceived product and production process; other activities serve only to slightly embellish a product.

In spite of the general impression given, manufacturing problems are not easily separated issues. Management organization does affect manufacturing; however, other issues, such as material management, shop floor control, and the like, affect a manufacturing system more directly. The major purpose of this book will be to identify a structure by which different manufacturing issues might be addressed. The majority of its content will focus on process planning systems, since process planning provides one of the major integration issues in a factory environment.

However, before embarking on a more technical discussion, it is worthwhile to trace some of the history of manufacturing. By viewing this history, one might glean a perspective of where present industry stands in the evolution of manufacturing.

The history of manufacturing can be said to have begun when human beings first tried to alter the geometry of a workpiece by rotating either a tool or a workpiece on a spindle to remove pieces of the material from the workpiece. This was important to create weapons to protect people against natural enemies as well as unfriendly tribes. The oldest evidence discovered so far is a fragment of an Etruscan wooden bowl found in the Tomb of the Warrior at Corneto in 700 B.C. [Rolt 1967]. However, it was not until the fifteenth century that people began machining metal. Eighteenth-century industrialization ushered in the demand for production-type machine tools. Machine shops were established to create more machines. Production systems became more organized, and metal processing became a trade carried out by experienced craftsman whose trade was passed from generation to generation. Small production volume with no standards made every product a unique one. A typical example of this era is that it took James Watt 25 years (after completing the design) to produce the first steam engine. The tolerance between the piston and cylinder was "no greater than a worn shilling"—a true feat for the time.

The advent of interchangeable parts can be attributed to the realization that we could not easily repair damaged firearms. This concept in manufacturing is credited to Eli Whitney (1765–1825). As the pioneer of this new form of manufacturing, he signed (in 1798) a contract with the U.S. government for 12,000 muskets—4000 to be delivered in the first year. Although only 500 muskets were delivered by 1801, and it was 1806 when he finally finished the contract, a new era in manufacturing history began.

Interchangeability in manufactured parts not only meant a new technique in machining and inspection, but also created a better, more uniform planning method. A conventional machine shop had previously used the skill of a machinist to determine the entire operation of a product. Until this new era began, as long as the product functioned as the original design specified, the product was acceptable. (No guarantee on the sameness of the parts constrained production.) However, the new manufacturing concept (interchangeability) demanded that every part be made the same with only a small variance. A more thorough plan for production was obviously necessary. Over the years, as the demand for a product grew (whether it be weaponry or consumer products), mass production became the standard for economically satisfying the demand.

Scientific study in metal cutting and mass production are products of the twentieth century, when increased market demand contributed to the development of mass-production techniques. Increased demand also promoted the scientific study of manufacturing. Scientific research and development focused on production processes, planning, and technology. Perhaps the greatest impact came from scientific management, pioneered by Frederick W. Taylor (1856–1915). "Methods" for production by machines as well as by people were studied. Standards for human operators and metal machining were established.

Taylor is best known for two major contributions: one is scientific management, and the other is his investigations of metal cutting. He conducted metal-cutting experiments, at Midvale Steel Company, which lasted for 26 years. His studies not only resulted in the invention of high-speed steel, which revolutionized metal-cutting efficiency, but also established machinability tables. In his 1907 paper, "On the Art of Cutting Metals," which was based on the results of some 50,000 experiments and 800,000 lb of metal chips, he proposed a relationship of tool life to feed and speed. A better understanding of how metal is cut and how to regulate these variables (feed and speed) in cutting was provided. The Taylor tool-life equation and his metal-cutting experiments still play an important role in process planning.

Although the manufacturing industries continue to evolve, it was not until the 1950s that the next major development occurred. For some time, strides to reduce human involvement in manufacturing were being taken. Speciality machines using cams and other "hardwired" logic controllers had been developed. The U.S. Air Force recognized the development time required to produce this special equipment and that the time required to make only small sequence changes was excessive. As a result, the Air Force commissioned the Massachusetts Institute of Technology to demonstrate programmable, or numerically controlled (NC) machines (also known as "softwired" machines). With this first demonstration in 1952 came the beginning of a new era in manufacturing. Since then, digital computers have been used to produce input in either a directed manner to many NC machines, direct numerical control (DNC), or in a more dedicated control sense, computer numerical control (CNC). Today, machine control languages such as APT (Automatic Programming Tool) have become the standard for creating tool control for NC machines.

It is interesting to note that much of the evolution in manufacturing has come as a response to particular changes during different periods of time. For instance, the technology that evolved in the nineteenth century brought with it the need for higher-precision machining. (This resulted in the creation of many new machine tools, a more refined machine design, and new production processes.) The early twentieth century became an era of prosperity and industrialization that created the demand necessary for mass-production techniques. In the 1950s it was estimated that as the speed of an aircraft increased, the cost of manufacturing the aircraft (because of geometric complexity) increased proportionately with the speed. The result of this stimulus was the development of NC technology.

A few tangential notes on this history include the following. As the volume of parts manufactured increases, the production cost for the parts decreases (this is generally known as "economy of scale"). Some of the change in production cost is due to fixed versus variable costs. For instance, if only a single part is to be produced (such as a space vehicle), all of the fixed costs for planning and design (both product and process) must be absorbed by the single item. If, however, several parts are produced, the fixed charges can be distributed over several parts. Changes in production cost, not reflected in this simple fixed- versus variable-cost relationship, are usually the result of different manufacturing procedures—transfer-line techniques for high-volume items versus job-shop procedures for low-volume items. Figure 1.1 illustrates the fundamental relationship of volume versus production system, and Figure 1.2 depicts cost versus volume for different types of systems.

Also of interest to note is that as the tolerance specification is tightened, the cost

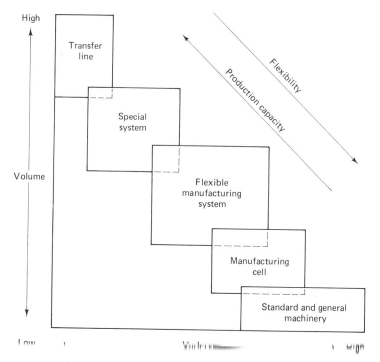

Fig. 1.1. System selection versus volume and variety of parts.

of manufacturing the product increases. This is either the result of requiring "finished machining operations" or because a reduced speed and feed rate is necessary to obtain the required geometric specification. This relationship is illustrated in Figure 1.3.

Finally, with these cost curves and figures, one can look ahead to the 1980s and 1990s. The U.S. Department of Commerce has pointed out that in the United States, 95% of all products are produced in lots of size 50 or fewer. This indicates that although high-volume techniques are desirable from a consumer standpoint (lower cost), these techniques are not appropriate from a manufacturing standpoint because the volume will not offset the setup expenses. The manufacturing alternative to produce those parts is through the use of flexible manufacturing systems (FMSs). These systems are nothing more than programmable job shops. However, a major economic expense still exists before one can begin employing such systems more fully. This obstacle is that a considerable setup (planning) expense is still required. The alternative to eliminate this expensive setup is through integration of computer-aided design and computer-aided manufacturing (CAD/CAM). In an integrated CAD/CAM system, parts will be detailed using a computer graphics system. This system will store the geometric information necessary to create process plans and generate the machine instructions necessary to control the machine tools. Some estimates suggest that this approach will reduce planning time for FMS parts by more than 95%.

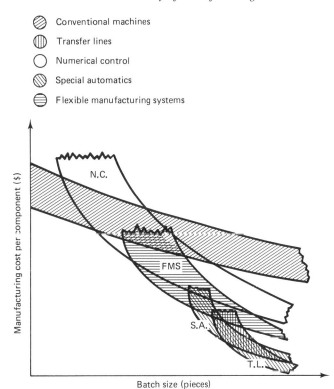

⊘ Conventional machines

⦀ Transfer lines

○ Numerical control

⊗ Special automatics

⊜ Flexible manufacturing systems

Fig. 1.2. Comparison of the average cost of various machining systems as a function of the number of pieces per production run.

1.2 BASIC TAXONOMY OF MANUFACTURING

1.2.1 Discrete versus Continuous Manufacturing

Manufacturing systems can be classified into two major categories: discrete part manufacturing and continuous process manufacturing. Continuous process manufacturing refers to the production of a continuous product, in which the entire process is controlled through valves, pumps, heaters, and so on. For instance, a chemical reaction transforms the raw material into final product. On the other hand, in discrete part manufacturing the product undergoes a finite number of production or assembly operations. This book focuses on discrete part manufacturing and more specifically, the manufacturing of machined parts.

1.2.2 Design for Production

Manufacturing is a means of physically transforming a design into reality. Two sets of input are required for manufacturing: design and resources. The resources include raw material, labor, and other utilities. The design includes symbols bearing the specifications and shape of the product. Since manufacturing is the only place

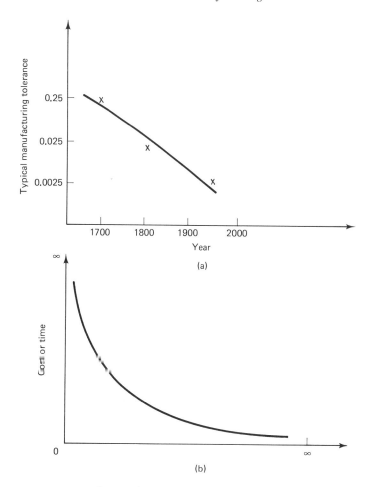

Fig. 1.3. History of (a) tolerance specification and (b) cost versus tolerance.

where value is added to raw material, the reduction of manufacturing cost implies a lower product cost. Unfortunately, designers often consider their job as one of designing the product for performance, appearance, and possibly reliability, and that it is the manufacturing engineer's job to produce whatever has been designed. Although the manufacturing engineer tries to find an applicable process to satisfy the design, a minor change in the design may reduce the manufacturing requirements without affecting the product's functionality.

For example, a nonfunctional surface with a surface tolerance specification simply adds an additional finishing operation (machining process). A flat bottom hole is more difficult to machine than a hole with a conic-shaped bottom (Figure 1.4). A flat-bottomed hole that is threaded its entire length is virtually impossible to produce. Little difference results in using these design alternatives; yet, entirely different problems result for the manufacturing engineer that must execute the process design.

A designer should always keep production efficiency in mind during design. Some general rules are [Boothroyd 1975] as follows:

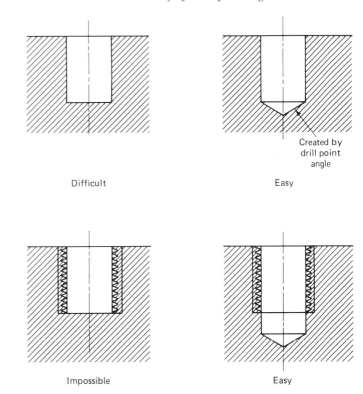

Difficult

Easy

Created by
drill point
angle

Impossible

Easy

Fig. 1.4. Design for machining.

1. Whenever possible, use standard components.
2. Whenever possible, take advantage of the work material shape to design the components.
3. Whenever possible, use the previous design of similar jobs.
4. Whenever possible, minimize the required machining.
5. In designing the shape of the component, consider the ease of material handling, fixturing, machining, and assembly.
6. Avoid overspecified tolerances and surface finish specifications.
7. Consider the kinematic principles during the initial steps of a design.

1.2.3 Material Processing

"Material processing" used in this text is a synonym for "machining." It is the basic procedure for transforming the workpiece into final component geometry by removing pieces of the workpiece material. Machine tools are employed for this purpose. Basic machining processes include:

1. Turning
2. Drilling
3. Reaming
4. Boring

5. Tapping
6. Milling
7. Grinding
8. Broaching
9. Sawing
10. EDM/ECM (electrodischarge machining/ electrochemical machining)
11. Laser processes

For the past 200 years, basic machining processes have changed little with the exception of EDM, ECM, and lasers. Only the material, structure of machine tools, power sources, and control methods have evolved from a very primitive form to today's standards. Some of the most common machining processes are illustrated in Figure 1.5. Turning and drilling are two of the most ancient machining processes. In turning, the workpiece is rotated by a stationary tool to peel off a thin layer of material. The components produced are symmetric in shape. In drilling, the tool is rotated at a high rpm and uses its sharp cutting edges (normally two) to remove material in chip form. The chip is removed via the drill flutes.

Reaming and boring are similar to drilling except that they do not produce a hole, but instead enlarge holes and improve the quality of an existing hole. Reaming improves the hole-diameter tolerance and surface finish. Boring provides positioning accuracy and also produces a better surface finish than does drilling.

Milling is probably the most versatile of all processes. It is used widely for external shape forming from the most simple flat surface to delicate surfaces such as a curved propeller surface.

Grinding is a finishing process that creates a very fine surface. When a fine surface finish is specified, grinding is normally used. Small amounts of metal are usually removed in grinding.

Broaching is a lesser used process that is normally efficient when machining a large volume of metal from a "flat or slotted" workpiece. Because of high tool cost, broaching is typically a high-volume production process.

ECM (electrochemical machining) and EDM (electrodischarge machining) are nonconventional processes. ECM is similar to electroplating (the difference being that the workpiece material is removed and washed away by an electrolyte). EDM, on the other hand, uses small sparks created by an electrode (the tool). The sparks vaporize a small spot on the workpiece material which is then washed away by an electrolyte. Both ECM and EDM are very effective in machining very hard materials such as casting dies. Very delicate parts can also be machined with high surface finish and a small or no burr. However, special tooling is required for different jobs.

Laser (light amplification by the stimulated emission of radiation) is a process using a light beam of high intensity and single frequency to burn and vaporize workpiece material. The laser was developed in 1958 and has been used in industry only in recent years. As mentioned earlier, laser machining is nonconventional. It can be used in place of drilling, cutting, and welding. Because of the efficiency of

Operation	Block Diagram	Most Commonly Used Machines	Machines Less Frequently Used	Machines Seldom Used
Shaping		Horizontal shaper	Vertical shaper	
Planing		Planer		
Milling	slab milling / face milling	Milling machine		Lathe (with special attachment)
Facing		Lathe	Boring mill	
Turning		Lathe	Boring mill	Vertical shaper / Milling machine
Grinding		Cylindrical grinder		Lathe (with special attachment)
Sawing		Contour saw		
Drilling		Drill press	Lathe	Milling machine / Boring mill / Horizontal boring machine

Fig. 1.5. Operations and machines for the machining of surfaces. [Reprinted with permission of Macmillan Publishing Company from *Materials and Processes in Manufacturing* by E. Paul Degarmo. Copyright © 1974, 1979 by Darvic Associates Inc.]

Operation	Block Diagram	Most Commonly Used Machines	Machines Less Frequently Used	Machines Seldom Used
Boring		Lathe Boring mill Horizontal boring machine		Milling machine Drill press
Reaming		Lathe Drill press Boring mill Horizontal boring machine	Milling machine	
Grinding		Cylindrical grinder		Lathe (with special attachment)
Sawing		Contour saw		
Broaching		Broaching machine		
ECM		ECM machine		
Laser		CO_2 laser YAG laser		

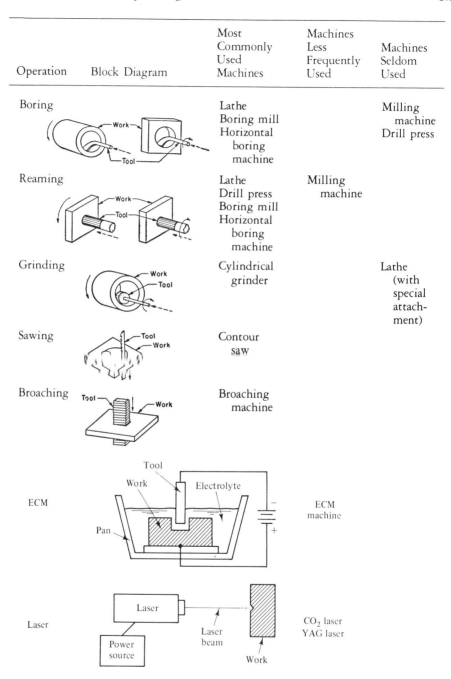

Fig. 1.5. (Continued)

laser-beam generation and the surface-reflection properties of the light beam, laser machining is not very (energy) efficient. It is typically used for special-purpose applications.

1.2.4 Material Handling

The major objective of material handling is to deliver the right material (raw material, workpiece, or finished part) at the right time to the proper location (with the right orientation). Economic considerations are extremely important since material handling is a zero-value-added operation. Reduction in material handling time results in an improvement in the total production efficiency. This saving must, however, offset additional handling costs.

1.2.4.1 *Material Handling Function.* In general, the material-handling function in a machine shop includes:

1. Receiving
2. In-process handling
3. In-process storage
4. Workplace handling
5. Finished-part storage

Receiving is the function that accepts raw material from vendors/suppliers. Transportation is necessary to move raw material from receiving storage to the machine tool. In-process handling is required to move the workpiece inside the shop among machines and to in-process storage locations. While in-process storage is used to locate parts in temporary storage areas (e.g., a bin, a box, or a pallet), workplace handling requires much more care and accuracy. Loading/unloading the workpiece directly affects the machining accuracy and thus requires high positioning accuracy. After the part has been completed, it is transported to the finished-part storage area (warehouse). This stage is the final material-handling stage in the machine shop.

1.2.4.2 *Material-Handling Methods.* Several properties of the material affect the material-handling method, such as

1. Material properties
2. Shape
3. Size
4. Weight

Small workpieces or parts are normally carried in boxes, bins, or trays. Large, heavy workpieces or parts are carried on pallets. The transportation of boxes, bins, trays, and pallets within the shop, such as the receiving and in-process handling, is done by either manual or mechanical equipment (Table 1.1).

Table 1.1. MATERIAL-HANDLING EQUIPMENT

Transportation	Handling
Dolly	Push rod
Pushcart	Robot
Forklift truck	
Gravity chute	
Conveyor	
Roller	
Belt	
Powered roller	
Crane	
Tow cart	
Monorail	
Automated guided vehicle (AGV)	
Transfer table	

1.2.5 Material Planning

Material planning is the process of choosing the appropriate material form for successive machining operations. Aside from the technological requirements (such as material properties), other factors involved in material planning include:

1. Component of shape and size
2. Quantity
3. Convenience of machining
4. Cost and availability

The component shape and size is a dominant factor in the final cost of a product. However, both economic as well as physical constraints must be considered. For instance, one can use a 4-in.-diameter bar stock to make a ¼-in.-diameter pin. The choice of a 4-in.-diameter bar to make a ¼-in.-diameter pin is a poor economic choice since the majority of material will be machined to chips and scrapped. Therefore, the processing time will be exceedingly long and costly. For a V-8 engine block, one can either machine directly from a "slab" of metal, or first cast the material into a rough form and then machine it to the final shape and finish. Since the first alternative requires excess machining of the material, it is obviously very inefficient. However, casting requires a large initial investment. Therefore, the quantity also plays an important role. The choice between standard stock and casting can be expressed by a break-even equation (see also Figure 1.6).

$$NC_1 + N \sum C_i V_i = C_m + N \sum C_i' V_i' + NC_1'$$

where C_1 = cost for preparing one workpiece from stock
    C_i = cost of machining a unit volume by process i
    V_i = volume being machined by process i from stock
    C_m = cost of mold

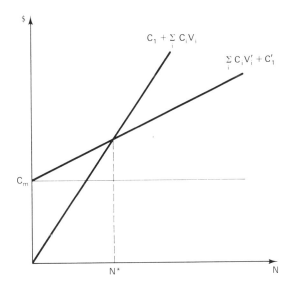

Fig. 1.6. Break-even quantity.

$N*$ = break-even quantity
C_1' = incremental cost of making one casting
V_i' = volume being machined by process i from the casting

N is the break-even quantity. When the batch size is larger than N, it is desirable to cast and then machine. If the batch size is smaller than N, it is more economical to fabricate the part from stock. If the batch size equals N, the two methods are indifferent.

1.2.6 Process Planning

Manufacturing planning, process planning, material processing, process engineering, and machine routing are only a few of the titles given to the topic referred to here as process planning. Similarly, material processors or process planners are only two of the titles given to people who actually perform this function. Since these titles and descriptions are so often confused, some time should be given to the definition of process planning and the use of this terminology throughout this book. "Process planning" is that function within a manufacturing facility that establishes which machining processes and parameters are to be used (as well as those machines capable of performing these processes) to convert (machine) a piece part from its initial form to a final form predetermined (usually by a design engineer) from an engineering drawing. Alternatively, process planning could be defined as the act of preparing detailed work instructions to produce a part. The initial material may take a number of forms, the most common of which are bar stock, plate, castings, forgings, or maybe just a slab (of any geometry) of metal (see Figure 1.7). The slab of material is normally a burnout, cut to some rough dimension. This metal slab can consist of almost any geometry.

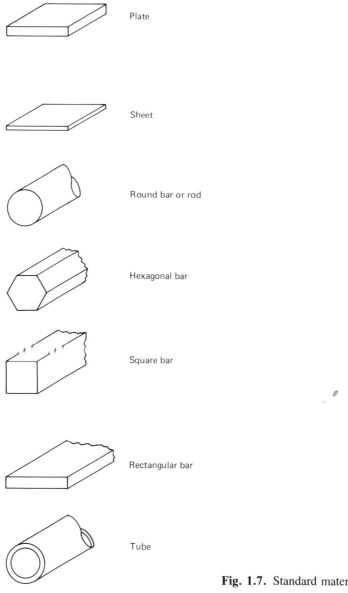

Fig. 1.7. Standard material shapes.

With these raw materials as a base, the process planner must prepare a list of processes needed to convert this normally predetermined material into a predetermined final shape. The processes used by a process planner in a discrete part metal manufacturing industry are shown in Figure 1.8. Some of the operations above are often considered subsets of some major category. Facing can be considered a subset of turning. Reaming can be considered a subset of drilling.

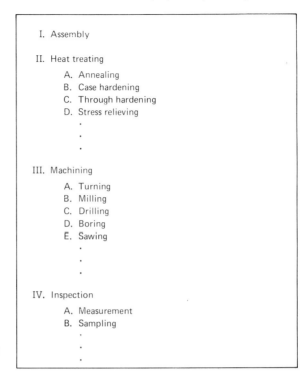

I. Assembly

II. Heat treating
    A. Annealing
    B. Case hardening
    C. Through hardening
    D. Stress relieving
        .
        .
        .

III. Machining
    A. Turning
    B. Milling
    C. Drilling
    D. Boring
    E. Sawing
        .
        .
        .

IV. Inspection
    A. Measurement
    B. Sampling
        .
        .
        .

Fig. 1.8. Processes used in discrete parts metal manufacturing.

The process plan (Figure 1.9) is frequently called an operation sheet, route sheet, operation planning summary, or another similar name. The detailed plan usually contains the route, processes, process parameters, and machine and tool selections. In a more general sense, a process is called an operation (including manual operations). (The route is the operation sequence.) The process plan provides the instructions for production of the part. These instructions dictate the cost, quality, and rate of production. Therefore, process planning is of utmost importance to the production system.

In a conventional production system, a process plan is created by a process planner, who examines a new part (engineering drawing) and then determines the appropriate procedures to produce it. The previous experience of the process planner is critical to the success of the plan. Planning, as practiced today, is as much an art as it is a formal procedure.

As mentioned previously, there are numerous factors that affect process planning. The shape, tolerance, surface finish, size, material type, quantity, the manufacturing system itself, and so on, all contribute to the selection of operations and the operation sequence. These factors are discussed in detail in Chapter 2.

In addition to operation sequencing and operation selection, the selection of tooling and jigs/fixtures is also a major part of the process planning function. The tooling portion includes selection of both the tool itself and the machine on which the tool is used. There are a limited set of commercially available tools, with different

OPERATION SHEET (Process Plan)				
Part No. *S576-67*			Material *Cast Iron 9lb/pc*	
Part Name *Eccentric Strap Cap Half*				
Orig. _____			Changes _____	
Checked _____			Approved _____	
No.	Operation Description	Machine	Setup Description	Operate Hr/Unit
5	Rough and finish mill 2 mating surfaces	Cinc. Mill (Kender #136)	Gang 6 castings in fixture	
10	Spotface and drill two holes 33/84 in. D; drill 27/84 in. D pipe hole; tap 1/4 in. pipe thread	Multispindle drill press	Piece on table Piece in 35° drill jig	
15	Rough and finish bore 6 1/4 in. D; bore 6 1/2 in. D X 3/8 in. wide groove	Bullard Vert. Boring Mill (Kender #335)	Clamp to Eccentric Connector Half (S563-5), then mount both parts in 4-jaw chuck	

Fig. 1.9. Process plan.

shapes, diameters, lengths, number of teeth, and alternative tool materials. The most commonly used tool materials are high-speed steel (HSS) and tungsten carbide (TC). TC can machine metal at higher cutting speed than HSS, but costs more and is difficult or impossible to regrind. TC is also brittle and is not recommended for interrupted cuts. All the conditions above need to be taken into account to select an appropriate tool.

Jigs/fixtures are devices to guide a tool or hold a workpiece for better machining. Very few standard devices are available. Even with standard devices, application is normally left to the machine operator. Process planning, however, should consider the effect of tooling and jigs/fixtures on the quality of the product during the selection of the production operations.

1.2.7 Computer-Aided Process Planning

Process planning is a task that requires a significant amount of both time and experience. According to an Air Force study, a typical process planner is a person over 40 years of age with significant experience in a machine shop. Although the U.S. industry requires about 200,000 to 300,000 process planners, only 150,000 to 200,000 are currently available. Automating process planning is an obvious alternative to eliminate this imbalance.

Early attempts to automate process planning consist primarily of building computer-assisted systems for report generation, storage, and retrieval of plans. When used effectively, these systems can save up to 40% of a process planner's time. A typical example can be found in Lockheed's CAP system [Tulkoff 1981]. Such a system can by no means perform the process planning tasks; rather, it helps reduce the clerical work required of the process planner.

Perhaps the best known automated process planning system is the CAM-I automated process planning system—CAPP (CAM-I stands for Computer-Aided Manufacturing–International, a nonprofit industrial research organization). In the CAPP system, previously prepared process plans are stored in a data base. When a new component is planned, a process plan for a similar component is retrieved and subsequently modified by a process planner to satisfy special requirements. The technique involved is called group technology (GT) or variant planning. Both GT and variant planning will be discussed in more detail later. The typical organization of a variant process planning is illustrated in Figure 1.10.

Recent developments in computer-aided process planning have focused on eliminating the process planner from the entire planning function. Computer-aided process planning can reduce some of the decision making required during a planning process. It has the following advantages:

1. It can reduce the skill required of a planner.
2. It can reduce the process planning time.
3. It can reduce both process planning and manufacturing cost.
4. It can create more consistant plans.
5. It can produce more accurate plans.
6. It can increase productivity.

The benefits of computer-aided process planning systems have been documented by several industries [Vogel 1980, Tulkoff 1981, Dunn and Marn 1978, Kotler 1980a,b]. Such systems can reduce planning time from hours to minutes.

Two approaches to computer-aided process planning are currently being pursued: variant and generative. The variant approach uses library retrieval procedures to find standard plans for similar components. The standard plans are created manually by process planners. The generative approach is considered more advanced as well as more difficult to develop. In a generative process planning system, process plans are generated automatically for new components without referring to existing plans. Details of these two approaches are discussed in Chapter 4.

Figure 1.11 represents the structure of a complete computer-aided process planning system. Although no existing turnkey system integrates all of the functions shown in Figure 1.11 (or even a goodly portion of them), the figure illustrates the functional dependencies of a complete process planning system. It also helps to illustrate some of the constraints imposed on a process planning system (e.g., available machines, tooling, jigs, etc.).

In Figure 1.11 the modules are not necessarily arranged based on importance or decision sequence. The system monitor controls the execution sequence of the individual modules. Each module may require execution several times in order to obtain the optimum process plan. Iterations are required to reach feasibility as well as a good economic balance.

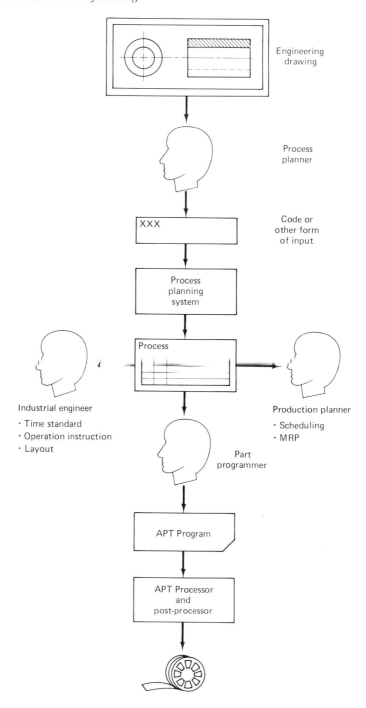

Fig. 1.10. Typical process planning system.

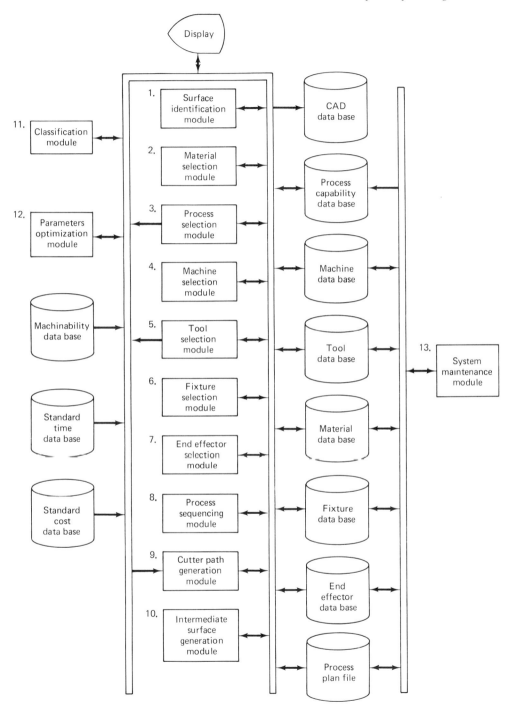

Fig. 1.11. Process planning modules and data bases [Chang 1983].

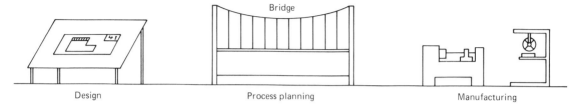

Fig. 1.12. Process planning bridges design and manufacturing.

The input to the system will most probably be a three-dimensional model from a CAD data base. The model will contain not only the shape and dimensioning information, but also the tolerances and special features. The process plan can be routed directly to the production planning system and production control system. Time estimates and resource requirements can be sent to the production planning system for scheduling. The part program, cutter location (CL) file, and material-handling control program can also be sent to the control system.

Process planning is the critical bridge between design and manufacturing (Figure 1.12). Design information can be translated into manufacturing language only through process planning. Today, both automated design (CAD) and manufacturing (CAM) have been implemented. Integrating or bridging these functions requires automated process planning.

1.3 GROUP TECHNOLOGY

Since the beginning of human culture, people have tried to apply reason to their actions. One important way to apply reason is to relate similar things. Biologists classify items into genus and species. We relate to such things as mammals, marsupials, batrachians, amphibians, fish, mollusks, crustacean, birds, reptiles, worms, insects, and so on. A chicken is a bird with degenerated wings. A tiger, jaguar, and domestic cat are all members of a single family.

The same concept applied to natural phenomena can also be applied to artificial ones. When a vast amount of information needs to be kept and ordered, a taxonomy is normally employed. Librarians use taxonomies to classify books in libraries. Similarly, in manufacturing, thousands of items are produced yearly. When one looks at the parts that construct the product, the number is exceptionally large. Each part has a different shape, size, and function. However, when one looks closely, one may again find similarities among components (Figure 1.13); a dowel and a small shaft may be very similar in appearance but different in function. Spur gears of different sizes need about the same manufacturing processes. It therefore appears that manufactured components can be classified into families similar to biological families or library taxonomies. Parts classified and grouped into families produce a much more tractable data base for management.

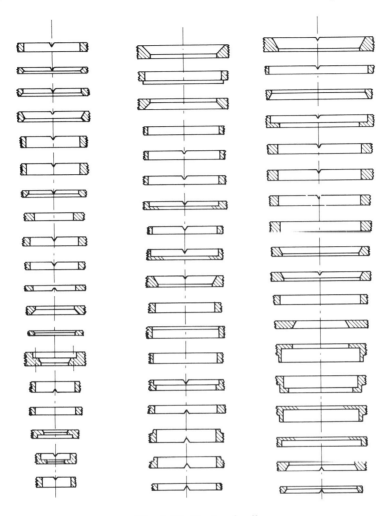

Fig. 1.13. Design family.

Although this simple concept has been in existence for a long time, it was not until 1958 that S. P. Mitrofanov, a Russian engineer, formalized the concept and put together a book entitled *The Scientific Principles of Group Technology*. Group technology (GT) has been defined [Solaja 1973] as follows:

> Group Technology is the realization that many problems are similar, and that by grouping similar problems, a single solution can be found to a set of problems thus saving time and effort.

Although the definition is quite broad, one usually relates group technology only to production applications. In production systems, group technology can be applied

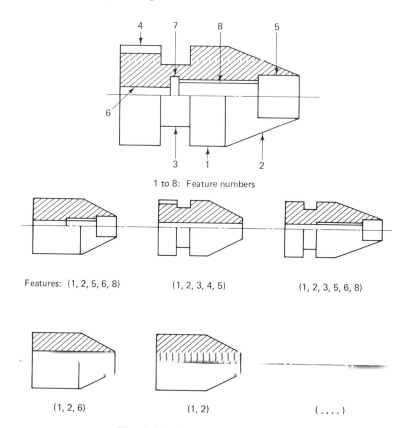

Fig. 1.14. Composite component.

in different areas. For component design, it is clear that many components have a similar shape (Figure 1.13). Similar components therefore can be grouped into design families. A new design can be created by modifying an existing component design from the same family. Using this concept, composite components can be identified. Composite components are parts that embody all the design features of a design family or design subfamily. An example is illustrated in Figure 1.14. Components in the family can be identified from features of the composite components.

For manufacturing purposes, GT represents a greater importance than simply a design philosophy. Components that are not similar in shape may still require similar manufacturing processes. For example, in Figure 1.15 most components have different shapes and functions; but all of them require internal boring, face milling, hole drilling, and so on. Therefore, it can be concluded that the components in the figure are similar. The set of similar components can be called a production family. From this, process planning work can be facilitated. Since similar processes are required for all family members, a machine cell can be built to manufacture the family. This makes

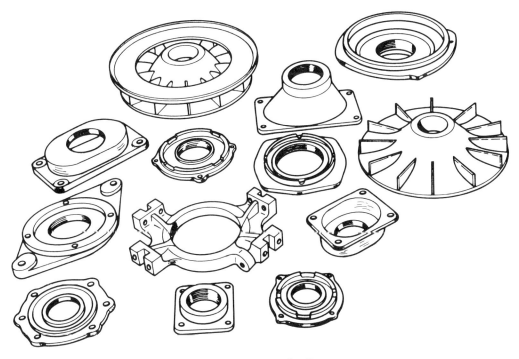

Fig. 1.15. Production family.

production planning and control much easier, since only similar components are considered for each cell. Such a cell-oriented layout is called a group technology layout.

The following techniques are employed in GT:

1. Coding and classification
2. Production flow analysis
3. Group layout

Although both production flow analysis and group layout are based on coding and classification methods, they can still be distinguished as different activities. Since group layout is not "directly" related to process planning, they will not be discussed further in detail.

1.3.1 Coding and Classification

Coding is a process of establishing symbols to be used for meaningful communication. Classification is a separate process in which items are separated into groups based on the existence or absence of characteristic attributes. Coding can be used for classification purposes, and classification requirements must be considered during the construction of a coding scheme. Therefore, the two topics are closely related.

Before a coding scheme can be constructed, a survey of all component features must be completed, then code values can be assigned to the features. The selection of relevant features is dependent on the application of the coding scheme. For example, tolerance is not important for design retrieval; therefore, it is not a feature in a design-oriented coding system. However, in a manufacturing-oriented coding system, tolerance is indeed an important feature.

Because the code structure affects its length, the accessibility and the expandability of a code (and the related data base) is of importance. There are three different types of code structures in GT coding systems: (1) hierarchical, (2) chain (matrix), and (3) hybrid.

A hierarchical structure is also called a monocode. In a monocode, each code number is qualified by the preceding characters. For example, in Figure 1.16, the fourth digit indicates threaded or not threaded for a 322x family. One advantage of a hierarchical structure is that it can represent a large amount of information with very few code positions. A drawback is potential complexity of the coding system. Hierarchical codes are difficult to develop because of all the branches in the hierarchy that must be defined.

A chain structure is called a polycode. Every digit in the code position represents a distinct bit of information, regardless of the previous digit. In Figure 1.17 a chain-structured coding scheme is presented. A "2" in the third position always means a cross hole, no matter what numbers are given to positions one and two. Chain codes are compact and are much easier to construct and use. The major drawback is that they cannot be as detailed as hierarchical structures with the same number of coding digits.

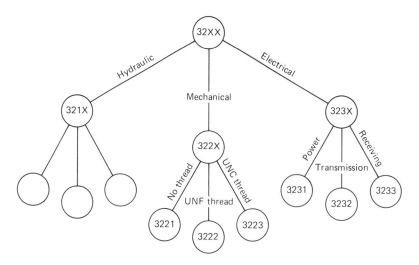

Fig. 1.16. Hierarchical structure.

Digit position	1	2	3	4
Class of feature	External shape	Internal shape	Holes	
Possible value 1	Shape 1	Shape 1	Axial	
2	Shape 2	Shape 2	Cross	
3	Shape 3	Shape 3	Axial and cross	
4				

Fig. 1.17. Chain structure.

The third type of structure, the hybrid structure, is a mixture of the hierarchical and chain structures (Figure 1.18). Most existing coding systems use a hybrid structure to obtain the advantages of both structures. A good example is the widely used Opitz code (Figure 1.19).

There are more than a hundred GT coding systems used in industry today. The structure selected is based primarily on the application. Table 1.2 provides comprehensive guidelines for code structure selection.

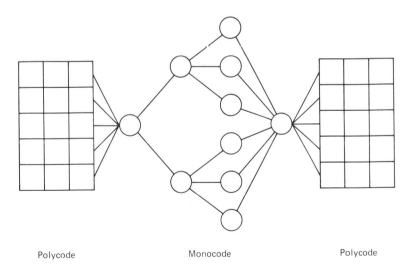

Polycode   Monocode   Polycode

Fig. 1.18. Hybrid structure.

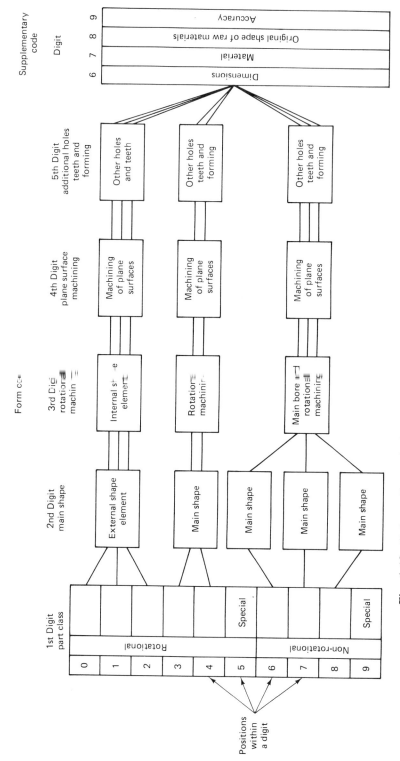

Fig. 1.19. Opitz coding and classification system. [Reprinted with permission from H. Opitz, *A Classification System to Describe Workpieces*, Pergamon Press.]

28

Table 1.2. CODE STRUCTURE SELECTION

Major Item Class	Resolution Required	Flexibility Needed	Code System Type[a]
Raw materials	Moderate	Low	Hybrid (H/C)
Commercial items	High	Low	H
Designed piece parts	Moderate	High	C
Assemblies models	Moderate	Moderate	Hybrid (H/C)
Machinery	Moderate	Moderate	Hybrid (H/C)
Technical information	Moderate	Low	H
Tools	Moderate	Low	H
Commercial			
Proprietary	Moderate	High	C
Gauges/fixtures	Moderate	Low	H
Supplies	High	Low	H

[a]H, hierarchical, C, chain.
Source: Krag [1978]. [Courtesy of Numerical Control Society.]

The physical coding of a component can be shown best by example. In Figure 1.20, a rotational component is coded using the Opitz system. Going through each code position, the resulting code becomes 01112. This code represents this component and all others with similar shape and diameter. Later, in Chapter 2, GT applications to process planning will be discussed.

1.3.2 Closing Remarks

A brief review of manufacturing history, coupled with a passing knowledge of today's economic situation, should lead one to believe that U.S. manufacturing industries are facing a very difficult period in their evolution. In view of the rapidly

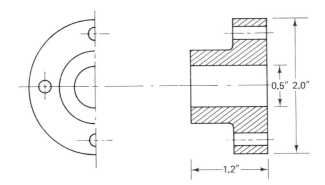

Fig. 1.20. Rotational component. [Reprinted with permission from H. Opitz, *A Classification System to Describe Workpieces*, Pergamon Press.]

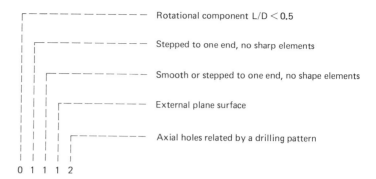

Fig. 1.20. (Continued)

developing international competition, one must utilize the most modern manufacturing technologies in order to keep pace. CAD and CAM have become a standard for improving productivity. However, neither CAD nor CAM have proven to be answers in themselves. Integrating CAD and CAM appears to be the key to larger productivity gains. Furthermore, the basis for this integration is automated process planning. The remainder of the book focuses on process planning technology and key integration issues that must be overcome before CAD/CAM can become a reality.

REVIEW QUESTIONS

1.1. Discuss the advantages and disadvantages of using transfer-line technology in a high-technology manufacturing facility.

1.2. Discuss the mechanical designer's role in a manufacturing facility.

1.3. Manufacturing systems planning and design are economically driven engineering functions. Discuss how classical engineering economic analysis is used and some of the problems related to "time-value" decisions.

1.4. Many manufacturing managers when they learn the principles of group technology comment, "We've been doing that for years!" Have they? Comment.

1.5. Discuss the Department of Commerce statistic that 95% of all parts made in the United States are produced in lots of 50 or less. Toward what focus should this statistic direct us?

1.6. You and a group of close friends have recently patented a small NC drilling machine (for home use). You are currently planning on starting your own manufacturing operation. A marketing analyst has come back to you and said that because of the newness of the product line, "demand for the next 10 years may be between 50 and 50,000 units per year." The selling price for the drill was placed in the range $1000 to $2500. If you were to manufacture the product yourself, the cost would range from $300 to $775 based on a production rate from $5000 for 50 units per year as well as the production system design. Discuss your approach to beginning this company. (Include advantages and disadvantages as well as financing.)

1.7. In order to store and retrieve household items (canned goods, boxed goods, towels, clothes, etc.) more efficiently at home, you have decided to develop a coding and classification system to characterize "geometric families." Discuss what types of code(s) might be appropriate and how you would classify these items into families.

PART DESIGN REPRESENTATION

Process planning, like other planning activities, has a very specific objective—to identify the detailed processes required for the production of a piece part. Product design is the input for the planning system. The operations planning summary is the output. Although several different input representations are used to describe a part, the most general input representation is referred to as an engineering design. This representation is input to the planning system, which interprets it in order to find the appropriate machining processes, process parameters, and so on, to satisfy the design.

In a computerized planning system, a formal structure and data base for this knowledge are required in order to transform the engineering design information into production design. In this chapter information requirements for process planning systems are discussed and ordered into a detailed data base.

2.1 ENGINEERING DESIGN

Engineering design is the partial realization of a designer's concept. The designer normally cannot directly transform a concept into a physical item. Instead, the designer conveys the idea to other people through an alternative medium such as an engineering drawing, and then a manufacturing engineer or machinist produces the design. When a farmer needed a tool prior to our industrialized age, he normally went

2

to a blacksmith and told the blacksmith the shape and size of the tool required. Because most tools were simple and did not require significant accuracy, the blacksmith would get a pretty good picture of a hoe or a plow through a verbal description. If the blacksmith still did not understand, the farmer could roughly sketch the tool on the dirt floor of the blacksmith shop.

As design became more complex, a picture became necessary to relate the information to others. Multiview orthographic drawing has long been adopted by engineers as the standard tool to represent a design. Design information can be passed from the designer to others who are well trained in reading such drawings. The object a designer draws on paper can be interpreted and reconstructed in the designer's image in a viewer's mind. The capability of transforming an object from one medium to another (e.g., from a two-dimensional three-view drawing to a three-dimensional picture in one's mind), and an understanding of the rules of drawing are prerequisite to pass design information from the designer to other people without error.

An engineering drawing therefore contains all the information necessary to represent a design (e.g., a component). Since process planning is the function that creates detailed plans for the production of a component, an engineering drawing is the basic input to the process planning function. Figure 2.1 illustrates the information flow for this process.

There are several methods available to represent an engineering drawing. The

34

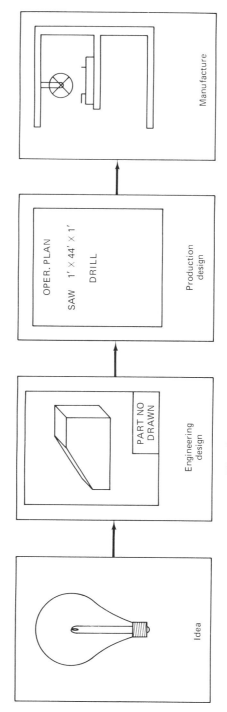

Fig. 2.1. Evolution—realization of a product.

most conventional is drafting on paper with pencil or ink. Manual drafting is tedious and requires a tremendous amount of patience and time. Recently, computer-aided drafting systems have been implemented to improve drafting efficiency. The major objective of these systems is to assist the draftsman with tedious drawing and re-drawing. Partially completed or completed drawings from a graphics tablet or screen can be digitized and stored in a computer, and can be retrieved when needed.

Most CAD systems store drawings in a three-dimensional representation. Points (vertices), lines (edges), and curves are represented in (X, Y, Z) space. When a drawing is requested, a series of transformations are performed on the data, and a drawing is presented either in two- or three-dimensional perspective or sectional views. The resultant drawing can then be drawn physically using a plotter, or simply displayed on a cathode ray tube (CRT). Such internal representations can be used not only for design drafting but also for engineering analysis, such as finite element (structural) analysis.

In recent years, the term "geometric modeling" in CAD has become common jargon. Geometric modeling is a technique for providing computer-compatible descriptions of the geometry of a part. Conventional CAD systems are geometric models that use surface-oriented three-dimensional models. Recent advances in CAD have focused on the development of bounded shape models for a three-dimensional representation. In these bounded shape models, individual surfaces are structured together to define the complete shell (boundary of a shape). Operators can then be applied to manipulate the shape.

2.2 DESIGN DRAFTING

Engineering drawing is a universal language used to represent a designer's idea to others. It is the most accepted medium of communication in all phases of industrial and engineering work. In ancient times before multiview drawing standards were adopted, perspective drawings were normally employed. The great master of art during the Renaissance, Leonardo da Vinci, designed several machines and mechanical components (which still amaze contemporary designers) using perspective sketches (Figure 2.2). Today, pictorial drawings are still used to supplement other design representations.

2.2.1 Multiview Drawing

In today's modern manufacturing industry, several types of drawings are acceptable. However, the standard is still the multiview drawing (Figure 2.3). A multiview drawing usually contains two or three views (front, top, and side). Each view is an orthographic projection of one plane. In the United States and Canada, the third-angle

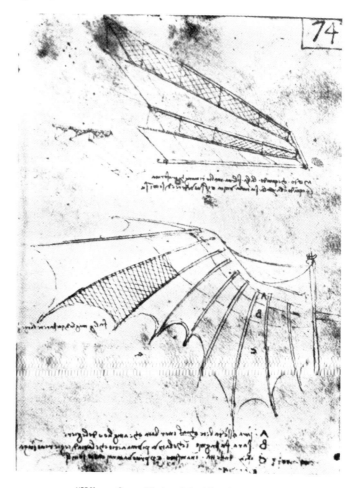

"Wings for a Flying Machine," c. 1488.

Fig. 2.2. Idea sketch prepared by Leonardo da Vinci (1452–1519). [Courtesy of Institut de France.]

projection is the system used (see Figure 2.4). In Figure 2.4 the four quadrants of the *YZ* plane (called the I, II, III, and IV angles) are illustrated. For the third-angle projection, we always place the object in the third angle and project the object in three planes [looking toward the frontal plane (*XY*) and rotating the horizontal plane (*XZ*) on the *X* axis (clockwise 90 degrees), the profile plan (*YZ*) on *Y* axis (clockwise 90 degrees) in order to obtain part (b)].

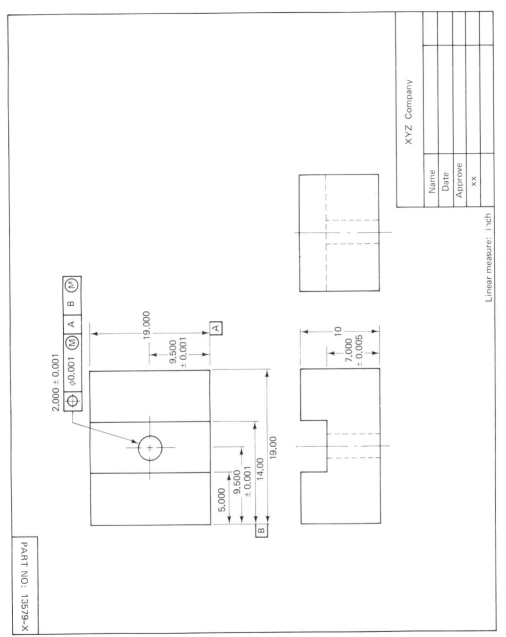

Fig. 2.3. Multiview drawing of a bracket.

Linear measure: inch

XYZ Company

Name
Date
Approve
xx

PART NO: 13579-X

37

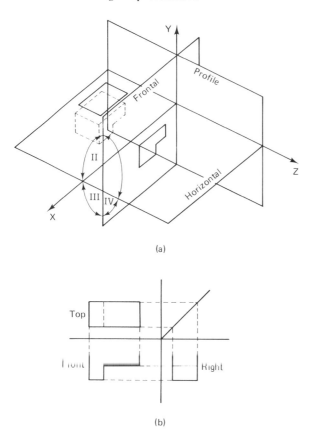

(a)

(b)   **Fig. 2.4.** Third-angle projection.

2.2.2 Partial View

When drafting a symmetrical object, two views are sufficient to represent the object (typically, one view is omitted). Sometimes a partial view is used to substitute one of the two views (Figure 2.5). Sectional and auxiliary views are also commonly used to present part detail. Sectional views (Figure 2.5b) are extremely useful in displaying the detailed design of a complicated internal configuration. Casting designers often employ sectional views. When a major surface is inclined to all three projection planes, only a distorted picture can be seen. An auxiliary plane that is parallel to the major surface (Figure 2.5a) can be used to display an undistorted view.

2.2.3 Dimensioning

A drawing is expected to convey a complete description of every detail of a part. However, dimensioning is as important as the geometric information. In manufacturing, a drawing without dimensions is worth as much as the paper on which it is drawn.

According to American National Standards Institute (ANSI) Standards, the fol-

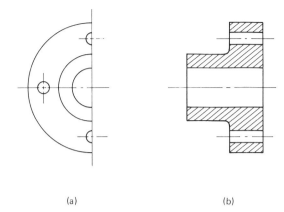

Fig. 2.5. Partial views.   (a)   (b)

lowing are the basic rules that should be observed in dimensioning any drawing:

1. Show enough dimensions so that the intended sizes and shapes can be determined without calculating or assuming any distances.
2. State each dimension clearly, so that it can be interpreted in only one way.
3. Show the dimensions between points, lines, or surfaces which have a necessary and specific relation to each other or which control the location of other components or mating parts.
4. Select and arrange dimensions to avoid accumulations of tolerances that may permit various interpretations and cause unsatisfactory mating of parts and failure in use.
5. Show each dimension only once.
6. Where possible, dimension each feature in the view where it appears in profile, and where its true shape appears.
7. Wherever possible, specify dimensions to make use of readily available materials, parts, tools, and gauges. Savings are often possible when drawings specify (a) commonly used materials in stock sizes, (b) parts generally recognized as commercially standard, (c) sizes that can be produced with standard tools and inspected with standard gauges, and (d) tolerances from accepted published standards.

2.2.4 Conventional Tolerancing

Since it is impossible to produce the exact dimension specified, a tolerance is also used to show the acceptable variation in a dimension. There are two types of tolerances: bilateral tolerance and unilateral tolerance (Figure 2.6). Bilateral tolerances, such as 1.00 ± 0.05, specify dimensional variation from the basic size (i.e., $0.95 - 1.05$). On the other hand, a unilateral tolerance expresses an increase (or decrease) in one direction in relationship to the basic size: for example,

$$1.00 \begin{array}{c} + \ 0.00 \\ - \ 0.05 \end{array} \quad \text{equals} \quad 0.95 - 1.00$$

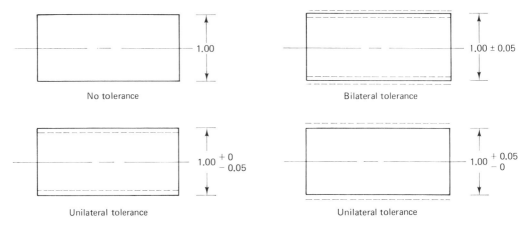

Fig. 2.6. Tolerancing: bilateral and unilateral. Dashed lines show the tolerance limits.

The basic location where most dimension lines originate is the reference location. For machining, the reference location provides the base from which all other measurements are taken. By stating tolerances from a reference location, cumulative errors can be eliminated.

On a component there are working surfaces and nonworking surfaces. Working surfaces are surfaces such as bearings, pistons, and gear teeth, for which optimum performance may require control of the surface characteristics. Nonworking surfaces,

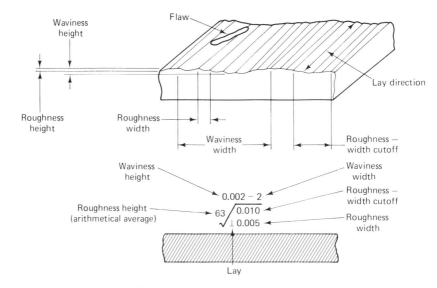

Fig. 2.7. Surface control symbols.

such as the exterior walls of an engine block, crankcase, or differential housings, seldom require surface control. For surfaces that require surface control, a control surface symbol can be used. Figure 2.7 shows how the symbol is used.

In the symbol, several surface characteristics are specified. The roughness height is the roughness value as normally related to the surface finish. It is the average amount of irregularity above or below an assumed centerline. It is expressed in microinches (μin.) (0.000001 in.) or, in the metric system, in micrometers (μm) (0.000001 m). Recommended roughness heights are given in Table 2.1. Lay is another property of a machined surface. It indicates the direction of the predominant pattern of surface irregularities produced by the tool. Lay symbols are listed in Figure 2.8. An example of using control surface symbols is shown in Figure 2.9.

Conventional methods of dimensioning only provide information concerning size and surface condition. A component can be produced without a guarantee of interchangeability. For example, in Figure 2.10, both components (b) and (c) satisfy the dimension specified in (a) [i.e., the diameter of components (b) and (c) is 0.501 in. over the entire length of the component]. Obviously, both (b) and (c) are not desirable. However, as specified, both (b) and (c) meet specifications.

Table 2.1. RECOMMENDED HEIGHT VALUES

Roughness Value (μin.)	Type of Surface	Purpose
1000	Extremely rough	Used for clearance surfaces only where good appearance is not required
500	Rough	Used where vibration, fatigue, or stress concentration are not critical and close tolerances are not required
250	Medium	Most popular for general use where stress requirements and appearance are essential
125	Average smooth	Suitable for mating surfaces of parts held together by bolts and rivets with no motion between them
63	Better-than-average finish	For close fits or stressed parts except rotating shafts, axles, and parts subject to extreme vibration
32	Fine finish	Used where stress concentration is high and for such applications as bearings
16	Very fine finish	Used where smoothness is of primary importance, such as high-speed shaft bearings, heavily loaded bearings, and extreme tension members
8	Extremely fine finish produced by cylindrical grinding, honing, lapping, or butting	Use for such parts as surfaces of cylinder
4	Superfine finish produced by honing, lapping, buffing, or polishing	Used on areas where packings and rings must slide across the surface where lubrication is not dependable

☰	Parallel to the boundary line of the nominal surface indicated by the symbol
⊥	Perpendicular to the boundary line of the nominal surface indicated by the symbol
✕	Angular in both directions to the boundary line of the nominal surface indicated by the symbol
M	Multidirectional
C	Approximately circular relative to the center of the nominal surface indicated by the symbol
R	Approximately radial relative to the corner of the nominal surface indicated by the symbol

Fig. 2.8. Lay symbols.

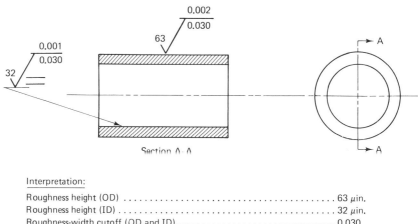

Section A-A

Interpretation:

Roughness height (OD) . . . . 63 μin.
Roughness height (ID) . . . . 32 μin.
Roughness-width cutoff (OD and ID). 0.030
Waviness height (OD) 0.002
Waviness height (ID). 0.001
Lay (OD) . . . . Circumferential
Lay (ID). . . . . Axial

Fig. 2.9. Application and interpretation of the surface roughness symbols.

2.2.5 Geometric Tolerancing

Geometric tolerancing is the method to specify the tolerance of geometric characteristics. Basic geometric characteristics include

Straightness	Perpendicularity
Flatness	Angularity
Roundness	Concentricity
Cylindricity	Symmetry
Profile	Runout
Parallelism	True position

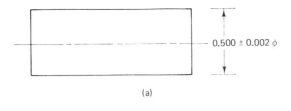

(a)

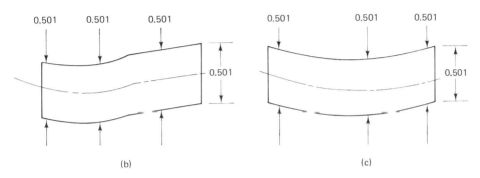

(b)   (c)

Fig. 2.10. Illustration of some addition part conditions.

Symbols that represent these features are shown in Table 2.2. To specify the geometric tolerances, reference features—either planes, lines, or surfaces—can be established. A datum is a plane, surface, point(s), line, axis, or other source of information concerning an object. Datums are assumed to be exact, and from them dimensions similar to the reference location dimensions in the conventional drawing system can be established. However, datums are used only for geometric dimensioning.

Symbolic modifiers are used to clarify implied tolerances. Maximum material condition (MMC) can be used to constrain the tolerance of the produced dimension and the maximum designed dimension. It can be defined as the condition of a part feature where the maximum amount of material is contained. For example, maximum shaft size and minimum hole size can be illustrated as shown in Figure 2.11. Least material condition (LMC) specifies the opposite of the maximum material condition. They can be applied only when both of the following conditions hold:

1. Two or more features are interrelated with respect to the location or form (e.g., two holes). At least one of the features must refer to size.
2. MMC or LMC must directly reference a size feature.

When MMC or LMC are used to specify the tolerance of a hole or shaft, it implies that the tolerance specified is constrained by the maximum or least material condition as well as some other dimensional features. The tolerance may increase when the actual produced feature size is larger (for hole) or smaller (for a shaft) than the MMC size. Because the increase in the tolerance is compensated by the deviate of size in production, the final combined hole size error and geometric tolerance error will still be larger than the anticipated smallest hole (see Figure 2.12).

Table 2.2. GEOMETRIC TOLERANCING SYMBOLS

Geometric characteristic symbols

——	Straightness	⊥	Perpendicularity
▱	Flatness	∠	Angularity
○	Roundness	◎	Concentricity
⌀	Cylindricity	=	Symmetry
⌒	Profile of a line	⟋	Runout
◠	Profile of a surface	⊕	True position
//	Parallelism		

Modifiers

(M)   MMC, Maximum material condition

(R)   RFS, Regardless of feature size

(L)   LMC, Least material condition

Datum identification

–A–   Datum A

Special symbols

(P)   Projected tolerance zone

⌀   Diameter

The third modifier is "regardless of feature size" (RFS). It is also the default modifier. When RFS is used, the tolerance does not change. Table 2.3 shows the application of three modifiers applied to the hole and shaft shown in Figure 2.11.

Figure 2.13 illustrates the use of form geometry symbols and their meaning. In all of the examples (except true position), RFS is assumed. The first drawing in each group of drawings represents the original drawing. The second drawing illustrates the interpretation of the geometric tolerance specified. All variations on surfaces have been exaggerated.

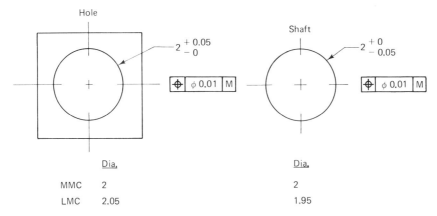

Fig. 2.11. Maximum material diameter and least material diameter.

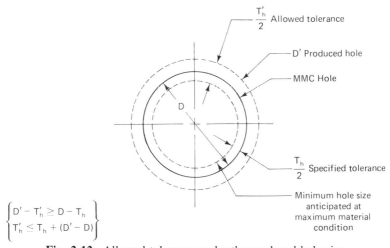

$$\begin{cases} D' - T'_h \geq D - T_h \\ T'_h \leq T_h + (D' - D) \end{cases}$$

Fig. 2.12. Allowed tolerance under the produced hole size.

In Figure 2.13a (where straightness is illustrated), straightness defines the maximum deviates on the assumed centerline over the entire length of a cylindrical component. It is useful in specifying the fit of shafts and holes. Flatness (Figure 2.13b) is the maximum deviation allowed on a flat surface. It is important for plane surface fit (e.g., gasket surfaces). Roundness (Figure 2.13c) defines the irregularity of the diameter at any given cross-sectional location of a cylindrical component. Cylindricity (Figure 2.13d) is similar to roundness except that it defines the irregularity over the entire length. Again, these symbols are useful in specifying the fit for shafts and holes. Profile of a line (Figure 2.13e) and profile of a surface (Figure 2.13f) both describe the deviation on the profile, except that profile of a line focuses on any cross-sectional

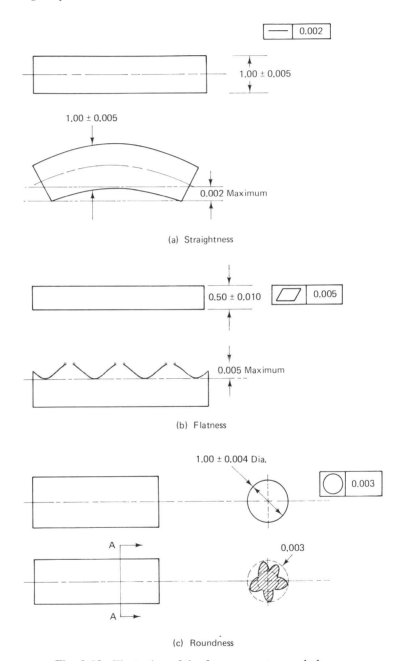

Fig. 2.13. Illustration of the form geometry symbols.

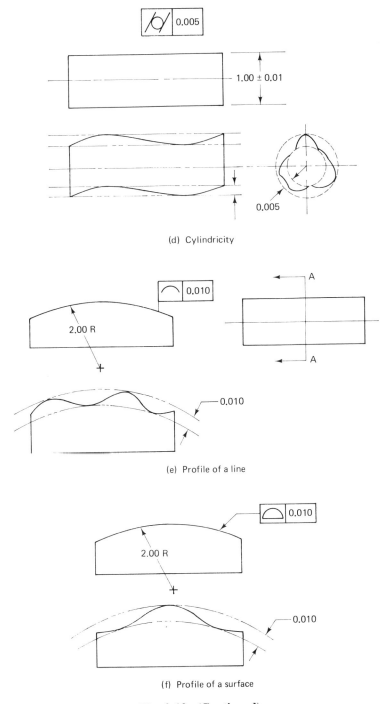

(d) Cylindricity

(e) Profile of a line

(f) Profile of a surface

Fig. 2.13. (Continued)

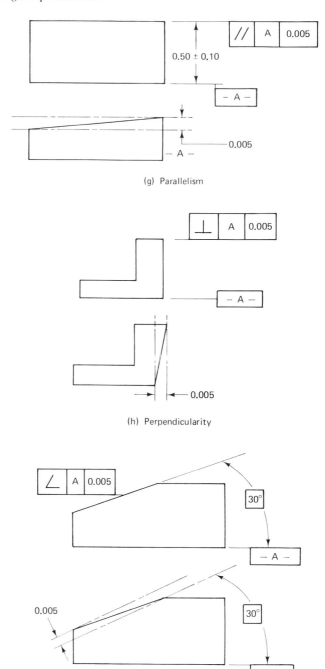

(g) Parallelism

(h) Perpendicularity

(i) Angularity

Fig. 2.13. (Continued)

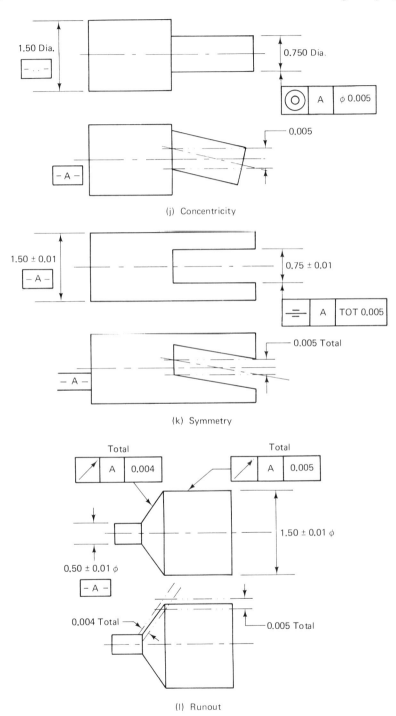

(j) Concentricity

(k) Symmetry

(l) Runout

Fig. 2.13 (Continued)

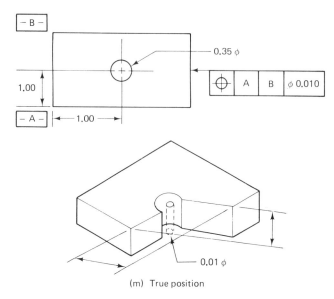

Fig. 2.13 (Continued)

Table 2.3. MAXIMUM OUT-OF-TRUE POSITION ALLOWABLE UNDER THREE MODIFIERS

	Maximum Out-of-True Position Allowable					
	Hole[a]				Shaft[b]	
Produced Size	MMC(M)	LMC(L)	RFS(S)	MMC(M)	LMC(L)	RFS(S)
1.95				0.06	0.01	0.01
1.96				0.05	0.02	0.01
1.97	Out-of-diameter tolerance range			0.04	0.03	0.01
1.98				0.03	0.04	0.01
1.99				0.02	0.05	0.01
2.00	0.01	0.06	0.01	0.01	0.06	0.01
2.01	0.02	0.05	0.01			
2.02	0.03	0.04	0.01			
2.03	0.04	0.03	0.01	Out-of-diameter tolerance range		
2.04	0.05	0.02	0.01			
2.05	0.06	0.01	0.01			

[a] $\phi 2 \pm \begin{smallmatrix} 0.05 \\ 0 \end{smallmatrix}$ ⊕ | φ | 0.01 | (M)

[b] $\phi 2 \pm \begin{smallmatrix} 0 \\ 0.05 \end{smallmatrix}$ ⊕ | φ | 0.01 | (M)

location and profile of a surface looks at the entire surface. Any feature of a component can be specified as being parallel to any given datum. Figure 2.13g shows the use of the parallelism symbol.

Perpendicularity (Figure 2.13h) defines the tolerance of a feature that is 90 degrees to a given datum. Angularity (Figure 2.13i) is similar to perpendicularity except that the relationship of a feature to a given datum need not be 90 degrees. The axis of a hole or cylindrical object can also be dimensioned with angularity. Concentricity (Figure 2.13j) is used to establish a relationship between the axes of two or more cylindrical parts of a component. Symmetry (Figure 2.13k) is a counterpart of concentricity for planes. Runout (Figure 2.13l) is the composite deviation from the desired form of a rotational part during full rotation (360 degrees) of the part on a datum axis.

True position (Figure 2.13m) expresses the location of the centerline with respect to a feature. Conventional tolerancing methods put tolerance area which is greater than the round tolerance area that true position ($\oplus$) specifies.

Thus far, basic drafting methods and symbols have been discussed. Using this knowledge of basic engineering geometry, dimensioning, and tolerancing symbols, any proper engineering design drawing can be interpreted precisely.

2.3 COMPUTER-AIDED DESIGN

Computer-aided design (CAD) can be most simply described as "using a computer in the design process." A wide range of applications can qualify as CAD (from engineering design analysis to drafting). Some narrower views of CAD have been taken to confine it to computer graphic applications in the design process. Some examples of CAD applications include mechanical part design, IC (integral circuit) chip layout, architectural design, and so on. Because of the nature of this text, the major focus will be placed on mechanical part design (input to process planning). Only drafting and geometric modeling of mechanical parts will be discussed. In this book the term "CAD" is equivalent to computer-aided drafting and the related geometric modeling of mechanical parts.

The development of CAD originated from early computer graphic systems. CAD first appeared in the late 1950s when a computer was first used to create graphic objects on a CRT. This, coincidentally, was about the same time that NC and APT first appeared. A bit later X-Y plotters were used as hard-copy output devices. An interesting note is that an X-Y plotter has the same basic structure as an NC drilling machine except that a pen is substituted for the tool on the NC spindle. Early CAD systems basically focused on improving the productivity of draftsmen. However, the more recent CAD systems have focused on modeling engineering objects. This approach is not limited to drafting, but also includes APT programming, engineering analysis, and so on.

2.3.1 CAD Input/Output Devices

Figure 2.14 depicts the typical input/output (I/O) devices of a CAD system. Input devices are generally used to transfer information from a human or storage medium to a computer where "CAD functions" are carried out. A keyboard is the standard input device used to transmit alphanumeric data to the system. In some systems, function keypads are also used to make input easier. Joysticks, track balls, and mouses

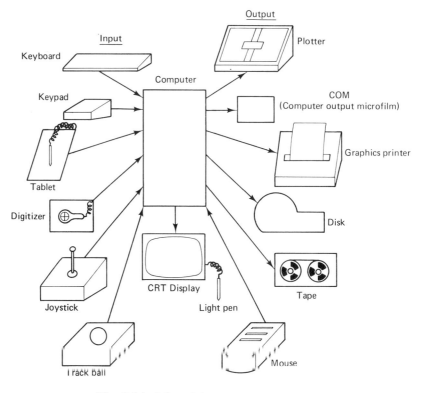

Fig. 2.14. I/O peripherals of a CAD System.

are also used to manipulate a cursor. They can manipulate the graphic cursor (e.g., cross hair) on a CRT and feed the location of an object on the CRT back to the computer. Using these devices allows an operator to address terminal locations interactively. A light pen can also be used for this type of interactive graphics (locational information is fed back discretely to the computer).

There are two basic approaches for the input of an existing drawing: (1) model the object on a drawing, or (2) digitize the drawing. Digitizing is usually much easier than modeling the object. A digitizer is a device that translates the X, Y locations on a drawing into a digital signal and feeds them to a computer. Another input device is a sketch pad called a graphics tablet. A graphic tablet is a special flat surface on which a user draws with a stylus. The location of the stylus is sent to a computer.

The standard output device for CAD is a CRT display. There are two major types of CRT displays: a random-scan-line-drawing display and raster-scan display. Random-scan-line-drawing displays use direct-view-storage tubes (DVSTs) as well as refresh tubes for displaying pictorial representations. On a DVST, a line written onto the screen will remain visible for some period of time (the tube itself stores the line in its memory). A refresh CRT does not continuously display a line on its tube. Rather, the line disappears right after it is drawn. Therefore, information on the screen must be redrawn very quickly, so that the human eye will have the illusion of continuity of the picture. Although the redraw speed is restricted (lower limit) by the number of lines that can be displayed without the screen appearing to flicker, the partial erasing capability of a refresh CRT display makes it more attractive than DVST.

A raster-scan display differs from the random-scan line-drawing display in the method of scanning. The scanning method of a raster-scan display is similar to that of television. Frequent scans are conducted from the top line of the screen to the bottom line. A frame buffer made of random access memory (RAM) is designated to correspond to one frame of picture on the screen. Each pixel (addressable dot on the screen) is controlled by a byte or a half-byte in the frame buffer. During the scan, a pixel can be (1) turned on/off or (2) change color, or (3) change intensity. Picture images are written into a frame buffer rather than directly onto the screen. Some advantages of the raster-scan display include: (1) a more continuous picture tone can be generated, and (2) the cost is usually lower than for random-scanning displays. However, the resolution of the display is also lower. Although the method of display is important, the display does not affect the computer graphics technique [Newman 1979].

2.3.2 Modeling Objects

A component must be modeled before it can be drawn. In a conventional drafting system, a component is modeled using simple geometry (Figure 2.15). A model can also be configured using an APT-like (circles, lines, points, etc.) language to define geometric features. This type of model is stored in a data structure (e.g., the structure in Figure 2.16). The drawing (Figure 2.17) obtained using such a system is basically the same as that which a draftsman would create.

Modeling a component using simple two-dimensional geometry (i.e., points, lines, circles, curves) is not sufficient for engineering drawing (information concerning their relationships is not represented). Any object can be modeled using a set of primitives. A convenient primitive is a polyhedron (Figure 2.18). A polyhedron is a bounded object with *n* faces. Each face is a planar polygon (Figure 2.19) which can be modeled by using an ordered list of the vertices (points) of the polygon or by a similar list of its edges (lines). Wire-frame displays can then be generated using the edges of the polyhedron. However, the hidden lines or hidden surfaces cannot be removed from the display without defining faces on the object. Faces hide the edges, not the other edges.

Another problem yet to be effectively resolved in CAD systems is detecting whether the inside or outside of a polyhedron is being displayed. The side of a plane facing the interior of a part cannot be seen. However, the side of a plane can be identified by the normal of a face. Any point (x, y, z) on a face can be represented by the equation

$$ax + by + cz + d = 0$$

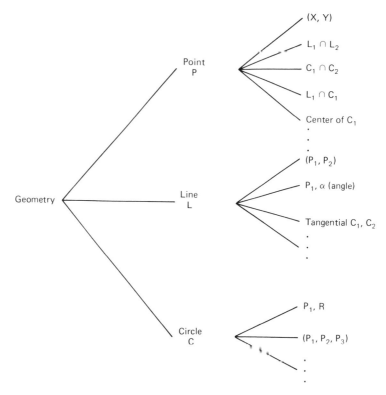

Fig. 2.15. Subset of the geometric definitions for drafting.

where a, b, c, and d are parameters of the face. If P represents the face, P can be characterized by its normal and a constant.

$$P = \begin{bmatrix} a \\ b \\ c \\ d \end{bmatrix}$$

We can also map a vertex (from three-dimensional space to four-dimensional space) in order to obtain a homogeneous representation. This can be written in vector form as

$$\mathbf{V} = (x, y, z, w)$$

where w can be any number. The inside or outside can then be represented by

$$\mathbf{V} \cdot \mathbf{P} \leq 0 \qquad \text{or} \qquad \mathbf{V} \cdot \mathbf{P} > 0$$

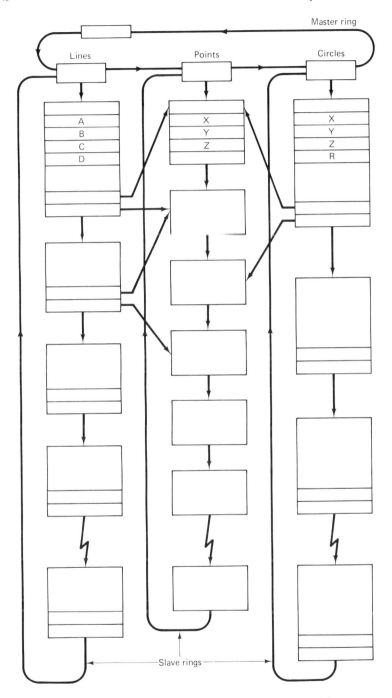

Fig. 2.16. Typical data structure for geometric entities.

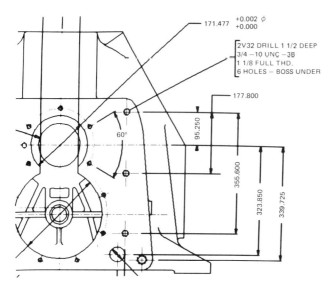

171.477 +0.002 φ
+0.000

2V32 DRILL 1 1/2 DEEP
3/4 –10 UNC –3B
1 1/8 FULL THD.
6 HOLES – BOSS UNDER

177.800

95.250

355.600

323.850

339.725

60°

Fig. 2.17. Drawing from a CAD system. [Courtesy of Applicon.]

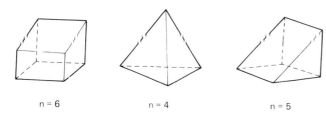

n = 6   n = 4   n = 5   **Fig. 2.18.** Polyhedrons.

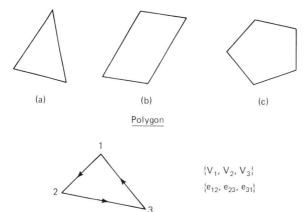

(a)   (b)   (c)

Polygon

$\{V_1, V_2, V_3\}$

$\{e_{12}, e_{23}, e_{31}\}$

Fig. 2.19. Polygons and their representation.

2.3.3 Topology

Surface topology represents the basic relationships of the geometries of an object. For example, in Figure 2.20, the topology of a tetrahedron is shown using a tree structure. The basic topological relationships will always remain the same for any tetrahedron even though tetrahedrons can be of different size and may be oriented differently. The analogy of the tetrahedron can be expanded to any polyhedron. Any polyhedron can be characterized by its

1. Geometry
2. Topology
3. Auxiliary information

Both the geometry and topology are necessary in order to manipulate and display the object. Some additional information may also be necessary to display the object or for other purposes (e.g., engineering analysis, manufacturing, etc.). Such additional information is typically stored in an auxiliary information buffer. A complete model for a polyhedron is shown in Figure 2.21.

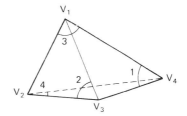

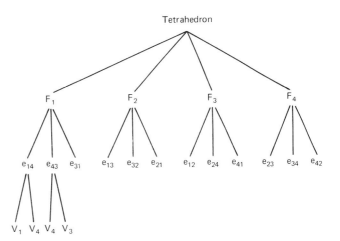

Fig. 2.20. Topology of a tetrahedron.

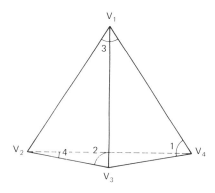

Geometry		$ax + by + cz + d > 0$ outside	
V_1	(x_1, y_1, z_1)	F_1	(a_1, b_1, c_1, d_1)
V_2	(x_2, y_2, z_2)	F_2	(a_2, b_2, c_2, d_2)
V_3	(x_3, y_3, z_3)	F_3	(a_3, b_3, c_3, d_3)
V_4	(x_4, y_4, z_4)	F_4	(a_4, b_4, c_4, d_4)

Topology

Faces	Edges
F_1 V_1, V_4, V_3	$V_1 V_2$ $V_1 V_4$
F_2 V_1, V_3, V_2	$V_2 V_3$
F_3 V_1, V_2, V_4	$V_3 V_4$
F_4 V_2, V_3, V_4	$V_1 V_3$
	$V_2 V_4$

Auxiliary information

Color

Dimensions

Etc.

Fig. 2.21. Complete representation of a tetrahedron.

2.3.4 Curves and Curved Surfaces

Thus far, only planar polygons have been discussed. The representation required for curved surfaces or curves is more complex. There are two ways to represent curves: as functions of the variables x, y, and z, or as functions of another parameter (such as t). In the first case, points on a curve can be defined,

$$X = x, \qquad y = f(x), \qquad z = g(x)$$

This representation poses many computational difficulties for computer applications (e.g., an infinite slope may be required at some point on a curve). It is also difficult to plot a smooth curve using finite relationships.

The parametric cubic curve is one in which x, y, and z are represented as a third-order polynomial of some parameter t. Because slope can be replaced with tangent vectors, some computational difficulties can be reduced. In this representation, a curve is represented as:

$$\left.\begin{array}{l} x(t) = a_x t^3 + b_x t^2 + c_x t + d_x \\ y(t) = a_y t^3 + b_y t^2 + c_y t + d_y \\ z(t) = a_z t^3 + b_z t^2 + c_z t + d_z \end{array}\right\} \ 0 \le t \le 1$$

or in vector form,

$$P(t) = \mathbf{C} \cdot \mathbf{T}^t$$

where

$$\mathbf{T} = \begin{bmatrix} t^3 & t^2 & t & 1 \end{bmatrix}$$

$$\mathbf{C} = \begin{bmatrix} a_x & b_x & c_x & d_x \\ a_y & b_y & c_y & d_y \\ a_z & b_z & c_z & d_z \end{bmatrix}$$

Tangent vectors can be

$$\frac{dx}{dt} = 3a_x t^2 + 2b_x t + c_x$$

$$\frac{dy}{dt} = 3a_y t^2 + 2b_y t + c_y$$

$$\frac{dz}{dt} = 3a_z t^2 + 2b_z t + c_z$$

which will never be infinite.

There are many methods to define parametric cubic curves. The most commonly used methods are Bezier [1972] and B-spline [Gordon 1974] methods. Both methods approximate a curve from n known points (a_x, b_x, c_x, . . ., are unknown). We call those points control points P_i. In the Bezier method, the curve is defined as

$$P(t) = \sum_{i=0}^{n} P_i B_{i,n}(t)$$

and $B_{i,n}(t)$ is called a blending function,

$$B_{i,n}(t) = C(n,i)t^i(1 - t)^{n-i}$$

and

$$C(n, i) = \frac{n!}{i!(n - i)!}$$

Figure 2.22 shows a curve drawn using the Bezier method. Since the end points are connected and the tangent vector of end point P_1 is the tangent of $P_1 P_2$, first-order

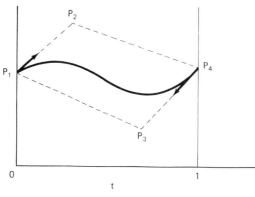

Fig. 2.22. Bezier curve and its four control points.

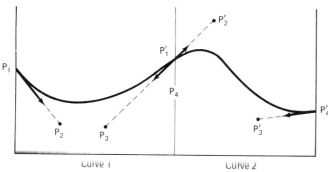

(a) First-order continuity at joint

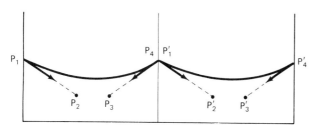

(b) Zero-order continuity at joint   **Fig. 2.23.** Continuity at the joint.

continuity of two Bezier curves can be obtained by making the end point of two curves coincide and the control points adjacent to the end point lie on the same line (Figure 2.23).

The B-spline method also uses a set of blending functions. However, with the B-spline method, the location of the curve depends only on a few neighboring control points. A B-spline curve can be defined as

$$P(t) = \sum_{i=0}^{n} P_i N_{i,k}(t) \qquad 0 \le t \le n - k + 2$$

where $N_{i,k}(t)$ = blending function
$\quad\quad k$ = parameter that controls the order of continuity

and

$$N_{i,1}(t) = \begin{cases} 1 & \text{if } u_i \leq t < u_{i+1} \\ 0 & \text{otherwise} \end{cases}$$

$$N_{i,k}(t) = \frac{(t - u_i)N_{i,k-1}(t)}{u_{i+k-1} - u_i} + \frac{(u_{i+k} - t)N_{i+1,k-1}(t)}{u_{i+k} - u_{i+1}}$$

where

$$u_i = \begin{cases} 0 & \text{if } i < k \\ i - k + 1 & k \leq i \leq n \\ n - k + 2 & i > n \end{cases}$$

and zero/zero = zero.

Both Bezier and B-spline curves can be drawn in a seemingly natural way (i.e., the curve is variation diminishing, axis independent, and multivalued). However, the B-spline has local control, which enables a user to define a shape without connecting many pieces of curve together. Figure 2.24 shows a comparison of two curves drawn by the Bezier and B-spline methods with the same set of control points.

Both the Bezier and B-spline methods can be extended to define curved surfaces. For surfaces, two parameters (t, s) are required. Using a Cartesian product method, a Bezier surface can be written as

$$P(t, s) = \sum_{i=0}^{n} \sum_{j=0}^{m} P_{i,j}B_{i,n}(t)B_{j,m}(S)$$

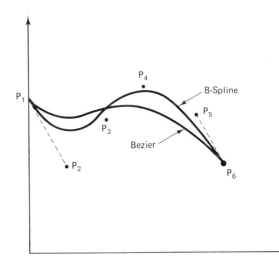

Fig. 2.24. Comparison of Bezier and B-Spline curves.

$B_{i,n}(t)$ and $B_{j,m}(s)$ are similar blending functions. In a Bezier surface, a total of $(n + 1) \times (m + 1)$ control points arranged in a mesh are necessary.

A B-spline surface also can be written as

$$P(t, S) = \sum_{i=0}^{n} \sum_{j=0}^{m} P_{i,j} N_{i,j}(t) N_{j,1}(S)$$

requiring the same constraints and allowing the same flexibility as the Bezier method.

2.3.5 Geometric Transformation

No matter how well an object is modeled, we still must display it in a manner that allows us easily to perceive its detail. Geometric transformations are an important tool for generating images and manipulating primitives. They can be used to define the location of an object relative to other objects. Generally, any image model can be viewed from any point and direction as a three-dimensional image or translated into a two-dimensional perspective view.

Basic transformations include translation, scaling, rotation, and mirror imaging. These transformations are represented mathematically in matrix form and pictorially in Figure 2.25. Any point, V, in the original coordinate system (x, y, z) can be transformed to some other point, V', in a new system (x', y', z') using the relationship

$$V' = V \cdot T$$

In viewing an object, we need to define two sets of coordinates: (1) the object's coordinates (the original coordinate definition), and (2) the "viewer's" coordinate position. In Figure 2.26a, the object is viewed at a distance. Figure 2.26b shows the object viewed from a standard eye location. The object in Figure 2.26c has been transformed using the following sequence:

1. Translate to location (a, b, c).
2. Rotate about x (-90 degrees).
3. Mirror image on X.

The concatenated transformation matrix can be written as follows. Let $\theta = -90$ degrees:

$$T = \begin{bmatrix} 1 & 0 & 0 & 0 \\ 0 & 1 & 0 & 0 \\ 0 & 0 & 1 & 0 \\ -a & -b & -c & 1 \end{bmatrix} \begin{bmatrix} 1 & 0 & 0 & 0 \\ 0 & \cos\theta & \sin\theta & 0 \\ 0 & -\sin\theta & \cos\theta & 0 \\ 0 & 0 & 0 & 1 \end{bmatrix} \begin{bmatrix} -1 & 0 & 0 & 0 \\ 0 & 1 & 0 & 0 \\ 0 & 0 & 1 & 0 \\ 0 & 0 & 0 & 1 \end{bmatrix}$$

2.3.6 Perspective Transformation

The next graphical issue to be discussed concerns the development of a methodology to display a three-dimensional object on a two-dimensional CRT or plotter. In engineering drawing, there are either multiview drawings or perspective drawings.

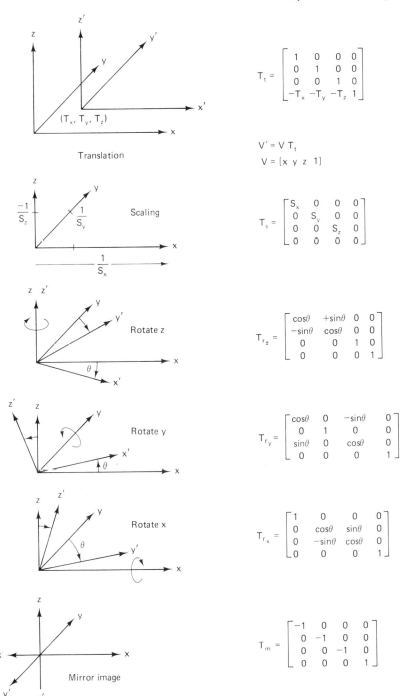

$$T_t = \begin{bmatrix} 1 & 0 & 0 & 0 \\ 0 & 1 & 0 & 0 \\ 0 & 0 & 1 & 0 \\ -T_x & -T_y & -T_z & 1 \end{bmatrix}$$

Translation

$V' = V\,T_t$
$V = [x \; y \; z \; 1]$

$$T_s = \begin{bmatrix} S_x & 0 & 0 & 0 \\ 0 & S_y & 0 & 0 \\ 0 & 0 & S_z & 0 \\ 0 & 0 & 0 & 0 \end{bmatrix}$$

Scaling

$$T_{r_z} = \begin{bmatrix} \cos\theta & +\sin\theta & 0 & 0 \\ -\sin\theta & \cos\theta & 0 & 0 \\ 0 & 0 & 1 & 0 \\ 0 & 0 & 0 & 1 \end{bmatrix}$$

Rotate z

$$T_{r_y} = \begin{bmatrix} \cos\theta & 0 & -\sin\theta & 0 \\ 0 & 1 & 0 & 0 \\ \sin\theta & 0 & \cos\theta & 0 \\ 0 & 0 & 0 & 1 \end{bmatrix}$$

Rotate y

$$T_{r_x} = \begin{bmatrix} 1 & 0 & 0 & 0 \\ 0 & \cos\theta & \sin\theta & 0 \\ 0 & -\sin\theta & \cos\theta & 0 \\ 0 & 0 & 0 & 1 \end{bmatrix}$$

Rotate x

$$T_m = \begin{bmatrix} -1 & 0 & 0 & 0 \\ 0 & -1 & 0 & 0 \\ 0 & 0 & -1 & 0 \\ 0 & 0 & 0 & 1 \end{bmatrix}$$

Mirror image

Fig. 2.25. Transformations.

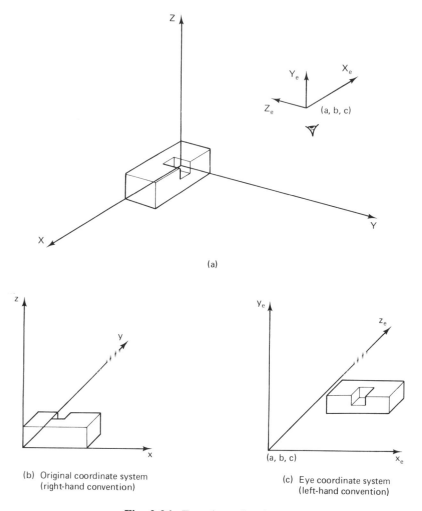

(a)

(b) Original coordinate system
(right-hand convention)

(c) Eye coordinate system
(left-hand convention)

Fig. 2.26. Transform the view.

The same basic approaches are applied to computer-generated drawings. For a multi-view (say three-view) display, each view is a simple two-dimensional orthographic drawing. The front, top, and side views can be generated by simply discarding y, z, and x coordinates, respectively. To construct a perspective drawing, a geometric transformation is required. A perspective drawing can be generated by projecting each point of an object onto a plane (called a display screen, shown in Figure 2.27) which is characterized by d, the distance from the eye. The X_s and Y_s axes of the display screen are parallel to the X_e and Y_e axes of the eye coordinate system. The transformed projection is shown in Figure 2.28. Point $P(x, y, z)$ in the eye coordinate system can

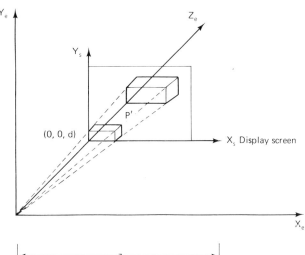

Fig. 2.27. Perspective projection of an object on a display screen.

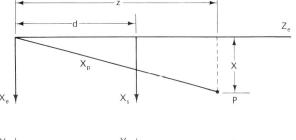

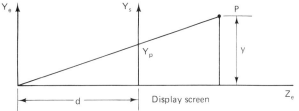

Fig. 2.28. Perspective projection of a point (x, y, z).

be projected onto the display screen as (x_p, y_p). By using the relationships of two similar triangles, x_p and y_p can be found.

$$\frac{x_p}{d} = \frac{x}{z} \qquad \frac{y_p}{d} = \frac{y}{z}$$

$$x_p = \frac{x}{z/d} \qquad y_p = \frac{y}{z/d}$$

All points in the eye coordinate system except those on the eye plane $(Z = 0)$ can be transformed. Clipping, a process to discard views outside the screen, is also necessary to eliminate invisible lines (line segments outside the drawing window and lines hidden by a surface).

2.3.7 Data Structure

Each geometric model of an object in a CAD system is represented by a set of data. The data consist of numerical values, names, codes, and symbols. These data are stored in computer memory in an organized manner. This organization represents the relationship of each data element to other elements: Included in these relationships is the topological relationship of the surface geometry. There are also other relationships, such as names and their associated geometries. A more complete survey on the different types of data structures for computer graphics can be found in two technical papers by Williams [1971] and Grays [1967]. In this section only a general data structure of CAD will be described.

As discussed in Section 2.3.3, an object can be represented by its geometry, topology, and ancillary information. This information can be stored in a list structure. (This list structure is discussed more fully in Chapter 4). By using data pointers, each element geometry (i.e., vertex, edges, faces, etc.) can be connected. A simple data structure is illustrated in Figure 2.29. Although data structures for operational CAD systems are more complicated [Baer 1979], the basic concept is similar. In the figure, a tetrahedron is modeled and stored in a specific data base. The object (a tetrahedron) has four faces which are pictorially and relationally linked via a link list. A pointer in the "face list" links a face with its edges. Face 1 points to location 1 in the "edge list." Since the faces are comprised of polygons, the number of edges for each face must be stored. The first item in the edge list, therefore, represents the number of edges. In the figure, edge 1 is represented by the data "3, 3, 4, 5," where the first 3 indicates that there are three edges: 3, 4, and 5. Each edge has two vertices (edge 3 has V_1 and V_3). Finally, a vertex may store all the coordinates of vertices.

When objects are represented by polyhedrons with planar polygons, the data structure in Figure 2.29 is sufficient. However, not all components in mechanical design can be modeled using such polyhedrons. Therefore, additional data elements must be stored. Holes are the most common shape in mechanical design and cannot be stored as a simple polyhedron. A hole can be represented as two circles and two virtual edges. The implication of virtual edges implies that they are the projection of a curved surface onto a two-dimensional display screen. For holes, circles, and other curves and curved surfaces, a code is necessary to distinguish them from polyhedron surfaces. To avoid redundant computation during some image manipulation, it is sometimes desirable to have "face" equations stored. An additional pointer is therefore necessary to link the parameter list. An example of the data structure for a research/commercial available system is shown in Figure 2.30. BUILD is a system written by Braid at Cambridge University. The commercial system Romulus, marketed by Evans and Sutherland, is also based on BUILD.

For manufacturing purposes, technological information, such as dimensions,

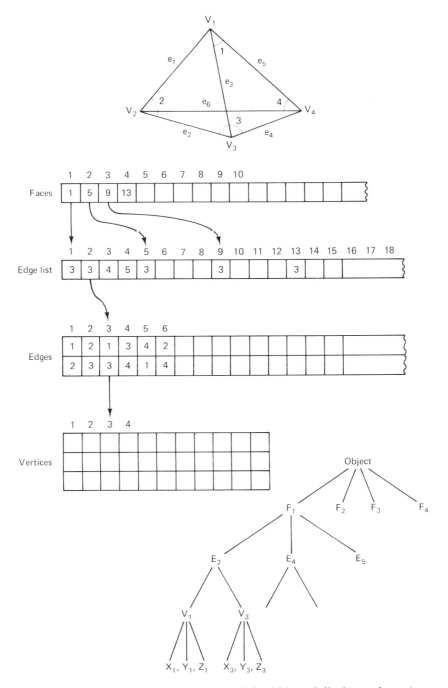

Fig. 2.29. Simple data structure. (The link within each list is not shown.)

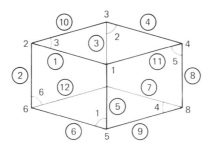

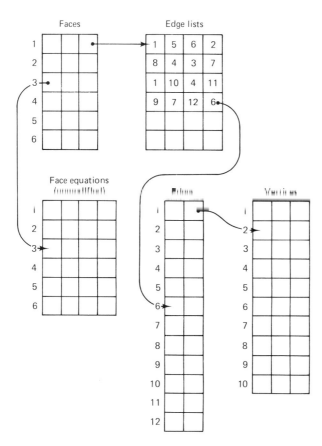

Fig. 2.30. BUILD data structure. [Baer 1979. This figure first appeared in Baer, A., Eastman, C. and Henrion, M. 'Geometric modelling: a survey' Computer-Aided Design, Volume II Number 5 (September 1979) Published by Butterworth Scientific Ltd., PO Box 63, Westbury House, Bury Street, Guildford, Surrey GU2 5BU, UK.]

tolerances, and geometric tolerances, are essential. They must also be included in constructing the CAD data structure. Most current systems explicitly (or more appropriately externally) define such information in a manner similar to the way in which a draftsman would. Dimensioning and tolerancing information is not implicit defined within the model. For explicit dimensioning another list is added to store the dimensioning information. However, some systems, such as PADL [Voelcker 1977], use symbolic dimensioning. In such systems, dimensions are measured directly from the model. However, geometric tolerances are not available directly from the model; that is, the model always shows perfect geometric tolerances. The data structure must be expanded to include space for storing tolerance information.

Since most CAD systems use different data structures, it is usually not possible to move data directly from one system to another. With the increasing need to develop a common data exchange, a joint effort was undertaken by industry and the National Bureau of Standards with the support of U.S. Air Force. The project resulted in a data exchange standard—IGES (Initial Graphics Exchange Specification) [Nagel 1980]. It was later adopted as an ANSI standard. Several existing commercially available CAD systems already have preprocessors and post processors to read and create IGES files. A survey of some three-dimensional modeling systems is shown in Table 2.4.

2.3.8 Geometric Modeling for Process Planning

In the preceding section, the fundamentals of computer-aided design were discussed. In this section a discussion of three-dimensional representation schemes and their application to process planning is presented.

There are seven different types of graphic representation schemes:

1. Wire frame
2. Primitive instancing
3. Spatial occupancy enumeration
4. Cell decomposition
5. Constructive solid geometry (CSG)
6. Boundary representation
7. Sweeping

Of these, wire-frame systems are the most commonly used display representation. Most commercially available computer-aided drafting systems are wire-frame representations. In such systems, objects are represented by points, lines, curves, circles, and so on (Figure 2.31c). A wire frame is not considered a solid model because it does not provide a complete or unambiguous representation of a part.

Pure primitive instancing is one kind of solid representation (Figure 2.31d). It can be used to represent a family of objects. One application of pure primitive instancing is GT coding [Requicha 1980].

Spatial occupancy enumeration (SOE) records all spatial cells that are occupied by the object (Figure 2.31e). SOE is equivalent to storing the physical object in sections. To describe the object accurately, very small cells must be used. The massive memory required for even small objects makes this representation virtually useless in engineering design.

Cell decomposition is a general class of spatial occupancy enumeration. The representation is difficult to create. A solid is decomposed into simple solid cells with no holes, whose interiors are pairwise disjoint (Figure 2.31f). A solid is the result of "gluing" component cells that satisfy certain "boundary-matching" conditions.

Constructive solid geometry (CSG) is a superior system for creating three-dimensional models. Using primitive shapes (Figure 2.32) as building blocks, CSG employs Boolean set operators to construct an object (Figure 2.31a). Because CSG

Table 2.4. SOME THREE-DIMENSIONAL MODELING SYSTEMS

Name	AD2000	BDS/GLIDE	BUILD-1	COMPAC	EUCLID(F)
Developer	Hanratty	Eastman et al	Braid	Spur et al	Brun et al
Institution	Manufacturing and Consulting Services Inc.	Carnegie-Mellon University	Cambridge University	Technical University of Berlin	LIMSI
Country	USA	USA	UK	Germany	France
Host/ Implementation Language	FORTRAN	BLISS	FORTRAN SAL	FORTRAN	FORTRAN FOCAL
Machine	Many different Machines	DEC PDP-10	TITAN PDP-7	DEC PDP-10	UNIVAC-1110
Interactive/ Batch	interactive	interactive	interactive	batch	either
Purpose/area	commercial: Engin. & NC	research: database for Arch. & Engin.	research: Engin. & NC	commercial: Engin. & NC	commercial: Engin. & Arch.
Shaded Graphics	-	-	Yes	Yes	-
Curved Surfaces	splines, toros and others	approximate cylinders & cones	cylinder	cylinder & others	circle & curve segments
Shape Operators	intersection (of faces)	union intersection difference	union intersection difference addition	union difference	-
Solid definition Method	generating lines and surfaces	Euler operations	primitive solids	generating lines, primitives	face list

Source: This table first appeared in Baer, A., Eastman, C. and Henrion, M. 'Geometric modelling: a survey' Computer-Aided Design, Volume II Number 5 (September 1979) Published by Butterworth Scientific Ltd., PO Box 63, Westbury House, Bury Street, Guildford, Surrey GU2 5BU, UK.

cannot directly link to a drawing procedure, a transform of CSG to another representation is required. Since the display is generated by another representation (usually a boundary representation, as shown in Figure 2.31b), and the reverse process of translating back to CSG is nontrival, direct manipulation of the graphics on the screen is difficult. The input to certain process planning systems (e.g., AUTAP) has been considered using a type of CSG model.

Boundary representations are also used to identify an object. In these systems, objects are represented by their bounding faces. Faces are further broken down and represented by edges and vertices. Boundary models are very difficult to create, but can provide easy graphic interaction.

Sweeping is another powerful modeling tool for certain types of geometry. There are two types of sweeping: translation and rotation (Figure 2.31g). Translation sweeping of a rectangle produces a box. Rotational sweeping of the same rectangle produces a cylinder. Rotation sweeping can be used to create turned parts. The best use of

Table 2.4. **(Continued)**

EUCLID(S)	GEOMED	GEOMAP	'HOSAKA'	PADL	TIPS-1
Engeli	Baumgart	Hosaka & Kimura	Hosaka & Kimura	Voelcker et al	Okino et al
Institution	Stanford University	University of Tokyo	University of Tokyo	University of Rochester	Hokkaido University
Switzerland	USA	Japan	Japan	USA	Japan
SYMBAL	ASSEMBLY	FORTRAN	GIL	FORTRAN	FORTRAN
CDC6500	DEC PDP-10	TOSBAC 5600 (GE635)	TOSBAC 5600 (GE635)	PDP-11/45	FACOM machines
batch	interactive	batch	batch	interactive	batch
commercial: Engin. & NC	research: visual shape recognition	research: Engin. & NC	research: Engin. & NC	commercial: Engin. & NC	commercial: Engin. & NC
-	-	-	Yes	-	-
(version: Bezier patches)	-	approx. cylinders cones	-	cylinders	cylinder sphere bicubic patch
union intersection difference addition	union intersection difference	union intersection difference	union intersection difference	union intersection difference	union difference
face list primitives solids	Euler operations	primitives	intersecting planes	primitive solids	primitive solids

translation sweeping is in cutter path simulation. Simulation can create intermediate surfaces, which can then be used to determine fixture clamping points and robot gripping points.

With the taxonomy of graphical representation described above, some general problems of current part representation systems can be identified. These problems include:

1. The lack of embedded tolerancing information
2. The inability to represent special manufacturing features (i.e., drill angles of a hole)
3. Poor graphical interaction
4. A lack of data interchange between representations
5. The lack of a method of identifying differences in two given models automatically (especially when they have different orientations in space)

Since there is no easy way to identify surfaces requiring machining using any of the geometric representations mentioned previously, the best immediate solution is to use a human–computer interactive system to identify the surface. Wire frame, boundary representation, and sweeping are candidate graphic systems for interactive sys-

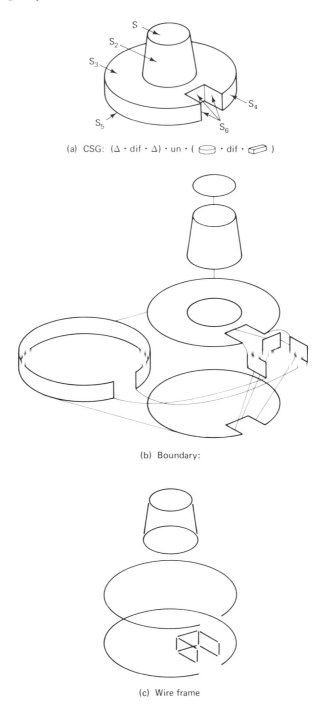

(a) CSG: $(\triangle \cdot \text{dif} \cdot \triangle) \cdot \text{un} \cdot (\ominus \cdot \text{dif} \cdot \square)$

(b) Boundary:

(c) Wire frame

Fig. 2.31. Three-dimensional representation schemes.

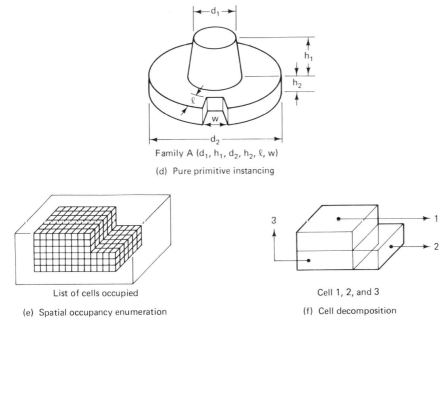

Family A (d_1, h_1, d_2, h_2, ℓ, w)

(d) Pure primitive instancing

List of cells occupied

(e) Spatial occupancy enumeration

Cell 1, 2, and 3

(f) Cell decomposition

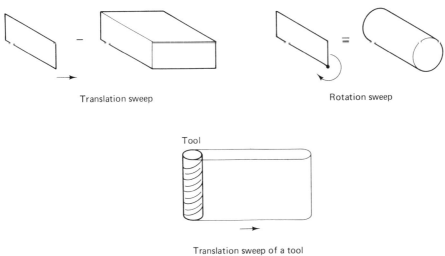

Translation sweep

Rotation sweep

Tool

Translation sweep of a tool

(g) Sweeping

Fig. 2.31. (Continued)

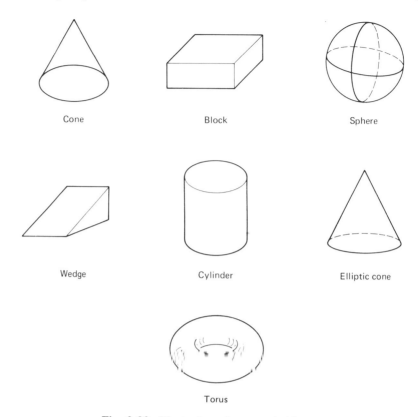

Cone   Block   Sphere

Wedge   Cylinder   Elliptic cone

Torus

Fig. 2.32. Illustration of some primitives.

tems. Since sweeping can only model a subset of objects in the object domain, it cannot be used independently. Most currently available commercial CAD systems are based on a wire-frame internal representation.

In order to use a CAD system as the frontend for computer-aided process planning, the following capabilities are required:

1. Location and interactive identification of lines and faces
2. Easy dimension retrieval
3. Tolerancing information storage and retrieval
4. Built-in special tags (i.e., drill angle for hole)
5. Capability of displaying multiple objects

The front-end interface should be designed so that it is independent of any representation or specific system. Therefore, any system can be modified to support the above mentioned five requirements in a single system; however, alphabetics must be stored separately in an array.

2.4 GROUP TECHNOLOGY CODING

Both drafting and geometric modeling are detailed representations of an engineering design. They provide detailed information concerning the component to be
made, and are essential in conveying the design for manufacturing. However, as with
many decision-making processes, too much information may make the decision more
difficult. For example, when one reads a magazine or journal, they seldom begin by
reading each sentence on successive pages. Instead, they peruse the table of contents
first in order to locate interesting technical information. By doing so, candidate articles
can be located more quickly. However, the title may not convey all of the necessary
information. Therefore, the reader would typically scan the abstract. The abstract is
a summary that represents the article without great detail. Reading the abstract of an
article normally provides us with the insight to continue the reading. Parts lists
corresponding to a table of contents have been around for a long time, and although
it is impractical to write abstracts for CAD model, a similar concept can be applied
using coding.

Group technology (GT) as described in Chapter 1 is an appropriate tool for this
purpose. Coding, a GT technique, can be used to model a component without all the
detail. When constructing a coding system for a component's representation, there are
several factors to be considered. They include:

1. The population of components (i.e., rotational, prismatic, deep drawn, sheet
   metal, etc.)
2. The detail the code should represent
3. The code structure: chain, hierarchical, or hybrid
4. The digital representation (i.e., binary, octal, decimal, alphanumeric, hexadecimal, etc.)

The population of components contributes to the variety of shapes. For example,
the population in the United States includes virtually all races which exist on earth.
In a sense, it is necessary to distinguish race, hair color, eye color, and so on.
However, in a nation such as China or Japan, it is not worthwhile to record skin color,
hair color, and so on, because these items are virtually invariant. In component
coding, it is also true that only those features that vary need to be included in the code.
When designing or using a coding scheme, two properties must hold true: The code
must be (1) unambiguous, and (2) complete.

We can define coding as a function H, which maps components from a population
space P into a coded space C (Figure 2.33). An unambiguous code can be defined (for
component i) as

$$i \in P \Rightarrow \exists \text{ only one } j \in C \Rightarrow j = H(i)$$

Completeness can be defined as

$$\forall i \in P \quad \exists j \in C \Rightarrow j = H(i)$$

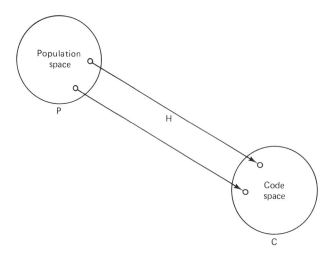

Fig. 2.33. Mapping from population space to code space.

The two properties on page 75 suggest that each component in a population has its own unique code. However, normally it is desirable to have several components in the population share one code.

The code need be concise. If a 100-digit code and a 10-digit code can both represent components in P completely and unambiguously, the 10-digit code is more desirable. However, when more detail is required, a longer code is normally necessary. For example, the basic Opitz code (shown in Figure 1.19) uses five digits to describe the shape. Five digits can represent 10^5 combinations. With this set it is not possible to show a large amount of detail of a component. Some codes are significantly longer: for example, the KK-3 of Japan [Japan Society 1980], which has 21 digits and contains multiple digits for single features, and MICLASS of TNO [Houtzeel and Schilperoort 1970], which has a 12-digit code. For some computer-aided process planning systems (e.g., APPAS [Wysk 1977]), a detailed surface code is used instead of a code for the entire component. The decision on how much detail the code should represent depends solely on the application. The selection of a code structure again depends on the application. Table 1.2 provides a comprehensive selection criterion.

The last consideration in coding system construction is the code digits. Several positional alternatives can be selected (from binary to alphanumeric). However, this selection yields different precision for the different schemes. For example, an N-digit code with different coding features yields the following combinations of code.

Binary	2	$(0, 1)$
Octal	8	$(0, 1, \ldots, 8)$
Decimal	10	$(0, 1, \ldots, 9)$
Hexadecimal	16	$(0, 1, \ldots, 9, A, \ldots, F)$
Alphanumeric	$(25 + 10)$	$(0, 1, \ldots, 9, A, \ldots, Z)$

Although alphanumeric systems are the most compact (the same amount of information can be represented by fewer digits), the difficulty of handling both numerical and alphabetical characters make alphanumerics less attractive. Furthermore, in many computer languages, a numeric can be stored in a single word, but alphabetics must be stored in an array.

2.4.1 Code Contents

When using a code to represent an engineering design, it is important to represent the basic features of the design. As a human being can be represented by his or her height, weight, color, hair, eye color, and sex, an engineering component can be represented by its basic shape, secondary features, size, tolerance, critical dimensions, material, and so on. For process planning, it is desirable to have codes that can distinguish unique production families (as discussed in Chapter 1).

Fortunately, most components of similar shape can be produced by the same set of processes. However, the opposite is not true as frequently. Shape elements normally dictate the manufacturing process. Secondary features such as auxiliary holes, gear teeth, threads, chamfers, and so on, are also important and can dictate a different set of process plans. From only the shape, there is no way of telling how large or small a component is. The production methods for a 2-cm^3 model airplane engine block are definitely different from those for the engine block of a 6-liter V-8 engine. Although similar processes may be applied to both engine blocks, the machines, tools, and material-handling methods will probably be very different. Size, tolerance, and surface finish can also affect the required processes. The price of a precision component (as was shown in Figure 1.3) increases as the tolerance is tightened. This is usually the result of a precision component requiring several more processes than a component of standard tolerance specification. For example, a milled workpiece will not require an addition finishing process if the specified surface finish is 125 μin. or above on a flat surface. However, if the surface-finish requirement is specified as 4 μin., a careful finishing cut on the last milling pass followed by grinding, polishing, and lapping may be necessary.

The workpiece material is also a factor that must be considered. Tools for machining aluminum are not appropriate for machining alloy steel. Feeds and speeds used for machining also depend on the material.

Since a coding system transforms the properties and requirements listed above into a code, this information should somehow be tied into a process planning system. Some of the systems that have been successfully implemented (process planning systems) are illustrated in the following sections.

2.4.2 The Opitz System

The Opitz coding system [Opitz 1970] is probably the best known coding system. It was developed by H. Opitz of the Aachen Tech University in West Germany. The Opitz code uses a mixed code structure. However, except for the first digit, it resembles a chain structure more closely (Figure 1.17).

The Opitz code consists of a geometric code and a supplementary code. The geometric code can represent parts of the following variety: rotational, flat, long, and cubic. A dimension ratio is further used in classifying the geometry; the length/diameter ratio is used to classify rotational components, and length/width and length/height ratios are used to classify nonrotational components. The Opitz geometric code uses five decimal digits, each representing component class, basic shape, rotational surface machining, plane surface machining, auxiliary holes, gear teeth, and forming. Primary, secondary, and auxiliary shapes can be represented using the five geometric digits.

A supplemental code containing four digits is usually appended to the Opitz code. The first digit represents the major dimension (either diameter or edge length). The approximate component size can then be determined by using the dimension ratio specified in the geometry. The dimension range is specified from 0.8 to 80. Dimensions of less than 0.8 and greater than 80 are represented by a 0 or 9 code, respectively. The material type, raw material shape, and accuracy are represented by digits 2, 3, and 4.

The Opitz code is concise and easy to use. It has been adopted by many companies as their coding subsystem. Several CAM-I CAPP systems currently use an Opitz-based coding system.

2.4.3 The CODE System

CODE is a coding and classification system developed by Manufacturing Data Systems, Inc. (MDSI) [Haan 1977]. CODE is an eight-digit code similar to the Opitz system. CODE however has a mixed code structure. Each digit of the code is represented by a hexidecimal value (most systems use decimal numbers). Using hexadecimal numbers allows more information to be represented with the same number of digits. The structure of the code is shown in Figure 2.34. CODE contains form and dimensional information, but does not include material or accuracy information.

CODE can be used to classify both rotational and nonrotational components. Because more digits in CODE are assigned to auxiliary shapes, better size information can be captured. Instead of classifying the ratio of dimensions, CODE directly classifies major dimensions. Since CODE uses two digits to classify dimensions, 16^2 sizes can be classified.

One distinct advantage of CODE is the ready-to-run software support system offered by MDSI. CODE is not only a coding and classification system, but also a data base system. Information related to the part, such as design data, process plan, and so on, can be stored and retrieved by CODE.

2.4.4 The KK-3 System

The KK-3 coding system is a general-purpose classification and coding system for machining parts. KK-3 was developed by the Japan Society for the Promotion of Machine Industry (JSPMI) [1980]. Parts to be classified are primarily metal cutting

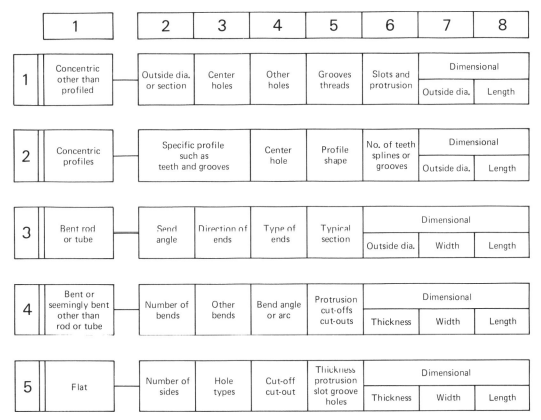

1	2	3	4	5	6	7	8

| 1 | Concentric other than profiled | Outside dia. or section | Center holes | Other holes | Grooves threads | Slots and protrusion | Dimensional | |
| | | | | | | | Outside dia. | Length |

| 2 | Concentric profiles | Specific profile such as teeth and grooves | Center hole | Profile shape | No. of teeth splines or grooves | Dimensional | |
| | | | | | | Outside dia. | Length |

| 3 | Bent rod or tube | Send angle | Direction of ends | Type of ends | Typical section | Dimensional | | |
| | | | | | | Outside dia. | Width | Length |

| 4 | Bent or seemingly bent other than rod or tube | Number of bends | Other bends | Bend angle or arc | Protrusion cut-offs cut-outs | Dimensional | | |
| | | | | | | Thickness | Width | Length |

| 5 | Flat | Number of sides | Hole types | Cut-off cut-out | Thickness protrusion slot groove holes | Dimensional | | |
| | | | | | | Thickness | Width | Length |

Fig. 2.34. Summary of CODE major divisions. [Courtesy of Manufacturing Data Systems Inc.]

and grinding components. KK-3 was first presented in 1976, and uses a 21-digit decimal system. The code structure for rotational components is shown in Figure 2.35. Because KK-3 is much greater in length than Opitz and CODE, more information can be represented. The KK-3 code includes two digits for component name (functional name) classification. The first digit classifies the general function, such as gears, shafts, drive and moving parts, fixing parts, and so on. The second digit describes more detailed functions. For example, included in a single family, there are spur gears, bevel gears, worm gears, and so on. With two digits, KK-3 can classify 100 functional names for rotational and nonrotational components. However, at times, this can be as confusing as complete. KK-3 also classifies materials using two-code digits. The first digit classifies material type, and the second digit classifies shape of the raw material. Dimensions and dimension ratios are also classified. Some redundancy can be found; that is, length, diameter, and length/diameter ratios are classified for rotation components. Shape detail and process type are classified in KK-3 using 13 digits of code (much more detail than either the Opitz or CODE systems). An example of

Digit	Items	(Rotational components)	
1	Parts name	General classification	
2		Detail classification	
3	Materials	General classification	
4		Detail classification	
5	Chief dimensions	Length	
6		Diameter	
7	Primary shapes and ratio of major dimensions		
8	Shape-details and kinds of processes	External surface	External surface and outer primary shape
9			Concentric screw threaded parts
10			Functional cut-off parts
11			Extraordinary shaped parts
12			Forming
13			Cylindrical surface
14		Internal surface	Internal primary shape
15			Internal curved surface
16			Internal flat surface and cylindrical surface
17		End surface	
18		Nonconcentric holes	Regularly located holes
19			Special holes
20		Noncutting process	
21	Accuracy		

Fig. 2.35. Structure of the KK-3 (rotational components). [Courtesy of the Japan Society for the promotion of Machine Industry.]

coding a component using KK-3 is illustrated in Figure 2.36. A modified version of KK-1 (an earlier version of KK-3) has been reported for use in computer-aided process planning (Japan Society 1980).

2.4.5 The MICLASS System

The MICLASS system was developed by TNO of Holland, and is currently maintained in the United States by Organization for Industrial Research [Houtzeel 1976a–c]. It is a chain-structured code of 12 digits. The code is designed to be universal; therefore, it includes both design and manufacturing information. Informa-

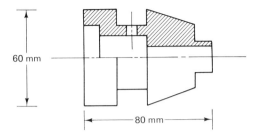

Code digit	Item	Component condition	Code
1	} Name	Control valve	0
2		(others)	9
3	} Material	Copper bar	7
4			
5	Dimension length	80 mm	2
6	Dimension diameter	60 mm	2
7	Primary shape and ratio of chief dimension	L/D 1.3	2
8	External surface	With functional tapered surface	3
9	Concentric screw	None	0
10	Functional cutoff	None	0
11	Extraordinary shaped	None	0
12	Forming	None	0
13	Cylindrical surface ≥ 3	None	0
14	Internal primary	Piercing hole with dia. variation, NO cutoff	2
15	Internal curved surface	None	0
16	Internal flat surface	None	0
17	End surface	Flat	0
18	Regularly located hole	Holes located on circumferential line	3
19	Spacial hole	None	0
20	Noncutting process	None	0
21	Accuracy	Grinding process on external surface	4

Fig. 2.36. Example of a KK-3 coding system.

tion such as main shape, shape elements, position of the elements, main dimension, ratio of the dimensions, auxiliary dimension, form tolerance, and the machinability of the material is included (Figure 2.37). An additional eighteen digits of code are also available for user-specified information (i.e., part function, lot size, major machining operation, etc.). These supplemental digits provide flexibility for the system expansion. MICLASS was also one of the earliest interactive coding systems (Figure 2.38 illustrates an interactive coding session). MICLASS has been adapted by many U.S. industries. Several application programs based on MICLASS are currently available, such as MIPLAN and MULTICAPP variant process planning systems.

Code position

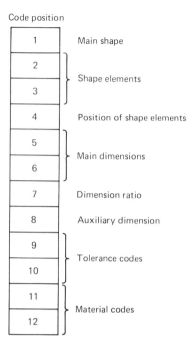

1	Main shape
2	Shape elements
3	
4	Position of shape elements
5	Main dimensions
6	
7	Dimension ratio
8	Auxiliary dimension
9	Tolerance codes
10	
11	Material codes
12	

Fig. 2.37. MICLASS code structure. [Courtesy of Organization for Industrial Research, Inc.]

2.4.6 DCLASS Systems

The DCLASS system was developed by Del Allen at Brigham Young University [Allen and Smith 1980]. DCLASS was intended to be a decision-making and classification system (thus the name DCLASS). DCLASS is a tree-structured system (Figure 2.39) which can generate codes for components, materials, processes, machines, and tools. For components, an eight-digit code is used:

Digits 1–3	Basic shape
Digit 4	Form feature
Digit 5	Size
Digit 6	Precision
Digits 7 and 8	Material

In DCLASS, each branch represents a condition, and a code can be found at the terminal (junction) of each branch. Multiple passes of the decision tree allow a complete code to be found. Figure 2.39 illustrates the process by showing a portion of the decision tree for components. One pass on this tree will generate the first three digits of the code. Code construction is established using certain roots (N nodes and E nodes). At N nodes, all branches can be true. At E nodes, only one branch can be true.

The DCLASS system is not only a coding system but also a decision support system. A generative process planning system using DCLASS has also been reported by Allen [Allen and Smith 1979, 1980].

```
RUN $MICLAS

    MICLAS  VERSION 2.0


ENTER THE CLASSIFICATION ROUTE (1 TO 9) >1

3 MAIN DIMENSIONS (WHEN ROT. PART D,L AND 0) >2.9375,2,0

   DEVIATION OF ROTATIONAL FORM >NO

   CONCENTRIC SPIRAL GROOVES >NO

TURNING ON OUTERCONTOUR (EXCEPT ENDFACES) >YES

   SPECIAL GROOVES OR CONE(S) OR PROFILE(S)  ON OUTERCONTOUR >NO

   ALL MACH. EXT. DIAM. AND ROT. FACES VISIBLE FROM ONE END
   (EXC. ENDFACES + GROOVE(S) >YES

TURNING ON INNERCONTOUR >YES

   INTERNAL SPECIAL GROOVES OR CONE(S) OR PROFILE(S) >NO

   ALL INT.DIA. + ROT.FACES VISIBLE FROM 1 END(EXC. GROOVES >YES

ALL DIA. + ROT.FACES VISIBLE FROM ONE END (EXCL. ENDFACES >YES

ECC. HOLING AND/OR FACING AND/OR SLOTTING >YES

   ON INNERFORM AND/OR FACES (INC. ENDFACES) >YES

   ON OUTERFORM >NO

ONLY ENCLOSED INTERNAL SLOTS >NO

ECC. MACHINING ONLY ONE SENSE >Y

   ONLY HOLES ON A BOLTCIRCLE (AT LEAST 3 HOLES) >YES

FORM-OR THREADING TOLERANCE >NO

DIAM. OR ROT. FACE ROUGHNESS LESS THAN 33 RU (MICRO-INCHES) >YES

   SMALLEST POSITIONING TOL. FIELD >.016

   SMALLEST LENGTHTOL. FIELD >.0313


CLASS.NR.= 1271 3231 3100 0000 0000 0000 0000 00
****************************************************

DIGIT TO CHANGE >
CONTINUE [Y/N]>N
TT0  --  STOP
>
```

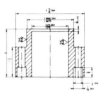

DRAWING TITLE	TOLERANCES	MATERIAL:
BUSHING	Fractional · 1:64	CC 15
DRAWING NO:	Decimal · .003	125 / (25)
7		ALL OVER EXCEPT AS NOTED

Drawing of Part

Fig. 2.38. Coding session of MICLASS. [Courtesy of Organization for Industrial Research, Inc.]

2.4.7 COFORM

COFORM (COding FOR Machining) was developed at Purdue University by Rose [1977]. COFORM is neither a commercial system nor a widely used system. COFORM is the coded input used by a generative process planning system (APPAS [Wysk 1977]) and is therefore different from other systems. Some of its specifics are worth discussing because of its uniqueness.

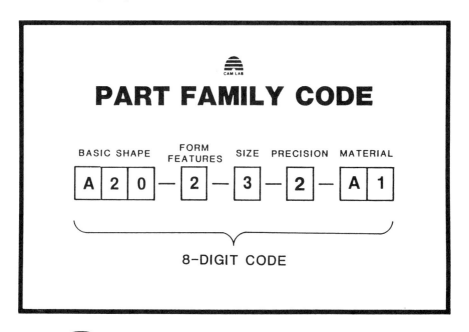

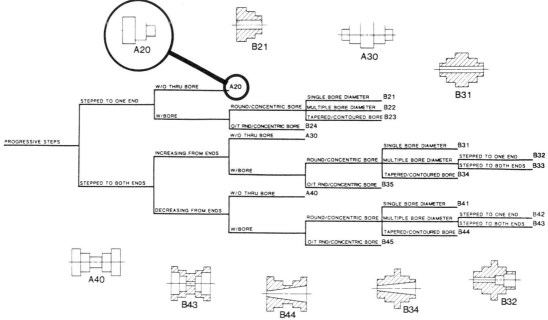

Fig. 2.39. DCLASS structure. [Courtesy of the CAM Lab., Brigham Young University.]

Rather than dealing with the entire part geometry, COFORM limits itself to the description of individuals machined surfaces (holes, slots, and general surfaces). The code describes each surface in terms of the attributes needed to select the appropriate machining process(es) and the related parameters (feed, speed, and depth of cut). Figure 2.40 contains a list of the attributes required to describe holes. The entire component can be described by decomposing it into several surfaces. However, COFORM does not contain a description of nonmachined features. Therefore, COFORM cannot be used for a CAD system even though it is quite detailed.

COFORM does not code each feature. Instead, it records the data values for some features (i.e., diameter, length, tolerances, etc). It is a component description system using mixed codes and data values.

ATRIB(1)   — Surface or hole identification number, ID number is user-assigned and can be between 1 and 99999

ATRIB(2)   — The type of surface of program entry being coded
    1 = round hole
    2 = plane or other surface
    3 = slot
    4 = symmetric turned surface
    5 = gear
    6 = spline
    7 = unround hole
    8 = other
    9 = end of information

ATRIB(3)   — ATRIB(3) is dependent on ATRIB(2). The following description is for (ATRIB(2) = 1):
    1 = simple, cylindrical hole
    2 = tapered or conic hole
    3 = threaded cylindrical hole
    4 = threaded tapered hole
    5 = cylindrical hole with keyway
    6 = noncylindrical hole with keyway
    7 = threaded hole with a keyway
    8 = hole used to locate a surface
    9 = hole used to locate another hole

ATRIB(4)   — The number of diameters or locating surfaces dependent on the current hole

ATRIB(5)   — Aterial type
    1 = gray cast iron
    2 = malleable iron
    3 = steel
    4 = steel forging

ATRIB(6)   — Material hardness (BHN)

ATRIB(7)   — Dimensionality of the hole-diameter

ATRIB(8)   — Tolerance on diameter-plus

ATRIB(9)   — Tolerance on diameter-minus

ATRIB(10)   — Surface finish — (side) — CLA

ATRIB(11)   — Length of diameter

ATRIB(12)   — Tolerance on length ± X

ATRIB(13)   — Direction cosine of surface

Fig. 2.40. Description of the attributes used in COFORM.

ATRIB(14) — Straightness

ATRIB(15) — Roundness

ATRIB(16) — Parallelism

ATRIB(17) — Perpendicularity

ATRIB(18) — Angularity

ATRIB(19) — Concentricity

ATRIB(20) — Symmetry

ATRIB(21) — True position

ATRIB(22) — Profile of a surface

ATRIB(23) — Profile of a line

ATRIB(24) — Cored hole indicator

ATRIB(25) — Maximum stock removal when hole is cored

ATRIB(26) — Initial surface condition indicator

ATRIB(27) — Chamfer code
        0 = no chamfer
        1 = chamfer
        2 = concave radius (inner fillet)
        3 = convex radius (outer fillet)

ATRIB(28) — Angle of chamfer or dimension of radius If ATRIB(28) = 1, $35° \leq$ angle $\leq 80°$

ATRIB(29) — Length of chamfer or radius (maximum)

ATRIB(30) — Tolerance of chamfer length

ATRIB(31) — Threads/inch (0 for no tapping operation)

ATRIB(32) — Thread tolerance

ATRIB(33) — Thread series
        1 = unified standard or American standard
        2 = others

ATRIB(34) — Bottom hole indication

ATRIB(35) — Bottom hole value

ATRIB(36) — Surface finish (bottom) — CLA

ATRIB(37) — Interrupter cut indicator

ATRIB(38) — Reference surface number

ATRIB(39) — Access surface indicator

ATRIB(40) — The number of holes to be produced by one tool; if ATRIB(40) is negating, minimum production time for each hole is to be obtained

Fig. 2.40 (Continued)

2.4.8 Closing Remarks

Process planning is necessary to plan the detailed processes for the production of a design. The input to a process planner or a process planning system is always a design. In this chapter various types of design representations have been discussed, from the most conventional design (drafting) to the modern CAD systems. An important design representation method which has been widely used in computer-aided process planning—GT coding—was also discussed.

It is necessary to understand the design data and its storage representation because the efficiency and accuracy of a system is greatly affected by the way information is represented and interpreted. Only after one understands the data can intelligent decisions be made. In Chapter 3 the knowledge needed to make these decisions in process planning will be discussed.

REVIEW QUESTIONS

2.1. Partial views in engineering drawing have long been used to clarify troublesome "detail areas" on a design. How difficult is it to generate partial views using a CAD system? Discuss the computational requirements.

2.2. Many computer scientists are overwhelmed by all of the tolerance specifications used on an engineering drawing, saying that the numerous specifications serve only to confuse the part description. Do these various methods of specification really serve a purpose? Defend or attack today's dimensioning and tolerance standard.

2.3. Gauges (*go/no go*) are frequently used to inspect parts. Create a set of gauges to determine the adequacy or inadequacy of the holes and pins shown in Figure P2.3.

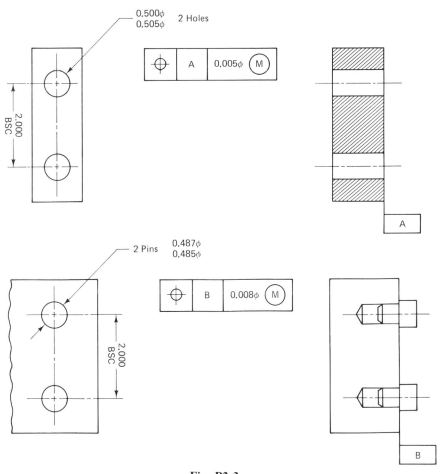

Fig. P2.3.

2.4. What are raster-scan and random-scan display systems? What is the difference(s) in the display systems?

2.5. Create a reduced graphics system that will draw and rotate a tetrahedron. How difficult would it be to expand this model into a general polyhedron? How user friendly is the model?

2.6. Code either the Bezier or the B-spline curve procedure into a computer-operable language. Will the computation requirements for either system be significant?

2.7. Describe a simple activity such as sorting as to the differences using binary, octal, decimal, hexidecimal, and alphanumeric codes. Are there advantages to any system?

2.8. The engineering drawings of six manufactured components are shown in Figure P2.8. Using the Opitz geometrical code, code each of the six parts. Assuming that these are to be only 6 to 10,000 items, propose a means of obtaining families besides a manual sort.

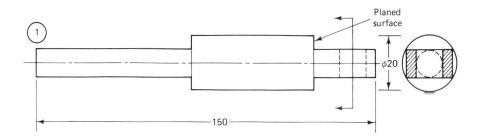

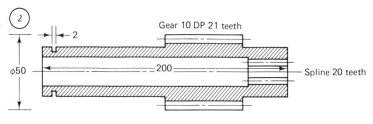

Fig. P.2.8

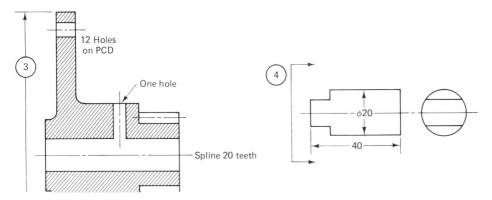

Fig. P.2.8 (Continued)

PROCESS ENGINEERING

Process planning is the activity that determines the appropriate procedures to transform a raw material into a final product. The final product is specified in the engineering design (either a drawing on paper or in a CAD model). Selecting the manufacturing processes to transform the raw material into finished specification is based on matching the design requirements with process capabilities. Process capability is the data base of knowledge for each process. It includes:

1. The shapes and size a process can produce
2. The dimensions and geometric tolerances that can be obtained by various processes
3. The surface finish attainable
4. The material removal rate
5. The relative cost
6. Other cutting characteristics/constraints

Process capability does not necessarily imply that all process selection is based on the information above. However, the more information considered in selecting a process, the more complete the result will be. For conventional process planning (where human planners are used), all process capability information comes either in the form of experience or in handbook lists and guides. A computer-aided process planning system functions based on this process capability information (see Section

3

1.3). A pure variant planning system is a pure retrieval system and is analogous to planning based on experience. In a variant planning system, standard plans are stored based on component shape. These plans are then retrieved based on the similarity of a coded part. Only some very basic information such as estimating machining time is calculated in the system. A generative system, however, makes processing, tooling, and other decisions via software program logic. To select an appropriate process(es), the process capabilities must be stored in the system.

The basic mechanisms of process selection are discussed in Chapter 4. Because the data structure of the process capabilities is planning method dependent, a discussion of process selection mechanisms and process capability information representations is presented in this chapter.

3.1 EXPERIENCE-BASED PLANNING

It is always true that the accumulation of experience is knowledge. Most of our knowledge comes either from our own experience or is passed on to us by others and is based on their experience. This is also true in the context of manufacturing processes. If we go back to the example of the farmer and blacksmith in Chapter 2, we can make a point of how experience works in a manufacturing environment. When the farmer verbally specified or drew a picture of the hoe he wanted, the blacksmith must have had a manufacturing method (process plan) in mind; otherwise, he would not have been able to make the hoe. The process plan the blacksmith created was neither a written one nor a complete one. However, in his mind he knew that he had some scrap iron in the back of his shop which he could use for the hoe. After retrieving the material, he heated it in his furnace until it reached red heat (hot working). He then completed the forging cycle by hand and hammer. Had the farmer asked "How do you know how to convert your scrap to my hoe?" the answer most assuredly would have been something like, "I've been in the trade for 30 years—experience told me."

Even in this space age, many process planning activities still rely on the experience of process planners. Where do process planners obtain their experience? From earlier training as machinists (most typical), from books, or from discussions with colleagues. This kind of information can be passed from person to person and generation to generation. However, there are some problems associated with such a planning base.

1. Experience requires a significant period to accumulate.
2. Experience represents only approximate, not exact knowledge.
3. Experience is not directly applicable to new processes or new systems.

Because of the problems noted above, we need to seek other ways to represent our process capability knowledge base so that it might be preserved and installed as a decision support system on a computer.

3.1.1 Machinist's Handbooks

One way to store process capability information is to print it in handbooks. This has long been a standard manufacturing practice. Process capability information is usually presented in tables, figures, or listed as guidelines. Large manufacturers typically prepare their own handbooks for internal use. Therefore, the knowledge is kept, but has traditionally been "proprietary." Handbooks can serve both as a reference and as a guide for process selection. Figure 3.1 represents some typical information of process capability (surface-finish ranges). The surface-finish chart shows the limiting extremes of several processes. For example, a flat surface of 8 μin. surface finish can be machined by grinding, polishing, and lapping. It can rarely be achieved by milling, yet a surface finish of 8 μin. is possible using a finish milling cut. Other information, such as process accuracy, can be found in similar tables or charts (see, Table 3.1). In Table 3.1, an accuracy class 10 for drilling is considered highly accurate, but for reaming, this is only considered moderately accurate.

Some process capability information is listed as guidelines, so process planners can follow some general rules. For example, the following guidelines can be applied to produce holes.

GENERAL MOTORS DRAFTING STANDARDS

SURFACE TEXTURE — ROUGHNESS, WAVINESS AND LAY

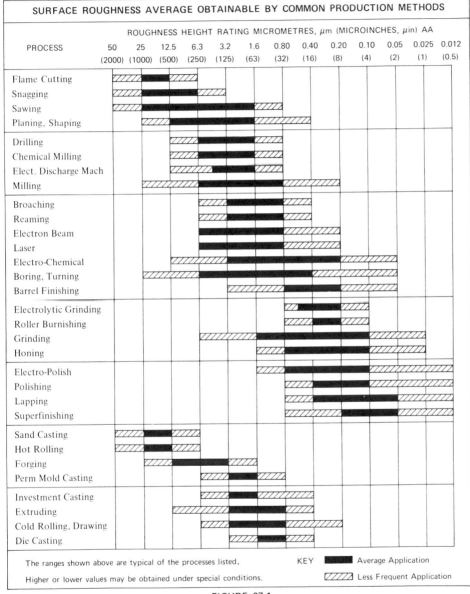

FIGURE 07.1

Fig. 3.1. Surface-finish ranges. [Courtesy of General Motors Corporation (taken from GM Drafting Standards.)]

Table 3.1. PRINCIPLES OF MACHINING BY CUTTING, ABRASION, AND EROSION

Classes (according to ISO) — columns 1 to 12 are "of accuracy"; columns 13 to 26 are "of surface quality".

Machining method	1 to 3	4	5	6	7	8	9	10	11	12	13	14 to 16	1	2	3	4	5	6	7	8	9	10	11	12	13	14
I. CHIP REMOVING PROCESSES																										
Turning				●	●	○	○	○	x	x	−	−		−	−	−	x	x	○	○	●					
Boring				●	●	○	○	○	x	x	−	−		−	−	−	x	x	○	○	●					
Drilling							●	○	x	x	−				−	−	x	x	○	●						
Reaming			●	●	○	○	x	x	−	−								−	x	○	○	●	●			
Peripheral milling				●	●	○	○	x	x	−	−			−	−	x	x	○	○	●	●					
Face milling				●	●	○	○	x	x	−	−			−	−	x	x	○	○	●	●					
Planing and shaping					●	○	○	○	x	x	−			−	−	x	x	○	○	●	●					
Broaching			●	●	○	○	x	x	−	−	−	−						−	x	○	○	●	●			
II. ABRASION PROCESSES																										
A. Using abrasive tools																										
Centre-type cylindrical grinding			●	○	○	x	x	−	−									−	x	x	○	●	●			
Centreless cylindrical grinding			●	○	x	x	x	−	−									−	x	x	○	○	●			
Internal grinding			●	○	○	x	x	−	−									−	x	x	○	●	●			
Surface grinding			●	○	○	x	x	−	−	−								−	x	x	○	○	●			
Abrasive belt grinding				●	○	○	x	x	−	−								−	x	x	○	○	●			
Surface honing		●	●	○	○	x	−	−											−	−	x	x	○	●		
Shaft and internal honing	●	●	●	○	○	x	−												−	−	x	x	○	○	●	
Superfinish	●	●	○	○	x	x	−												−	−	x	○	○	●	●	
B. Using loose abrasive																										
Lapping		●	●	○	○	x	x	−											−	−	x	○	○	●	●	
Mechanical polishing	●	●	○	○	x	x	−	−											−	−	x	x	○	○	●	●
Vibratory and barrel finishing				●	●	●	○	○	x	x	−					−	−	x	x	○	●					
Abrasive-blast treatment				●	●	●	○	○	x	x	−	−				−	−	x	○	○	●	●				
Ultrasonic machining				●	●	○	○	x	x	−							−	x	○	○	●	●				

Accuracy
- − rough
- x fairly accurate
- ○ accurate
- ● highly accurate

Surface quality
- − rough
- x fairly smooth
- ○ smooth
- ● very smooth

[Courtesy of Peter Peregrinus Limited, taken from J. Kaczmarek, *Principles of Machining by Cutting, Abrasion, and Erosion* 1977.]

I.   Diameter ≤ 0.5 in.
    A.   True position > 0.010
        1.   Tolerance > 0.010
            Drill the hole.
        2.   Tolerance ≤ 0.010
            Drill and ream.
    B.   True position ≤ 0.01
        1.   True position ≤ 0.01
            Drill, then finish bore or ream.
        2.   Tolerance ≤ 0.002
            Drill, semifinish bore, then finish bore.
II. 0.5 in. < diameter ≤ 1.00
    etc.

3.2 DECISION TABLES AND DECISION TREES

Decision tables and decision trees are methods of describing or specifying the various actions (decision) associated with combinations of (input) conditions. Both methods have been used for a long time to help systematize decision making. With the advent of the digital computer, an increased use of these tools has occurred. Both of these methods are described using the following example. The activity deals with a weekend decision that can be described as follows:

> "If it is raining, I will go to the arcade and play video games";
> "If it is not raining and hot, I will go to the beach";
> "If it is not raining and cool, I will go on a picnic with my friend."

The plan above can also be represented as either a decision table or a decision tree (see Figure 3.2).

In our decision table, T implies true to a specified condition, F implies false, and

Raining	T	F	F
Hot		T	F
Go to the arcade	X		
Go to beach		X	
Go to picnic			X

(a) Decision table

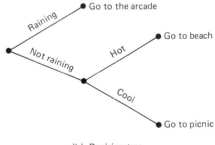

(b) Decision tree

Fig. 3.2. Decision table and decision tree representation.

a blank entry implies that we do not care. Only when all conditions in a decision table column are met is the marked action taken.

In a decision tree, the conditions are specified on the branches of the tree. When all of the branches leading to an action hold true, the action at the terminal point is taken. This system can be used to represent the decision for the personal recreation plan above, as well as a knowledge base for process planning.

Both decision tables and decision trees are tools to assist in decision making. Since decision rules must cover all possible situations, they must be well thought out before such a tool can be used for process planning. For a given set of decision rules, one can list the conditions and actions verbally as shown in the example, and then translate the actions into decision table or decision tree form. Whatever can be represented by a decision table can certainly be represented by a decision tree. The primary difference is the ease and elegance of presentation and programming if a computer is used.

3.2.1 Decision Tables

A decision table is partitioned (conditions and decisions) by vertical and horizontal lines (Figure 3.3). The portion of the table above the horizontal line specifies the condition, while the portion below that line indicates the action. The left portion of the vertical line contains the stub (or tag), and the right portion, the entries. Decision rules are identified by columns in the entry part of the decision table. Based on the rule representation, decision tables can be classified as follows:

1. *Limited-entry decision tables*
   The condition stub/tag specifies exactly what the conditions are [the value of the input variable(s)]. Condition entries can only be T, F, or do not care (see Figure 3.2).
2. *Extended-entry decision tables*
   The condition stub/tag specifies the identification of the condition, but not the value. Values are specified in the condition entries (see Figure 3.4).
3. *Mixed-entry decision tables*
   Sequenced as well as unsequenced actions can be identified using mixed-entry decision tables. A portion of a decision may be made then refined to compute the decision using mixed-entry systems. For sequenced actions a sequence number is assigned to each applicable action entry (Figure 3.5). Unsequenced actions do not require a sequence number. Therefore, only an "×" is used in the table (blank action entries imply that no operation was performed).

When constructing a decision table, the following factors must be considered: completeness, accuracy, redundancy, consistency, loops, and size. Completeness is somewhat obvious and is required for every specification. This rule must always be satisfied. An incomplete decision table will lead to uncertain actions. Decision table accuracy is always important. A decision table must represent the original rules that were specified. Redundancy occurs when two rules have the same action(s) and their

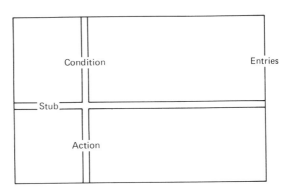

Fig. 3.3. Decision table partitions.

Temperature			≥ 80	< 80
Weather		Raining	Not raining	Not raining
Go to the arcade		X		
Go to beach			X	
Go to picnic				X

Fig. 3.4. Extended-entry decision table.

True position	> 0.01	T	T	
True position	≤ 0.01			
Dimensional tolerance > 0.1		T		
Dimensional tolerance ≤ 0.1			T	
Drill		X	1	
Ream			2	
Bore				

Fig. 3.5. Sequenced action.

condition sets overlap. For example, in Figure 3.6, rules A and B are redundant. When conditions 1 and 3 are true and condition 4 is false, both rules result in the execution of action 1. However, when conditions 1 and 3 are true, rule A will conclude action 1, and rule C will conclude actions 2 and 3. The conflict is called an inconsistency, and an inconsistent decision table produces erroneous decisions.

When an action is used to change conditions, and recurrent calls to the table are used, an endless loop can result. The process will never terminate with a conclusion from the table. For example, the surface condition specification of a machined hole denotes a diameter of 2 in., a surface finish of 40 μin., and a dimensional tolerance of ±0.005 in. Using the decision table given in Figure 3.7 and a backward planning

		A	B	C
Condition	1	T	T	T
	2			
	3	T	T	
	4		F	
Action	1	X	X	
	2			X
	3			X

Fig. 3.6. Redundant rules.

		A	B	C	D
True position	> 0.01	T			
Tolerance	> 0.01	T	F	F	
S.F.	≥ 60		T		
Dia.	= 0	F	F	F	T
Drill		X			
Ream			X		
Bore				X	
Dia. = 0		X			
S.F. = 60				X	
Terminate					X

S.F.: 40
Dia.: 2
Tol.: 0.005

Fig. 3.7. Endless loop.

method, the following processes can be found. For this example, rule C is first satisfied; therefore, a boring process is selected as the "final operation" and the surface finish is changed to 60 μin. Rule B is then executed and the remaining process is selected. Since the tolerance does not change, rule B is always satisfied, and the process never ends.

The size of the decision table is also important. If a decision table requires several pages of print, it is difficult for a human to read and interpret. The same also holds true for a computer-augmented decision table. A "large" decision table in a computer will not only require excessive memory, but also reduces the efficiency of the decision making. To reduce the table size, the following steps can be used.

1. Merge those rules with a common action and only one different condition (Figure 3.8). The merged rule has a "do not care" in that different condition entry.
2. If the table is still too large, it can be split; decision table parsing can be used to connect the separate tables (Figure 3.9).

A more detailed discussion on decision table techniques can be found in Metzner and Barnes [1977] and Montalbano [1974].

Several existing process planning systems use decision table techniques. Since most process knowledge can be represented by "If . . . THEN . . . process, AND . . ." rules, this information can be implemented using decision tables. Figure 3.10 shows a partial decision table for hole making process selection.

		A	B	C
Condition	1	T		F
	2		F	
	3	F	T	F
	4	F	T	F
Action	1	X		X
	2		X	
	3		X	

Merge A, C

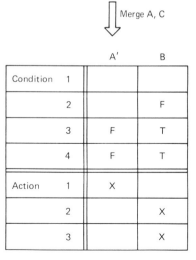

		A'	B
Condition	1		
	2		F
	3	F	T
	4	F	T
Action	1	X	
	2		X
	3		X

Fig. 3.8. Rule merge.

	A	B	C	D	E
Condition 1	T	T	F	F	F
2	F	T			
3			T	F	F
4				T	F
Action 1	X		X		
2		X	X		X
3				X	X

Split (A, B) (C, D, E)

Condition 1	T	F
Table 1	X	
2		X

	A	B
Condition 2	F	T
Action 1	X	
2		X

	C	D	E
Condition 3	T	F	F
4		T	F
Action 1	X		
2	X		X
3		X	X

Fig. 3.9. Table splitting and parsing.

3.2.2 Decision Trees

A decision tree is a graph with a single root and branches emanating from the root. Each branch communicates a value. In probability, decision trees are used to represent the outcome of events or the probability of a state transition. Figure 3.11 illustrates a decision tree that represents the transition probabilities from state A to other states in a three-state Markov process. The value on the branches are the one-stage transition probabilities. When used in decision making, branches usually carry values or expressions (Figure 3.12). Each branch represents an "IF" statement,

Dia. ≤ 0.5	T	T	T	T	F	F	F	F	F	F	F	F	F
0.5 < Dia. ≤ 1.0	F	F	F	F	T	T	T	T	T	F	F	F	F
1.0 < Dia. ≤ 2.0	F	F	F	F	F	F	F	F	F	F			
10 < Dia.	F	F	F	F	F	F	F	F	F	F			
T.P. ≤ 0.002	F	F			F	F	F	F	T	F	F		
0.002 < T.P. ≤ 0.01	F	F			F	F	T	T	F	F			
0.01 < T.P.	T	T	F	F	T	T	F	F	F	F	T		
Tol ≤ 0.002	F		F	T	F		F	T	T	F	F	T	
0.002 < Tol ≤ 0.01	F			F	F		T	F	F	F	T	F	
0.01 < Tol	T	F		F	T	F	F	F	F	T	F	F	
Drill	1	1	1	1	1	1	1	1	1	1	1	1	1
Ream		2											
Semifinish bore				2				2	2				2
Finish bore			2	3		2	2	3	3			2	3
Rapid travel			3								4	3	4

Fig. 3.10. Decision table for a hole-making process.

T.P., true position.

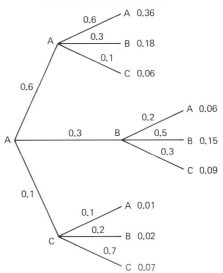

	To		
	A	B	C
A	0.6	0.3	0.1
B	0.2	0.5	0.3
C	0.1	0.2	0.7

Markov chain transition matrix

Fig. 3.11. Decision tree to show the probabilities.

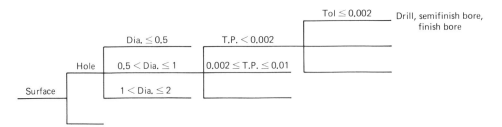

Fig. 3.12. Decision tree.

and branches in series represent a logical "AND." Therefore, a path from the root to the terminal can represent a rule similar to that in the decision table. The action is listed at the junction of each terminal branch.

Decision trees are composed of a root, nodes, and branches (Figure 3.13). The root is the source of the tree, and each tree can have only a single root. However, there are nodes that have properties similar to roots, except that nodes are preceded by other branches. Both roots and nodes have branches emanating from them. Branches can only have two logical values—True or False. When a branch is True in a specific situation, it can be traversed to the next node. There are two types of nodes, mutually excursive and nonmutually excursive [Allen 1981]. A mutually excursive node allows at most one of its successive branches to be true. But a nonmutually excursive node allows all the successive branches to be traversed concurrently. By using both types of nodes, we can construct a decision tree to select actions. A decision tree representation of process knowledge can be found in Figure 3.14.

There are few other methods for decision making except decision tables and decision trees. We show some of these methods in Chapter 4. Next, we will discuss the knowledge that is built into the decision logic.

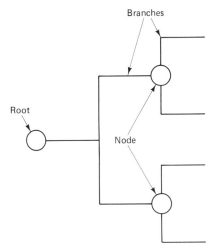

Fig. 3.13. Roots, nodes, and branches.

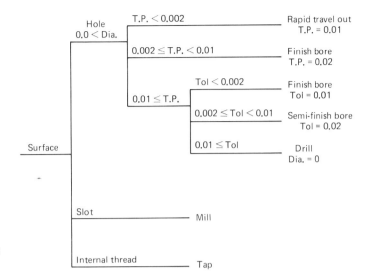

Fig. 3.14. Decision tree for process
selection.

3.3 PROCESS CAPABILITY ANALYSIS

Now that different process knowledge representation methods have been discussed, we can return our focus to the "knowledge" that will be represented in our system. This knowledge is the process capabilities which we began discussing earlier in the chapter. Again, this knowledge base will be limited to chip-metal removal processes.

Before any decision can be made (whether it be experience, table, or tree based), the information required to make the decision must be completed. This information includes a process-by-process breakdown of the following elements:

1. Shape(s) that a process can generate
2. Size limitation (boundaries of the tooling, machine tools, fixtures)
3. Tolerances (both dimensional and geometric)
4. Surface finish (as a limiting value or functional expression)
5. Cutting force
6. Power consumption

The first four elements are capabilities and the last two are limitations. The limitations form the constraints that the machinery is bounded by during processing. The shape elements imply/define the basic geometry producible by a process (see Table 3.2). With little training, virtually anyone can develop a set of shapes that can be produced by a process. However, this feature is perhaps the most difficult task to achieve using a computer, that is, reasoning the shape capability in its natural form (geometry and topology), especially for sophisticated components. A feasible alternative is to represent shape by a code. Human judgment can be used to identify machined surfaces and assign codes to them. The matching of shape capability and machined surface may not be automatic but can be significantly simplified.

Table 3.2. SHAPE CAPABILITY

Process	Shape Capability
Turning	External surfaces which can be generated by rotating a line or curve around an axis
Boring	Hole
Drilling	Hole
Reaming	Hole
Face milling	Flat surface
Peripheral milling	Flat surface, slot
Shaping and planing	Flat surface
End milling	Hole, flat surface, curved surface, slot
Grinding	Flat surface, hole, external cylindrical surface
Honing	Hole
Taping	Internal thread

For internal machining processes (holes, etc.), the size capability is constrained by the available tool size. In external machining, size is constrained by the available machine table size (machine cube). The other capabilities and limitations can be expressed mathematically. These expressions are straightforward to program on a computer if the "exact" equations and constraints can be found.

3.3.1 Process Boundaries

One way to represent process capabilities is to use process boundaries. A process boundary is interpreted as the limiting size, tolerances, and surface finish for a process. It is expressed as the best (or worst) case result of a process. Such a result can be obtained by careful control of the cutting condition and process parameters (feed, speed, depth of cut). Figure 3.15 contains a typical process boundary table.

Size boundaries are determined by available tool sizes or machine table sizes. This limitation is purely a function of the production system. In a small custom machine shop, the largest chuck for their lathes may be 10 in. in diameter. Therefore, the upper boundary for turning is a 10 in. diameter workpiece. However, in a shipyard, the largest lathe may be able to accommodate up to a 3-ft-diameter component. The upper boundary for turning would be 3 ft instead of 10 in. Other process boundaries are also system dependent.

For instance, dimensional tolerance is affected by many variables (e.g., tool diameter, machine tool accuracy, vibration, etc.). Several sources [Trucks 1974, Eary 1962] have developed tables, charts, or functions which show a tolerance dependency as a function of surface size and perhaps other variables such as material or operational parameters. Scarr [1967] suggested that the tolerance for all hole-making processes can be expressed in a general form:

$$Tol = A(D)^N + B \tag{3.1}$$

Boundary	Hole-producing processes	Plane-producing processes
Smallest tool size	S_h	S_s
Largest tool size	L_h	L_s
Negative tolerance	$A_1 (\text{Dia.})^{n_1} + B_1$	$A_1 (\text{Dia.})^{n_1} + B_1$
Positive tolerance	$A_2 (\text{Dia.})^{n_2} + B_2$	$A_2 (\text{Dia.})^{n_2} + B_2$
Straightness (holes)	$A_3 (\text{Len./Dia.})^{n_3} + B_3$	$A_3 = \dfrac{\text{depth of cut} \times \text{length}}{\text{Dia.}} + B_3$
Parallelism	$A \left(\dfrac{\text{Len.}}{\text{Dia.}} \right)^{n_5} + B$	$A_5 \left(\dfrac{\text{Len.}}{\text{Dia.}} \right)^{n_5} + B_5$
Roundness (holes); angularity (planes)	$R_h \; A_4$	$A_s \; A_4$
Depth limit	$D_h \; A_6 \cdot \text{Dia.}$	$A_6 (\text{Dia.}) + B_6$
True position	A_7	
Surface finish	A_8	A_8

Fig. 3.15. Process boundary table [Wysk 1977].

where Tol = tolerance
     A = coefficient of the process
     N = exponent describing the process
     B = constant describing the best tolerance attainable by the process
     D = hole diameter

This general form can also be used to represent other processes. The values of the coefficients A, B, and N in the equation can be obtained by experimentation. Again, it is worth noting that A, B, and N are system dependent (i.e., no universal parameters can be found).

Straightness and parallelism tolerances for holes define the axial tolerance. The major cause of error on straightness and parallelism is tool deflection. A tool can most simply be modeled as a cantilever beam (Figure 3.16). The deflection of the beam is

$$\delta = \frac{Pl^3}{3EI} \qquad (3.2)$$

where E = modulus of elasticity
     I = moment of inertia
     l = beam length
     P = force

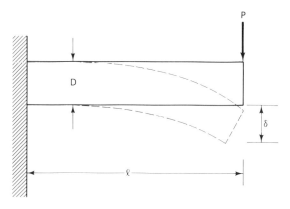

Fig. 3.16. Cantilever beam.

$$I = \frac{\pi D^4}{64} \qquad \text{for cylindrical beam or tool} \tag{3.3}$$

$$\delta = \frac{64Pl^3}{3ED^4} = \frac{CP}{D}\left(\frac{l}{D}\right)^3 \tag{3.4}$$

where C is a constant.

Roughly, the error caused by deflection can be expressed as a coefficient multiplied by the length/diameter ratio raised to some exponential power. Since no machine is perfect, a constant is necessary to represent the effect of other errors. The final form of straightness and parallelism tolerances can be written as

$$\text{Tol} = A\left(\frac{\ell}{D}\right)^N + B \tag{3.5}$$

where A, N, and B are experimentally determined values.

Flatness error, in surface production, is generally caused by the deflection of the tool and machine inaccuracy. Machining accuracy is a function of the machine tool repeatability, backlash, deflection, distortion, and machine spindle/tool alignment. If the machine is rigid, the tool can again be assumed to be a cantilever beam. Given this assumption, the flatness error can be represented as shown in Figure 3.17. In this system, the flatness error f is calculated as

$$h_1 = r \sin a \tag{3.6}$$

$$h_2 = R \sin a \tan a \tag{3.7}$$

$$f = h_1 - h_2 \tag{3.8}$$

For small a, $\sin a \simeq \tan a \simeq a$,

$$f = ra - Ra^2 = a(r - Ra) \tag{3.9}$$

For this cantilever system with a discrete bend,

$$a \simeq F_t k_1 R^{-3} \tag{3.10}$$

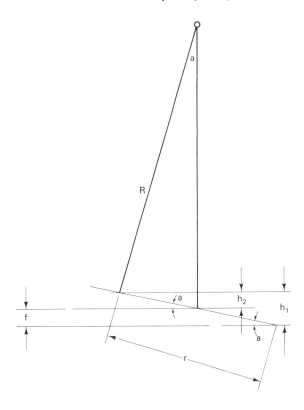

Fig. 3.17. Flatness error produced
by tool deflection.

and

$$f = F_t r k_1 R^{-3} - R F_t^2 k_1^2 R^{-6}$$

or

$$f = \frac{F_t k_1 (r - F_t k_1 / R^2)}{R^3} \tag{3.11}$$

The constant k_1 is determined by the material and its hardness (in this case, k_1 is the force required to remove a cubic measure of a material of this type). This equation can be expanded further to fit the lower limit of flatness error by making a number of assumptions, such as minimum cutting feed, minimum cutting width and depth, and so on. This equation, however, becomes quite cumbersome and may (or may not) become inaccurate because of all of the approximations made throughout.

Because of the complexity of the derivation, the dependence on the cutting force variables (width and depth cut, feed, number of cutter teeth), the length and diameter of the cutter, as well as today's shop practices, a general equation of form

$$\text{flatness} = A \left(\frac{a_p l d}{w} \right)^n + B \tag{3.12}$$

where a_p = depth of cut
    l = cutter length
    d = cutter diameter
    w = width of cut

was selected to quantify flatness error.

Roundness error of a hole-making process is a function of the machine rigidity, material, tool geometry, and so on. Little quantifiable information is available. However, experimental results can be used to find the boundaries for each process. The same is true for angularity and true position. Constant values or functional values can be used to model these characteristics.

Surface finish can be analytically expressed as a function of tool geometry and feed. The theoretical surface-finish height for different tool geometries is shown in Figure 3.18. In the figure, h is the maximum height irregularity and f is the feed. The arithmetic mean value of surface finish, R_a, is defined as the sum of the areas above and below a line which equally divide these two areas (Figure 3.18). For a pointed tool,

$$R_a = \frac{h}{4} = \frac{f}{4(\tan C_s + \cot C_s)} \qquad (3.13)$$

For a rounded tool (tip radius r) with small feed,

$$R_a = \frac{0.0321f^2}{r} \qquad (3.14)$$

For a rounded tool with a large feed, (3.14) also provides a reasonable approximation.

However, the equations above only estimate the surface finish under perfect cutting conditions; no consideration was given to other factors that affect cutting. Cook [1964] showed that surface finish is also affected by cutting speed as well as depth of cut. The actual surface-finish value may be more than twice the theoretical value. The surface-finish boundary, however, should be the best attainable surface finish.

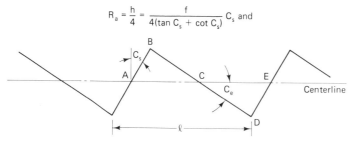

Fig. 3.18. Arithmetic mean surface finish.

3.3.2 Machining Force and Power Requirements

Machining force and power is not a limiting value in process selection, but becomes an important consideration in selecting process parameters (feed, speed, and depth of cut). Force and power are functions of process parameters. Using the same tool, machine, and workpiece material, in general, the greater the volume of work material removed per unit time, the greater the power required. A reduced feed, speed, or depth of cut can reduce both cutting force required and the power consumed. Since force and power are constrained by the machine output, it is necessary to know the power requirements of a cutting process as a function of the process parameters.

In orthogonal cutting, the resultant force F_r applied to the chip by the tool lies in a plane normal to the tool cutting edge (Figure 3.19). F_c is the major cutting force and F_t is the thrust force. The cutting force can be expressed roughly as a product of the specific cutting resistance k_s and the cross sectional area of undeformed chip.

$$F_c = w a_p k_s \qquad (3.15)$$

$$F_t = b w a_p k_s \qquad (3.16)$$

where b = coefficient empirically determined by the tool geometry

The cutting-power consumption, P_m, can be calculated as the product of the cutting speed v and the cutting force F_c. Thus

$$P_m = F_c V \qquad (3.17)$$

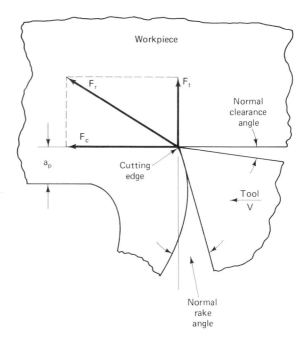

Fig. 3.19. Cutting-force geometry.

Table 3.3a. SUMMARY OF EQUATIONS FOR CUTTING OPERATIONS[a]

OPERATION	Machining time t_m	Tool Life t	Cutting Force F_c	Power P_m	Surface Finish R_a (4)
Turning Boring	$\dfrac{l_w}{f \cdot n_w}$	$K_T \cdot v^{\alpha_T} \cdot f^{\beta_T} \cdot a_p^{\gamma_T}$	$K_F \cdot f^{\beta_F} \cdot a_p^{\gamma_F}$	$\dfrac{F_c \cdot v}{6120 \, n_m}$	$\dfrac{32 \cdot f^2}{r_\epsilon}$
Facing	$\dfrac{D_m}{2 \cdot f \cdot n_w}$				
Parting Shaping & Planing	$\dfrac{b_w}{f \cdot n_r}$				
Drilling & Reaming	$\dfrac{l_w}{f \cdot n_t}$	$K_T \cdot v^{\alpha_T} \cdot f^{\beta_T} \cdot a_p^{\gamma_T} \cdot D^{\delta_T}$	$K_F \cdot f^{\beta_F} \cdot a_p^{\gamma_F} \cdot D_t^{\delta_F}$ (2)	$\dfrac{M \cdot n_s}{9.74 \times 10^5 \, \eta_m}$	$\dfrac{64 \cdot 2 f^2}{D_t}$ (5)
Slab Milling[a] Side & Face Milling	$\dfrac{l_w + k\sqrt{a(D_t - a)}}{f \cdot n_t}$ (1)	$K_T \cdot v^{\alpha_T} \cdot a_f^{\beta_T} \cdot a^{\delta_T} \cdot D_t^{\delta_T} \cdot b_w^{\epsilon_T} \cdot z^{\xi_T} \cdot \lambda_\beta^{\eta_T}$	$K_F \cdot f^{\beta_F} \cdot a_e^{\gamma_F} \cdot D_t^{\delta_F} \cdot b_w \cdot z$		$\dfrac{64 \, 2 f^2}{D_t + e}$
Face Milling	$\dfrac{l_w + D_t}{f \cdot n_t}$		$K_F \cdot v^{\alpha_F} \cdot a_f^{\beta_F} \cdot a_p^{\gamma_F} \cdot d_t^{\delta_F} \cdot b_w^{\epsilon_F} \cdot z^{\xi_F}$	$\dfrac{F_c \cdot v}{6120 \, \eta_m}$	$K_R \cdot a_f^{1.4}$
Broaching	$\dfrac{l_t}{v}$	$K_T \cdot v^{\alpha_T} \cdot a_f^{\beta_T}$	$K_F \cdot a_f^{\beta_F} \cdot D_m \cdot z_c$ (3)		$\cdots$

(1) $k = \begin{cases} 1, \text{ case (a)} \\ 2, \text{ case (b)} \end{cases}$

(2) same formula holds for torque M

(3) valid for broaching of round holes only

(4) valid for ideal conditions only; however, empirical formulas are available for specific cases in turning operations

(5) eccentricity e will be equal to zero in ideal conditions

$$n_w = \frac{v}{n D_w} \qquad n_t = \frac{v}{n D_t}$$

[†]from Armorego 1968, Boothroyd 1975, and Kaczmarek 1976.

[a]An explanation of the notation used in this table is given in Table 3.3b.

Source: Coelho [1980].

However, the equations for force and power above do not consider compound affects of f and a_p to force and power. A more general expression can be found in Kaczmarek [1976]. Equations for cutting force, power, surface finish, tool life, and machine time are summarized in Tables 3.3a and 3.3b. The equations for F_c contain an empirically determined coefficient, K_F, to account for all possible factors that affect cutting force. K_F must be determined for all tool–work material combinations, process types, tool-wear conditions, workpiece hardness, tool geometry, and speed.

3.3.3 Process Parameters

So far we have discussed process capabilities, cutting force, and power. However, surface finish, force, and power constraints are directly affected by the process parameters—feed, speed, and depth of cut. Therefore, process selection becomes an iterative procedure: first a process is selected and then the machining parameters adjusted to accommodate the system constraints. The selection of the machining parameters, however, affects the time and cost required to produce a component. These parameters are not arbitrary, nor are they constant for different operations.

Process parameters are the basic control variables for a machining process. The earliest study on the economical selection of process parameters was conducted by F. W. Taylor in 1906. As a result of his effort and later the efforts of many others, machining data handbooks [Metcut Research Associates] and machinability data systems [Parsons 1971] have been developed to recommend process parameters for efficient machining. These handbooks contain recommended feeds and speeds for

Table 3.3b. NOTATION FOR TABLE 3.3

a, a_e, a_f, a_p	depth of cut
b_w	width of workpiece
D_m	diameter of the machined surface
D_t	diameter of the tool
f	feed
K_F	constant for cutting-force, tool-life, and surface-roughness empirical equations, respectively
ℓ_t	length of tool or broach
ℓ_w	length of surface to be machined
n_r	frequency of reciprocation (strokes/min)
n_t	tool spindle speed (rpm)
n_w	rotational frequency of the workpiece (rpm)
r_ϵ	tool nose radius
v	cutting speed
z	number of teeth on the cutting tool
z_c	number of teeth cutting simultaneously in a tool
α_T, β_T, γ_T, ϵ_T, ξ_T, Y_T, n_T, δ_T	cutting speed, feed, depth of cut, tool diameter, machined surface width, number of teeth in the cutting tool, and tool cutting edge inclination (L^0) exponents for cutting-force, surface-roughness, and tool-life equations, respectively
n_m	overall efficiency of the machine tool motor and drive systems
e	tool cutting edge inclination

different tooling, work material, tool diameter, depth of cut, and so on, combinations. The parameters recommended are "good," but not necessarily the best or the most appropriate. An example is shown in Figure 3.20. In the figure, feeds and speeds for a 30- to 60-min tool life for high-speed-steel (HSS) tools (for carbide insert, 1 to 2 hr) are recommended.

Several machinability systems are currently marketed that recommend sets of parameters that either optimize machining cost, time or production rate, or simply retrieve data table or calculated values. The FAST system [Parson 1971] is an example of a table-value retrieval system. An early General Electric (GE) system used a mathematical model developed by W. W. Gilbert [1950] to calculate one parameter given all others. In Gilbert's model, speed, material, coolant, workpiece surface condition, tool geometry, flank wear, workpiece hardness, tool life, feed, depth of cut, and so on, was represented as a mathematical function. A so-called machinability computer (analog) using Gilbert's model was marketed by GE in the late 1950s [GE 1957].

More recently (1960 to present), machinability systems have become computer based to take advantage of the computational power to include optimization models. For example, a later version of the GE data system contains optimum feed and speed for minimum cost and time using an unconstrained optimization procedure [Parsons 1971]. The EXAPT system [Budde 1973] also uses an unconstrained optimization scheme to identify the optimal tool life. Although most commercial machinability data systems use unconstrained optimization, several research papers have appeared which focus on constrained models. This class of problems is discussed in the following sections.

3.3.4 Process Optimization

Before we begin discussing process optimization, we must first understand the basic tool-life equation. A faster metal removal rate will result in both reduced tool life and reduced machining time. However, whenever a tool has been worn past some practical limits, it must be replaced. Therefore, there is a trade-off between increased machining rate and machine idle time which results in frequent tool changes.

A tool's useful life can be achieved through one of two mechanisms: erosion (or wear) and breakage (catastrophic failure). Catastrophic tool failure is usually quite unpredictable and a phenomenon that one tries to minimize; therefore, tool life is usually defined as the cut time a new tool undergoes before a certain flank wear is reached. Permissible values of flank wear have been recommended by the International Organization for Standardization (ISO) [1972]. They appear in Table 3.4.

Taylor was the first to develop a generalized tool-life equation. In his work he produced an empirical equation which can be written as follows:

$$\frac{V}{V_r} = \left(\frac{t_r}{t}\right)^n \tag{3.18}$$

where n = constant
   V = cutting speed
   t = tool life
   V_r = reference cutting speed given tool life t_r

By rearranging equation (3.18), we obtain

$$t = \frac{t_r V_r^{1/n}}{V^{1/n}} \tag{3.19}$$

$$= \frac{C}{V^{\alpha}}$$

where $\alpha = 1/n$
   $C = t_r V_r^{1/n}$

Later research confirmed that feed and depth of cut also contributed to the tool life. An expanded Taylor tool-life equation of the following form resulted:

$$t = \frac{\lambda C}{V^{\alpha_T} f^{\beta_T} a_p^{\gamma_T}} \tag{3.20}$$

where λ, C = constants for a specific tool/workpiece combination
   α_T, β_T, γ_T = exponents for a specific tool/workpiece combinations

3.3.5 Cost and Time Models

Machining optimization models can be classified as single-pass and multipass models. In a single-pass model, we assume that only one pass is needed to produce the required geometry. In this case, depth of cut is fixed. In a multipass model, this assumption is relaxed and a_p also becomes a control variable. Any multipass model can be reconstructed into a single-pass model.

3.3.5.1 *Single-Pass Model.* In a single-pass model, processing time per component, t_{pr}, can be expressed as the sum of machining time t_m, material-handling time t_h, and tool change time t_t.

$$t_{pr} = t_m + t_h + t_t \left(\frac{t_m}{t}\right) \tag{3.21}$$

where $\left(\frac{t_m}{t}\right)^{-1}$ represent the number of parts can be produced before tool requires changing.

Equations for t_m and t can be found in Table 3.3. Depth of cut, a_p, in the equations is constant. The production cost per component, C_{pr}, can be written as

$$C_{pr} = \frac{C_b}{N_b} + C_m \left[t_m + t_h + \frac{t_m}{t} \left(t_t + \frac{C_r}{C_m} \right) \right] \tag{3.22}$$

Material	Hardness Bhn	Condition	Speed fpm	Speed m/min	1/16 in 1.5 mm	1/8 in 3 mm	1/4 in 6 mm	1/2 in 12 mm	3/4 in 18 mm	1 in 25 mm	1-1/2 in 35 mm	2 in 50 mm	Tool material grade ASI or C / ISO
Alloy steels, wrought high carbon	50 R_C to 52 R_C	Quenched and tempered	10		—	.0005	.001	.002	.002	.003	.003	.004	T15, M42*
				3	—	.013	.025	.050	.050	.075	.075	.102	S9, S11*
	52 R_C to 54 R_C	Quenched and tempered	75		—	—	.001	.001	.0015	—	—	—	C-2
				23	—	—	.025	.025	.038	—	—	—	K10
	54 R_C to 56 R_C	Quenched and tempered	60		—	—	.001	.001	.0015	—	—	—	C-2
				18	—	—	.025	.025	.038	—	—	—	K10
High strength steels, wrought	225 to 300	Annealed	50		.001	.003	.004	.007	.010	.012	.015	.018	M10, M7, M1
300M 4340Si H11	300			15	.025	.075	.102	.18	.25	.30	.40	.45	S2, S3

Feed† ipr / mm/rev — Nominal hole diameter

Material	Hardness (Bhn or Rₒ)	Condition	Speed									Tool material
4330V, 98BV40, H13, 4340, D6ac	300 to 350	Normalized	35	—	.002	.004	.006	.008	.010	.014	.017	M10, M7, M1
			11	—	.050	.102	.15	.23	.25	.36	.45	S2, S3
	350 to 400	Normalized	30	—	.002	.004	.006	.008	.010	.012	.015	T15, M42*
			9	—	.050	.102	.15	.20	.25	.30	.40	S9, S11*
	43 Rₒ to 48 Rₒ	Quenched and tempered	20	—	.002	.003	.004	.004	.004	.004	.004	T15, M42*
			6	—	.050	.075	.102	.102	.102	.102	.102	S9, S11*
	48 Rₒ to 50 Rₒ	Quenched and tempered	15	—	.001	.002	.003	.003	.004	.004	.004	T15, M42*
			5	—	.025	.050	.075	.075	.102	.102	.102	S9, S11*
	50 Rₒ to 52 Rₒ	Quenched and tempered	10	—	.0005	.001	.002	.002	.003	.003	.004	T15, M42*
			3	—	.013	.025	.050	.050	.075	.075	.102	S9, S11*
	52 Rₒ to 54 Rₒ	Quenched and tempered	75	—	—	.001	.001	.0015	.0015	.0015	.0015	C-2
			23	—	.025	.025	.025	.038	.038	.038	.038	K10

†For holes more than 2 diameters deep, reduce speed and feed.
*Any premium HSS (T15, M33, M41-M47) or (S9, S10, S11, S12).

Fig. 3.20. Example of drilling data from the *Machining Data Handbook*, 3rd Edition [by permission of the Machinability Data Center. © 1980 by Metcut Research Associates Inc.]

Table 3.4. AVERAGE PERMISSIBLE VALUES OF LATHE TOOL (FLANK) WEAR

Tool point material	Tool type	Workpiece material	Type of turning	Permissible values of VB in mm	
				In dry turning	*In turning with coolant*
High-speed steel	For external straight turning	Steel and malleable cast iron	Rough	0.5–1.0	1.5–2.0
			medium accurate and accurate	0.3–0.5	
		grey cast iron	Rough	3–4	—
			medium accurate and accurate	1.5–2.0	
	Boring and undercutting tools	Steel and malleable cast iron	Rough, medium accurate and accurate	0.3–0.5	1.5–2.0
		grey cast iron	Rough, medium accurate and accurate	1.5–2.0	—
	Cut-off and parting tools	Steel and malleable cast iron	Rough, medium accurate and accurate	0.3–0.5	0.8–1.0
		grey cast iron	Rough, medium accurate and accurate	1.5–2.0	
	Form tools	Steel	Rough medium accurate and accurate		0.4–0.5
	Threading tools	Steel	Rough finish	—	2.0
				—	0.3
Sintered carbides	All types of tools	Steel	Rough, medium accurate and accurate	0.8–1.0	—
		Grey cast iron	Rough and medium accurate ($s > 0.3$)	0.8– 1.0	—
			accurate ($s < 0.3$)	1.4–1.7	—
Sintered metal oxides	All types of tools	Steel and cast iron	Medium accurate and accurate	0.8	—

Source: ISO [1972]. [Courtesy of Peter Peregrinus Limited, taken from J. Kaczmarek, *Principles of Machining by Cutting, Abrasion, and Erosion*.]

where C_b = setup cost for a batch
       C_m = total machine and operator rate (including overhead)
       C_r = tool cost (for a HSS tool, it is the cost of regrinding for tungsten carbide tool steel (TCT), it is the cost of one insert cutting edge)
       N_b = batch size

An optimization model for machining would look as follows:

$$\min t_{pr} \quad \text{(for time)} \tag{3.23a}$$

or $$\min C_{pr} \quad \text{(for cost)} \tag{3.23b}$$

subject to:

1. Spindle-speed constraint:

$$n_{\min} < n_w < n_{\max} \quad \text{(for workpiece)} \tag{3.24a}$$

$$n'_{t\,\min} < n_t < n'_{t\,\max} \quad \text{(for tool)} \tag{3.24b}$$

2. Feed constraint:

$$f_{\min} < f < f_{\max} \tag{3.25}$$

3. Cutting-force constraint:

$$F_c < F_{c\max} \tag{3.26}$$

4. Power constraint:

$$P_m < P_{\max} \tag{3.27}$$

5. Surface-finish constraint:

$$R_a < R_{a\max} \tag{3.28}$$

Equations for n_w, n_t, F_c, P_m, and R_a are given in Table 3.3.

Many solution procedures can be used to solve the model above. Berra and Barash [1968] and later Wysk [1977] used an iterative search procedure which approached optimum. Groover [1976] used a "evolutionary operations" procedure, which is somewhat similar to a Hooke–Jeeves search procedure. Hati and Rao [1976] applied a sequential unconstrained minimization technique (SUMT) [Fiacco and McCormick 1968] in conjunction with the Davidson–Fletcher–Powell (D-F-P) algorithm to solve the problem. Dynamic programming (DP) and other mathematical programming methods have also been used.

3.3.5.2 *Multipass Model.* Multipass models also consider depth of cut as a control variable. Let a_p be the height of material to be removed, and n the number of passes. The time required per component can be written as

$$t_{pr} = t_h + \sum_{i=1}^{n_p} \left(t_m^i + \left(\frac{t_m^i}{t} \right) t_t \right) \tag{3.29}$$

where $= t_m^i$ is the time required for machining pass i.

The cost per component

$$C_{pr} = \frac{C_b}{N_b} + C_m t_h + \sum_{i=1}^{n_p} C_{pr}^i \tag{3.30}$$

where

$$C_{\mathrm{pr}}^i = C_m \left[t_m^i + \frac{t_m^i}{t} \left(t_t + \frac{C_r}{C_m} \right) \right] \tag{3.31}$$

$$a_t = \sum_{i=1}^{n_p} a_p^i \tag{3.32}$$

and the superscript i represents the ith pass.

An additional constraint is also required in the formulation.

(6) Depth-of-cut constraint:

$$a_{p\mathrm{min}} < a_p^i < a_{p\mathrm{max}} \tag{3.33}$$

The additional variable a_p makes the solution procedure more difficult than for a single-pass problem. In solving this class of problems, Challa and Berra [1976] used a modified Rosen's gradient search method. Philipson and Ravindron [1978] and Subbarao and Jacobs [1978] both used goal programming to deal with the problem. Iwata et al. [1977] introduced a dynamic programming (DP) procedure to solve a multistage machining optimization problem. Hayes et al. [1981] and Chang et al. [1982] transformed certain variables, such as depth of cut, into the discrete domain. The number of passes can then be obtained iteratively using a DP procedure to optimize the feed and speed. There is no general solution method that can be used for all problems.

Figure 3.21 shows the contours of unit cost and feasible region for an example single-pass problem. In the figure, the bounding constraints as well as the objective function are plotted. The bounding constraint for the example is the surface finish. If the surface-finish constraint is relaxed, the force constraint becomes binding.

3.3.6 Closing Remarks

There are two types of information that go into a process planning system: design and process knowledge. The design representation was discussed in Chapter 2. In this chapter the process knowledge was discussed. Process planning can be said to be a procedure that matches the knowledge of the processes with the requirements of the design. Process capability is the producibility knowledge for a process. It is the basic mechanism of the process planning system. However, a logical structure is necessary in order to carry out the matching procedure. This chapter provides both process capability and decision logic. In the next chapter, a discussion on combining process planning and product design will be given.

Tool: ISO SNMA 120408-P20

Holder: ISO PBSNR 2525

Material: SAE 1045 CD

Machine: Engine lathe

feed ~ 0.05 − 2.5 mm/rev
speed ~ 20 − 1600 rpm
power = 7.5 kW
machine efficiency = 0.80

C_m = \$0.25/min	t_h = 1.35 min/pc
C_e = \$0.50/edge	t_i = 0.2 min/pass
C_b = \$7.20/batch	t_c = 1 min/edge

D = 100 mm L = 250 mm

e = 50 mm N_b = 25

p = 0.1 a_p = 3 mm K = 0.3

$$v t^{0.2} f^{0.3} a_p^{0.18} = 220$$

$$F_c = 250\, V^{-0.12} f^{0.75} a_p\, f\, 170\, kp$$

$$P_e = F_c v / 6120 \leqslant 6\ kW$$

$$R_a = 2.43 \times 10^4\, v^{-1.52}\, f \leqslant 1.25\ \mu m$$

$$t^* = \left(\frac{1}{n} - 1 \right) \frac{L}{L + e} \left(t_c + \frac{C_e}{C_m} \right) = 10\ min$$

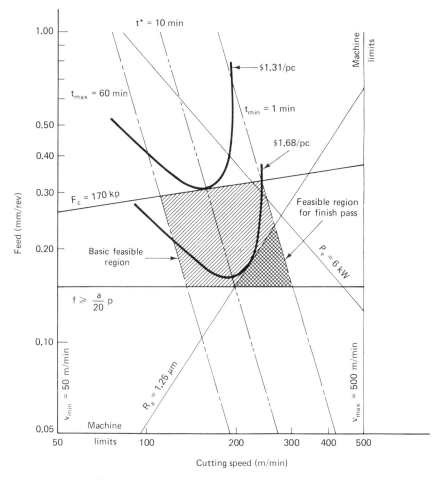

Fig. 3.21. Contours of unit cost and feasible region .

REVIEW QUESTIONS

3.1. Create a decision table model for the following course scheduling activity. Calculus is required before statistics can be taken, and two semesters of statistics are required before graduation. However, Professor Smith is the best statistics instructor and unless it postpones graduation, you will wait until he teaches the course.

3.2. Create a decision tree for the activity described in Problem 3.1.

3.3. Create a decision table for selecting a machine and manufacturing process based on part features.

3.4. Convert the decision table shown in Figure P3.4 into a decision tree.

Dia. ≤ 0.5	T	T	T	T	F	F	F	F	F	F
0.5 < Dia. ≤ 1.0	F	F	F	F	T	T	T	T	T	F
1.0 < Dia. ≤ 2.0	F	F	F	F	F	F	F	F	F	
10 < Dia.	F	F	F	F	F	F	F	F	F	
T.P. ≤ 0.002	F	F			F	F	F	F	T	F
0.002 < T.P. ≤ 0.01	F	F			F	F	T	T	F	F
0.01 < T.P.	T	T	F	F	T	T	F	F	F	T
Tol ≤ 0.002	F		F	T	F		F	T	T	F
0.002 < Tol ≤ 0.01	F			F	F		T	F	F	F
0.01 < Tol	T	F		F	T	F	F	F	F	T
Drill	1	1	1	1	1	1	1	1	1	1
Ream		2								
Finish bore			2	3		2	2	3	3	
Rapid travel			3						4	

T.P. = true position

Fig. P3.4.

3.5. Derive the ideal surface roughness (either Arithmetic Average or Root Mean Square) for a pointed tool.

3.6. Derive the ideal surface roughness (either AA or RMS) for a tool with a round nose.

3.7. Develop a "simple" search procedure to find the optimum cutting speed for a rough-turning operation on a 3-hp lathe. The feed rate is set at 0.007 in./rev and depth of cut at 0.12 in.

3.8. Embellish the optimization procedure developed in Problem 3.7 so that the feed rate can range from 0.005 to 0.10 in./rev. (An optimum feed as well as speed should be determined.)

3.9. The processing time for a single pass model is given in Equation (3.21). The depth of cut a_p is a constant; therefore, the tool life equation can be rewritten as:

$$t = \frac{C'}{V^\alpha f^\beta}$$

Let the length of cut be L. If there is no constraint on spindle speed, feed, etc., what is the optimum cutting speed and feed? t_h and t_t are constant.

3.10. Which machining process(es) can be used to create the following surface? (unit in μin)

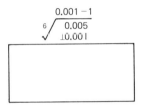

Fig. P3.10.

3.11. Use Figure 3.20 to answer the following questions. The workpiece material is quenched alloy steel, 53 *Rc* hardness.
  a. What are the recommended feed and speed for each hole?
  b. All three holes are 2″ deep. How long does it take to drill each hole?

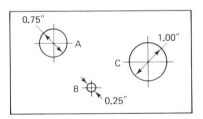

Fig. P3.11.

3.12. Table 3.2 gives the shape capability for some commonly used machining processes. Explain how those shapes are generated (i.e., by sweeping two cutting edges and translating along the axial direction, the drill can generate a hole).

PROCESS PLANNING

In the preceding chapters, design data and production/process information representations were discussed. They are the input to a process planning system, along with the information knowledge base necessary for decision making. The ultimate goal of an automated process planning system is to integrate design and production data into a system that generates usable process plans. An analogy can be drawn for military actions. The goal of the action is like the design. It defines what is to be achieved. To accomplish the goal, intelligence reports are gathered to provide knowledge on the goal itself, possible resistance, and other factors that may result from the action. No matter how well the goal is defined and how detailed and accurate the intelligence reports are, without a good general staff to prepare an ingenious operation plan, the action is not likely to be carried out smoothly. The general staff in a process planning system is the control and decision-making mechanism. A process plan is prepared based on the design data (the goal) and process knowledge (the intelligence).

As mentioned in Chapter 1, there are two approaches used in computer-aided process planning systems: variant and generative. The variant process planning approach uses a data retrieval system to retrieve existing process plans. Systems using this approach are similar in their basic logic. However, this is not the case of generative planning systems. The logic employed by generative planning systems varies both in detail and procedure.

In this chapter we discuss the structure of process planning systems using the variant and generative approaches for process planning. The structures discussed

4

represent some existing methods. They do not necessarily cover all existing or possible methods.

4.1 VARIANT PROCESS PLANNING

A variant process planning system uses the similarity among components to retrieve existing process plans. A process plan that can be used by a family of components is called a standard plan. A standard plan is stored permanently in the data base with a family number as its key. There is no limitation to the detail that a standard plan can contain. However, it must contain at least a sequence of fabrication steps or operations. When a standard plan is retrieved, a certain degree of modification is usually necessary in order to use the plan on a new component.

The retrieval method and the logic in variant systems is predicated on grouping of parts into families. Common manufacturing methods can then be identified for each family. Such common manufacturing methods are represented by standard plans.

The mechanism of standard plan retrieval is based on part families. A family is represented by a family matrix which includes all possible members. The structure of this family matrix will be discussed later.

In general, variant process planning systems have two operational stages: a preparatory stage and a production stage.

4.1.1 The Preparatory Stage

During the preparatory stage, existing components are coded, classified, and subsequently grouped into families. A family matrix is also constructed. The process begins by summarizing process plans already prepared for components in the family. Standard plans are then stored in a data base and indexed by family matrices (Figure 4.1). The preparatory stage is a labor-intensive process. (Reports indicate that it can take 18 to 24 person-years to complete preparation [Planning Institute 1980].)

4.1.2 The Production Stage

The operation stage occurs when the system is ready for production. New components can now be planned. An incoming component is first coded. The code is then input to a part family search routine to find the family to which the component belongs. The family number is then used to retrieve a standard plan. The human planner may modify the standard plan to satisfy the component design. Figure 4.2 shows the flow of the production stage. Some other functions, such as parameter selection and standard time calculations, can also be added to make the system more complete.

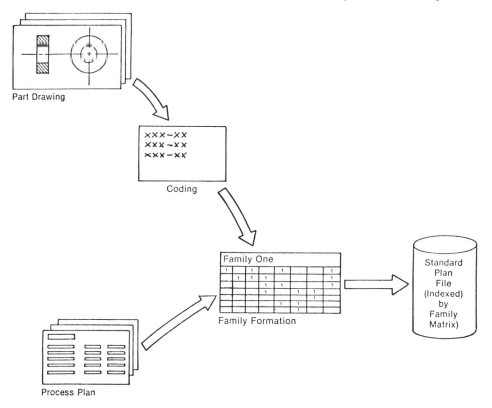

Fig. 4.1. Preparatory stage.

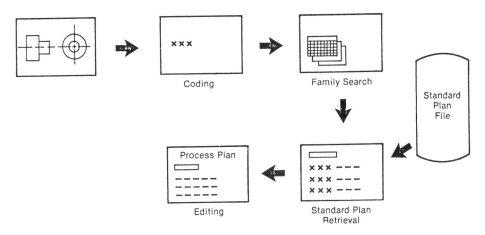

Fig. 4.2. Production stage.

4.2 AN EXAMPLE OF A VARIANT PLANNING SYSTEM

An example will be used to show the step-by-step construction of a variant process planning system. In our example, a simplified coding system will be used. The code table is shown in Figure 4.3. Because it is overly simplified for illustration, this system will lack detail and will not be appropriate for actual application. However, it is sufficient to represent the principles of coding for process planning. We will call

		Digit 1	Digit 2		Digit 3		Digit 4
		Primary shape	Secondary shape		Auxiliary shape		Initial form
0		$\frac{L}{D} \leq 0.05$	No shape element		No shape element		Round bar
1	Rotational	$0.05 < \frac{L}{D} < 3$	Steps with round cross section	No shape element	Holes	No shape element	Hexagonal bar
2		$\frac{L}{D} \geq 3$		With screw thread		With screw thread	Square bar
3		$\frac{L}{D} \leq 2$ with deviation		With functional groove		With functional groove	Sheet
4		$\frac{L}{D} > 2$ with deviation	Rotational cross section		Drill with pattern		Plate and slabs
5	Nonrotational	Flat	Rectangular cross section		Two or more from 2–4		Cast or forged
6		Long	Rectangular with chamfer		Stepped plane surface		Welded assembly
7		Cubic	Hexagonal bar		Curved surface		Premachined

Fig. 4.3. S-CODE.

our coding system S-CODE (Simple CODE) and the process planning system VP (Variant Planning).

VP will be used in a machine shop that produces a variety of small components. These components range from simple shafts to delicate hydraulic pump parts. We will discuss the construction of VP in the following sequence:

1. Family formation
2. Data base structure
3. Search algorithm
4. Plan editing
5. Process parameter selection

4.2.1 Family Formation

In a process planning system, family formation is based on production parts or, more specifically, their manufacturing features. Components requiring similar processes are grouped into the same family.

Since a part family is loosely defined, there is no rigid rule that can be applied to form families. Users must set their own definitions of what a family is or should be. A general rule for part family formation is that all parts must be related. For process planning purposes, all parts in a family must require similar process plans; therefore, a standard process plan can be shared by the entire family. A user may want to put only those parts having exactly the same process sequence into a family. Minimum modification on the standard plan will be required for such family members. However, few parts will qualify for family membership. On the other hand, if one groups all the parts requiring a common machine into a family, extensive plan modification will be required for every part.

Before grouping can start, information concerning the design and processing of all the existing components must be collected from existing part and processing files. Each component's design is coded using the S-CODE, and the associated process plan is represented in another coded form, called an operation plan code (OP code) (Figure 4.4a). An OP code represents a series of operations on one machine and/or one workstation. For example, we can use DRL01 to represent the sequence: load workpiece onto drill press, attach a drill, drill holes, change drill to a reamer, ream holes, and unload workpiece from drill. Operations represented by an OP code are called an operation plan. An OP code does not necessarily include all operations required on a machine for a component. It is used to represent a logical group of operations on a machine, so that a process plan can be represented in a much more concise manner. Such a representation is called an OP code sequence (Figure 4.4b). Since we do not want to lose the detail of a process plan, operation plans and OP code sequences must be stored properly.

The basic premise of an OP code is to simplify the representation of process plans. A simplified process plan can be stored and retrieved by a computer easily when

Operation code	Operation plan
01 SAW 01	Cut to size
02 LATHE 02	Face end
	Center drill
	Drill
	Ream
	Bore
	Turn straight
	Turn groove
	Chamfer
	Cutoff
	Face
	Chamfer
03 GRIND 05	Grind
04 INSP 06	Inspect dimensation
	Inspect finish

(a) Operation plan code (OP code) and operation plan

01   SAW 01
02   LATHE 02
03   GRIND 05
04   INSP 06

(b) OP code sequence

Fig. 4.4. Operation plan, OP code, and OP code sequence.

represented in this way. It can also contribute to the family formation process. For example, we have a total of 24 components in our minishop. After coding them, we can obtain a summary in table form as shown in Figure 4.5. There are two methods that we can use to group parts into families: (1) observation, or (2) computerized methods such as production flow analysis. It is obvious that when we have many components, the first method (observation) will be difficult to use.

Production flow analysis (PFA) was introduced by J. L. Burbridge to solve the family formation problem for manufacturing cell design [Burbridge 1971, 1975]. Many researchers have subsequently developed algorithms to solve the problem. In PFA, a large matrix (incidence matrix) is constructed. Each row represents an OP code, and each column in the matrix represents a component (Figure 4.6). We can define the matrix as M_{ij}, where i designates the OP codes and j designates components ($M_{ij} = 1$ if component j has OP code i; otherwise, $M_{ij} = 0$). The objective of PFA is to bring together those components that need the same or a similar set of OP codes in clusters.

King [1979] presented a rank order cluster algorithm which is quite simple in nature. We will use his method to show how component families can be determined in our shop. King's algorithm can be stated as follows:

Component	Code	Processes	(OP code sequence)		
A-112	1110	SAW01,	LATHE02,	GRIND05,	INSP06
A-115	6514	MILL02,	DRL01,	INSP03	
A-120	2110	SAW01,	LATHE02,	GRIND05,	INSP06
A-123	2010	SAW01,	LATHE01,	INSP06	
A-131	2110	SAW01,	LATHE02,	INSP06	
A-212	7605	MILL05,	INSP03		
A-230	6604	MILL05,	INSP03		
A-432	2120	SAW01,	LATHE02,	INSP06	
A-451	2130	SAW01,	LATHE02,	INSP06	
A-510	7654	MILL05,	DRL01,	GRIND06,	INSP06
A-511					
A-511					
A-512					
A-550					
A-556					
B-105					
B-107					
B-108					
B-109					
B-110					
B-116					
B-117					
B-118					
B-119					
B-120					

Fig. 4.5. Partial component process summary table.

Step 1. For $\forall_j$ calculate the total weight of column w_j:

$$w_j = \sum_{\forall^i} 2^i M_{ij}$$

Step 2. If w_j is in ascending order, go to step 3. Otherwise, rearrange the columns to make w_j fall in an ascending order.

Step 3. For $\forall_i$, calculate the total weight of row w_i:

$$w_i = \sum_{\forall^j} 2^j M_{ij}$$

Step 4. If w_i is in descending order, stop. Otherwise, rearrange the rows to make w_i fall in an ascending order. Go to step 1.

King's algorithm can only handle problems with a few machines as well as

	A-112	A-115	A-120	A-123	A-131	A-212	A-230	A-432	A-451	A-510
SAW01	/		/	/	/			/	/	
LATHE01				/						
LATHE02	/		/			/			/	/
DRL01		/								/
MILL02		/								
MILL05						/	/			/
GRIND05										
GRIND06	/		/							/
INSP03		/					/	/		
INSP06	/		/	/	/			/	/	/

Fig. 4.6. PFA matrix.

components. The number of rows and columns are constrained by the computer word size (i.e., 16 rows and columns for a 16-bit word computer). However, the limitation can be remedied by partial sorting [King and Nakornchai 1982].

Figure 4.7 shows the procedure of rearranging the PFA matrix in Figure 4.6. Note that the last two rows in Figure 4.6 were not used in Figure 4.7 in order to simplify the example.

After we obtain the final matrix, we can determine (arbitrary) that components A123, A120, A131, A432, A451, and A112 form a family that needs SAW01, LATHE01, LATHE02, and GRIND05. A115, A212, A230, and A510 form the second family.

This family must then be represented in a manner that is consistent with the S-CODE. The representation used is called a part family matrix. A part family matrix is a binary matrix similar to a PFA matrix. We can use P_{ij}^{ℓ} to represent a part family matrix for family ℓ i = 1, . . . , I, where I is the number of possible values in each code position, and j = 1, . . . , J, where J is the code length. In the S-CODE, I is equal to 8 and J is equal to 4. $P_{ij}^{\ell} = 1$ implies that code position j is allowed to have a value i.

A part family matrix can be constructed in the following manner. Let

$C_j^{k\ell}$ be the value of code position j for
      component k in family ℓ,   k = 1, . . . , k
      (k = the number of components)

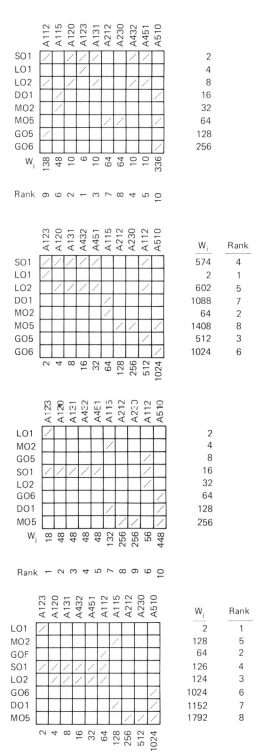

Fig. 4.7. Rank order cluster algorithm.

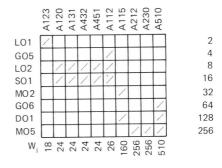

Fig. 4.7. (Continued)

Stop

```
For k := 1 to k
  For j := 1 to J
    i := C_j^{kℓ}
    P_{ij}^1 := 1
  enddo
enddo
```

Using the procedure above, we can obtain a part family matrix for family one (Figure 4.8). Thus far, we have a complete set of OP code sequences, OP plans, and

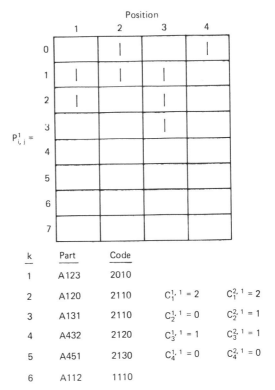

k	Part	Code		
1	A123	2010		
2	A120	2110	$C_1^{1,1} = 2$	$C_1^{2,1} = 2$
3	A131	2110	$C_2^{1,1} = 0$	$C_2^{2,1} = 1$
4	A432	2120	$C_3^{1,1} = 1$	$C_3^{2,1} = 1$
5	A451	2130	$C_4^{1,1} = 0$	$C_4^{2,1} = 0$
6	A112	1110		

Fig. 4.8. Part family matrix.

a family matrix. The next step is to store them in a computer-interpretable manner so that we can use this information later for new components.

4.2.2 Data Base Structure

The VP system contains only a small amount of information as opposed to an industrial application where thousands of components and process plans need to be stored and retrieved. Because of the large amount of information, data base systems play an important role in variant process planning. A data base is no more than a group of cross-referenced data files. The data base contains all the necessary information for an application, and can be accessed by several different programs for specific applications. There are three approaches to construct a data base: hierarchical, network, and relational. Although the concept and structure for these approaches is very different, they all can serve the same purpose.

For commercial programming, there are several available data base management systems, such as CODASYL, MARKIV, SPIRES, and so on. These systems are high-level languages for data base construction and manipulation. Of course, a data base can always be written using procedural languages such as COBOL, FORTRAN, or PL/I. No matter what approach and language is used, the basic structure of the data base keeps the same form.

The hierarchical approach will be used to construct the data base in the design of the VP system. Figure 4.9 shows the hierarchy of the data. Each family is accessed by its family number. A standard plan is associated with each family and is represented by an OP code sequence. In the sequence each OP code has an associated OP plan stored on a lower level. Data for each level are stored in a file; therefore, VP requires three files: (1) a family matrix file, (2) a standard plan file, and (3) an OP plan file.

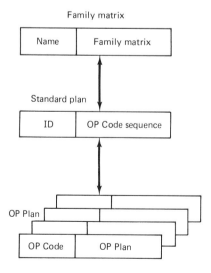

Fig. 4.9. Data hierarchy.

The family name and family matrix are stored as a record in the data base. A forward pointer is used to link the next record and another pointer is used to locate the associated standard plan in the standard plan file. We can assign two words for the family name, two words for pointers, and I × J (8 × 4) words for the family matrix. A total of 36 (8 × 4 + 4) words are required for each record. Figure 4.10 illustrates the structure of a family matrix file.

Because the OP code sequence has variable length, the structure for a standard plan file must include variable record lengths. In the file, a directory is used to locate OP code sequences. The rest of the file is divided into segments which can store up to five OP codes. The last word is used to indicate the continuation of the sequence. Expansion, deletion, and modification of a record are made possible by pointers in the directory and the continuation flag.

The OP plan file has a structure similar to the standard plan file except that it maintains link pointers to the standard plan file. Since records in the standard plan file have a one-to-many relationship with those in the OP plan file, it is necessary to keep "where it comes from pointers" in the OP plan file. This organization makes file maintenance easier.

Figure 4.11 shows the overall structure of the VP data base. The storage of families one and two is shown in Figure 4.12.

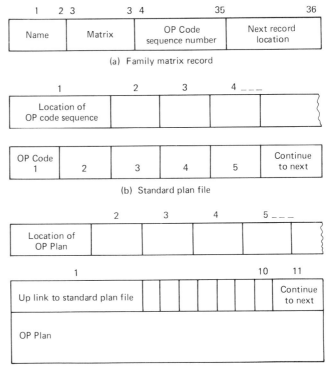

(a) Family matrix record

(b) Standard plan file

(c) OP Plan file

Fig. 4.10. Data records contents.

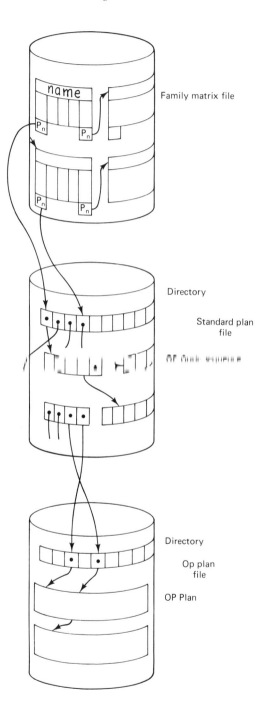

Fig. 4.11. Data base structure.

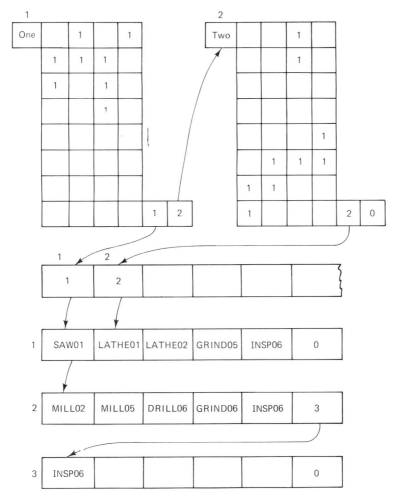

Fig. 4.12. VP system data.

4.2.3 Search Procedure

Once the preparatory stage has been completed, the variant planning system is ready for production. The spirit of a variant system is to retrieve process plans for similar components. The search for a process plan is based on the search of a part family to which the component belongs. When the part family is found, the associated standard plan can be easily retrieved.

A family matrix search can be seen as the matching of the family matrix with a given code. Family matrices can be considered as masks. Whenever a code can pass through a mask successfully, the family is found. The search procedure can be described as follows:

Let C_j be a value of code position j for the given component.

P_n^ℓ is a pointer for family matrix ℓ, which links to the next family matrix.

P_s^ℓ is a pointer for family matrix ℓ, which links to the directory of the standard plan file.

P_{ij}^ℓ is defined as in Section 4.2.1.

The following algorithm can be used to find a standard plan.

Step 1. For all ℓ, do step 2. End stop.

Step 2. For j = 1 to J, do step 3; end, go to step 5.

Step 3. i = C_j; if $P_{ij}^\ell \neq 0$; end step; otherwise,

Step 4. $\ell = P_n^\ell$; go to step 2.

Step 5. Standard plan found; P_s^ℓ is the pointer to the standard plan. Terminate process.

In some commercial systems, a "matrix search" is also used. In a matrix search, C_j is allowed to be a range of values instead of a single value. The algorithm above can be modified to perform a matrix search as follows:

Let C_j^* be a range $C_j^* = C_j \pm \epsilon$.

Step 3. $\sum_{i \in c_j} P_{ij}^\ell \neq 0$, end step; otherwise, next j.

We can demonstrate this search procedure by the use of an example. For the example, the mounting bracket shown in Figure 4.13 will be planned using the VP system. Based on the S-CODE table in Figure 4.3, a code (6514) can be developed for the component. (To make VP even more effective, we could develop an interactive

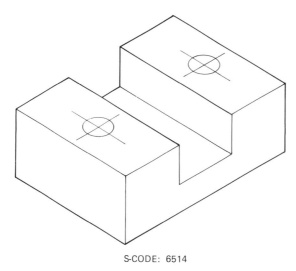

S-CODE: 6514

Fig. 4.13. Component to be planned: workpiece.

$$C = 6514$$

Step 1	$\ell = 1$
2	$j = 1$
3	$i = C_1 = 6,\ P_{6,1}^1 = 0$ next
4	$\ell = P_n^1 = 2$, go to 2
2	$j = 1$
3	$i = C_1 = 6,\ P_{6,1}^2 = 1$ end step
2	$j = 2$
3	$i = C_2 = 5,\ P_{5,2}^2 = 1$ end step
2	$j = 3$
3	$i = C_3 = 1,\ P_{1,3}^2 = 1$ end step
2	$j = 4$
3	$i = C_4 = 4,\ P_{4,3}^2 = 1$ end step
2	$j = 5$ go to step 5
5	plan found
	$P_s^2 = 2$

	OP Code
1	Mill 02
2	Mill 05
3	Drill 01
4	Grind 06
5	Insp 03
6	Insp 06

Fig. 4.14. Search procedure.

coding system for component coding.) This interactive system could eliminate the use of the manual table. ($C_1 = 6$, $C_2 = 5$, $C_3 = 1$, and $C_4 = 4$.) Referring to Figure 4.12, we can start the family search. Figure 4.14 shows the step-by-step search procedure. The search results in the retrieval of standard plan represented by an OP code sequence. This standard plan normally requires some modification before it can be used. OP plans can be retrieved and substituted for OP codes in the OP code sequence. Manual modification of the final process plan is also needed.

4.2.4 Plan Editing and Parameter Selection

Before a process plan can be issued to the shop, some modification of the standard plan is necessary, and process parameters must be added to the plan. There are two types of plan editing: One is the editing of the standard plan itself in the data base, and the other is the editing of the plan for the component. Editing a standard plan implies that a permanent change in the stored plan be made. This editing must be handled very cautiously, because the effectiveness of a standard plan affects the process plans generated for the entire family of components. Aside from the technical considerations of file maintenance, the structure of the data base must be flexible enough for expansion, additions, and deletions of data records. As a result, the pointer system in VP may prove to be efficient.

Editing a process plan for a component requires the same expertise as editing a standard plan. However, it is a temporary change and therefore does not affect any other component in the family. During the editing process, the standard plan needs to be modified to suit the specific needs of the given component. Some operations or entire OP records need to be removed, while others must be changed. Additional operations may also be required to satisfy the design. A text editor is usually used at this stage.

A complete process plan includes not only operations but also process parameters. As discussed in Chapter 3, process parameters can be found in machining data handbooks or can be calculated using optimization techniques. The first approach is easier and more appropriate for the VP system.

Figure 4.15 shows the structure for the parameter file. Data in the file are linked so that we can go through the tree to find the feed and speed for an operation. For example, MILL02 for the mounting bracket in Figure 4.13 uses a face milling process. The workpiece material is cast iron (BHN = 180). The depth of cut for roughing is

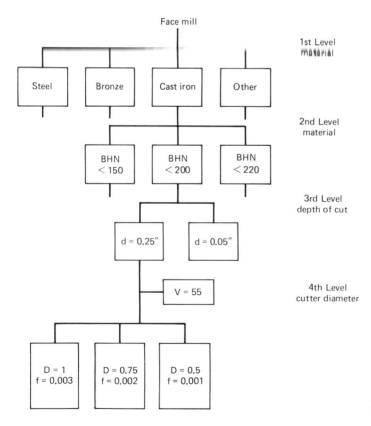

Fig. 4.15. Process parameter file.

0.25 in. and the cutter used is 0.5 in. in diameter. We can then locate using pointers from this information, a velocity (V = 55 sfm) and a feed (f = 0.001 ipt).

This parameter file can be integrated into VP to select process parameters automatically. Information such as depth of cut and cutter diameter can be retrieved directly from the OP plan for each operation. The same approach is also appropriate for standard time selection.

With this example we have completed our discussion of the variant process planning approach. A review of the current systems and a discussion on the pros and cons of this approach are presented in Chapter 5.

4.3 THE GENERATIVE APPROACH

Generative process planning is a second type of computer-aided process plan ning. It can be concisely defined as a system that synthesizes process information in order to create a process plan for a new component automatically. In a generative planning system, process plans are created from information available in a manufacturing data base without human intervention. Upon receiving the design model, the system can generate the required operations and operations sequence for the component. Knowledge of manufacturing must be captured and encoded into efficient software. By applying decision logic, a process planner's decision-making process can be imitated. Other planning functions, such as machine selection, tool selection, process optimization, and so on, can also be automated using generative planning techniques.

The generative planning approach has the following advantages:

1. It can generate consistent process plans rapidly.
2. New components can be planned as easily as existing components.
3. It can potentially be interfaced with an automated manufacturing facility to provide detailed and up-to-date control information.

Decisions on process selection, process sequencing, and so on, are all made by the system. However, transforming component data and decision rules into a computer-readable format is still a major obstacle to be overcome before generative planning systems become operational. Successful implementation of this approach requires the following key developments:

1. The logic of process planning must be identified and captured.
2. The part to be produced must be clearly and precisely defined in a computer-compatible format (e.g., three-dimensional model, GT code, etc.).
3. The captured logic of process planning and the part description data must be incorporated into a unified manufacturing data base.

Today, the term "generative process planning" is relaxed from the definition given above to a less complete system. Systems with built-in decision logic are often called generative process planning systems. The decision logic consists of the unusual ability to check some conditional requirements of the component and select a process. Some systems have decision logic to select several "canned" process plan fragments and combine them into a single process plan. However, no matter what kind of decision logic is used and how extensively it is used, the system is usually categorized as a generative system.

There are several generative process planning systems (based on the relaxed definition) used in industry (e.g., AUTOPLAN of Metcut [Vogel 1979, Vogel and Adlard 1981], CPPP of United Technology [Dunn and Mann 1978].

Ideally, a generative process planning system is a turnkey system with all the decision logic contained in the software. The system possesses all the necessary information for process planning; therefore, no preparatory stage is required. This is not always the case, however. In order to generate a more universal process planning system, variables such as process limitations and capabilities, process costs, and so on, must be defined prior to the production stage. Systems such as CPPP [Kotler 1980 a, b] require user-supplied decision logic (process models) for each component family. A wide range of methods have been and can be used for generative process planning. In the following sections, we discuss a few methods that have been implemented successfully.

4.3.1 Forward and Backward Planning

In variant process planning, process plans are retrieved from a data base. A direction for the planning procedure does not exist since plans are simply paired to a code. However, in generative process planning, when process plans are generated, the system must define an initial state in order to reach the final state (goal). The path taken (initial → final or final → initial) represents the sequence of processes. For example, the initial state is the raw material (workpiece), and the final state is the component design. If a planner works on modifying the raw workpiece until it takes on the final design qualities, the type of component is shown in Figure 4.16. The raw workpiece is a $6.0 \times 3.0 \times 2.5$ block. Using forward planning, we start from the top surface, S_1. A milling process is used to create the final dimension for S_1. After S_1 has been planned, S_2 can be planned. For S_2, a chamfering process is first selected, and then the hole is drilled and tapped. The progression begins from the raw material and proceeds to the finished requirements.

Backward planning uses a reverse procedure. Assuming that we have a finished component, the goal is to fill it to the unmachined workpiece shape. Each machining process is considered a filling process. A drilling process can fill a hole; a reaming process can fill a thin wall (cylinder); and so on. When applied to the example component, the bottom-most surface is planned first. A tapping process is selected (this reduces the threaded surface to a smaller-diameter hole with a rough surface finish). Drilling is then selected to fill the hole, and so forth, until we finally obtain the block.

Forward and backward planning may seem similar; however, they affect the programming of the system significantly. Planning each process can be characterized

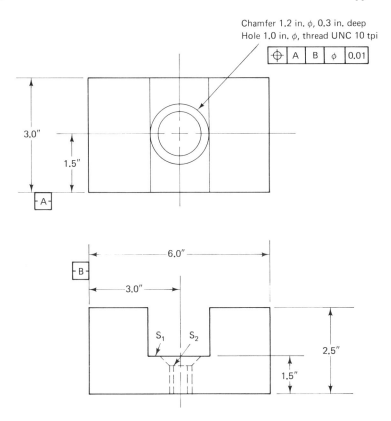

Fig. 4.16. Component to be planned: final design.

by a precondition of the surface to be machined and a postcondition of the machining (its results). For forward planning, we must know the successor surface before we select a process, because the postcondition of the first process becomes the precondition for the second process. For example, when we selected drilling, for the threaded hole, we knew that the thread was going to be cut. Therefore, we rough-drilled the hole using a smaller drill. Otherwise, we might have chosen a larger drill and no thread could be produced. Backward planning eliminates this conditioning problem since it begins with the final surfaces form and processes are selected to satisfy the initial requirements. The transient surface (intermediate surface) produced by a filling process is the worst precondition a machining process can accept, (i.e., depth of cut left for finish milling, etc.). Any filling process that can satisfy the transient surface can be selected as the successor process.

In forward planning, the objective surface must always be maintained even though several operations must be taken to guarantee the result. On the other hand, backward planning starts with the final requirements (which helps to select the predessor process) and searches for the initial condition or something less accurate (which is easy to satisfy).

4.3.2 The Input Format

The input format of a process planning system affects the ease with which a system can be used, and the capability of the system. A system using a very long special description language as its input is more difficult to use. The translation from the original design (either an engineering drawing or a CAD model) to a specific input format may be tedious and difficult to automate. In this case it is probably easier and faster to plan a component manually than to prepare the input. However, such input can provide more complete information about a component, and more planning functions can be accomplished using the input. This does not imply that a system using a long and special descriptive language always provides more planning functions.

Many different input formats have been used in process planning systems. Although no/few systems use the same input format, we can categorize the input for these systems into the following classes.

4.3.2.1 *Code.* As discussed in the variant approach, GT codes can be used as input for variant process planning systems. Some generative systems such as APPAS [Wysk 1977] and GENPLAN [Tulkoff 1981] also use part codes as input. Codes used in generative systems are more detailed, and sometimes mix code digits with explicitly defined parameter values (refer to Section 2.4). Since a code is concise, it is easy to manipulate. When process capabilities are represented by a code, a simple search through the process capability to match the component code will return the desired process. In order to determine the process sequence, a code for the entire component is appropriate, because it provides global information. However, when processing detail is required, surface coding is unavoidable. A surface code normally describes the surface shape, dimensions, surface finish, and tolerances (both dimensional and geometric) rather than characterizes the entire part.

Although a surface code is easy to manipulate and store, it is difficult to generate this code automatically through software. A human interface between design and process planning facilitates the translation of information from one system to another.

4.3.2.2 *Description Language.* Specially designed part description languages can provide detailed information for process planning systems. A language can be designed to provide all of the information required for the necessary functions of a process planning system. The format can be designed such that functions can easily accomplish their task from the information provided.

AUTAP system [Eversheim et al. 1980a] uses a language similar to a solid modeling language (Section 2.3.2). A component is described by the union of some primitives and modifiers. Figure 4.17 shows the description of a rotational component. CYLE (cylinder), CHAL (chamfer left), CHAR (chamfer right), UNCUL (undercut), and RADIR (radius right-curved chamfer) are primitives and modifiers. A process planner can model a component using the language. Material, processes, machine selection, and time estimates can be selected by the system using the input model. Although reasonably complex components can be modeled, this language lacks a

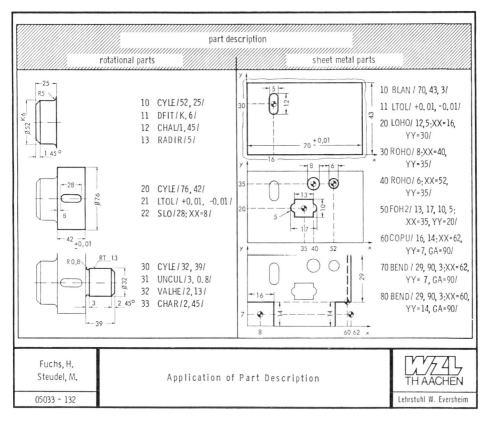

Fig. 4.17. AUTAP data input. [Eversheim and Fuchs, 1980] [Courtesy of the Laboratory for Machine Tools and Production Engineering of Technical University of Aachen.]

complete set of Boolean operators, and modeling a complex component may be difficult. The process sequence is also affected directly by the sequence with which a component is modeled. Although the system models a component from left to right, it does not reduce the number of possible models for a component to a single description.

Another system CIMS/PRO developed by Iwata et al. [1980] uses an input language called CIMS/DEC [Kakino et al. 1977]. In the CIMS/DEC system, component shape is modeled by sweeping (translation or rotation) to generate surfaces (Figure 4.18). In CIMS/PRO, a pattern-recognition module automatically identifies machined surfaces, such as planes, cylinders, threaded shafts, holes, and grooves. Twenty-six different types of machined surfaces can be characterized. Tool approach can also be determined (every machined surface has a set of approach directions predefined). This input language can model both rotational (by rotation sweep) and boxlike (by translation sweep) components. It is most powerful for modeling rotational components without axial shape elements. However, if the component is very complex, it can be difficult to model.

GIRI [Descotte and Latombe 1981] is an artificial intelligence (AI) problem

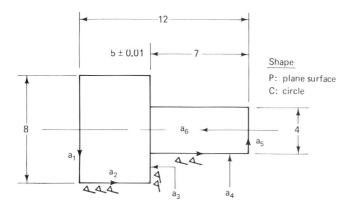

	Shape code	Dimensions		S.F.	Tol.	Adjacent shape
a_1	P	0	4		± 0.01	a_6
a_2	C	5	0	P P P		a_1
a_3	P	0	−2	P P		a_2
a_4	C	7	0	P P		a_3
a_5	P	0	2			a_4
a_6	*	−12	0			a_5

Fig. 4.18. CIMS/DEC component modeling.

solver. It is one of the earliest attempts to use AI in process planning. A component can be described by some system words such as diameter, surface finish, and so on (Figure 4.19). Rules can then be applied to determine the processes and machines needed to produce a part. The knowledge base (where process and machine capabil-

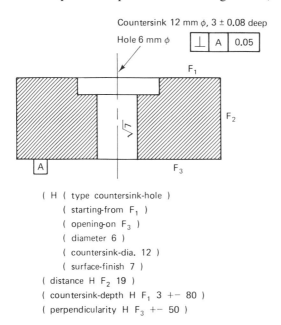

(H (type countersink-hole)
   (starting-from F_1)
   (opening-on F_3)
   (diameter 6)
   (countersink-dia. 12)
   (surface-finish 7)
(distance H F_2 19)
(countersink-depth H F_1 3 +− 80)
(perpendicularity H F_3 +− 50)

Fig. 4.19. GIRI component model.

ities are stored) uses the same set of system words; therefore, decisions can be reached by searching the knowledge base in order to satisfy the input description. The input description must, however, be prepared by a human operator. For a complex component, the translation of the original design to this input language can be very tedious and difficult.

There are many other systems (such as CPPP [Kotler 1980a, b], AUTOTECH [Tempelhof 1980], etc.) which use their own special description language. Basically, all of these systems contain a surface shape code, dimensions, and technological data. Although description languages can provide complete information for process planning functions, the main problem (the difficulty to generate the original design automatically) is still unresolved. The next class of input format is aimed at eliminating this problem.

4.3.3 CAD Models

Since a design can be modeled effectively in a CAD system, using a CAD model as input to a process planning system can eliminate the human effort of translating a design into a code or other descriptive form. The increased use of CAD in industry further points to the benefits of using CAD models as process planning data input.

A CAD model contains all the detailed information about a design. It can provide information for all planning functions. However, an algorithm to identify a general machined surface from a CAD model does not currently exist. Additional code is needed to specify the machined surface shape from raw material shape.

CADCAM [Chang and Wysk 1981] uses a CAD model as its input. Several other systems (AUTOPLAN [Vogel and Adlard 1981], GENPLAN, etc.) also use a CAD data base interactively for tool and fixture selection. There is tremendous potential for using CAD data for process planning input. However, this frontier must still be developed.

4.3.4 Decision Logic

In a generative process planning system, the system decision logic is the focus of the software and directs the flow of program control. The decision logic determines how a process or processes are selected. The major function of the decision logic is to match the process capabilities with the design specification. As discussed in Chapter 3, process capabilities can be described by "IF . . . THEN . . ." expressions. Such expressions can be translated into logical statements in a computer program. Perhaps the most efficient way to translate these expressions is to code process capability expressions directly into a computer language. Information in handbooks or process boundary tables can be easily translated using a high-level computer language. However, such programs can be very long and inefficient. Even more disadvantageous is the inflexibility (difficulty of modification) of such software—this inflexibility leaves customized codes of this type virtually useless in process planning.

In Chapter 3 we also discussed process capability representation methods. Several methods can be used to describe the decision structure of process planning.

The knowledge representation methods are related directly to the decision logic in these systems. The static data are the representation and the dynamic use of the data becomes the decision logic. In the remainder of this section, we discuss the following decision logic as applied to process planning systems:

1. Decision trees
2. Decision tables
3. Artificial intelligence

This list is by no means complete. However, this classification forms a handy framework for discussion.

4.3.4.1 *Decision Trees*. A decision tree is a natural way to represent process information. Conditions (IF) are set on branches of the tree and predetermined actions can be found at the junction of each branch.

A decision tree can be implemented as either (1) computer code, or (2) presented as data. When a decision tree is implemented in computer code, the tree can be directly translated into a program flowchart. The root is the start node (Figure 4.20), and each branch is a decision node. Each branch has a decision statement (a true condition, and a false condition). At each junction, an action block is included for the true condition. For a false condition, another branch might be taken or the process might be directed to the end of the logic block. When the false condition includes another branch, these two branches are said to branch from an OR node. When the false condition goes directly to the end of an action block (which is rooted from the same decision statement), the current branch and the following branch are part of the same AND node. A decision statement can be a predicate or a mathematical expression.

Figure 4.21 shows a sample decision tree and its flowchart representation. It can be written in a programming language (pseudolanguage) as follows:

```
;root
;
    IF E1 then do N1 enddo
    else if E1 then do A5 enddo
    else endif endif stop
; node N1
;
procedure N1
If E2 then do N2 enddo
    else if E3 then do A4 enddo
    else endif endif return
: node N2
;
procedure N2
If E4 then do A1 enddo
    else if E5 then do A2 enddo
    else if E6 then do A3 enddo
    else endif endif endif return.
```

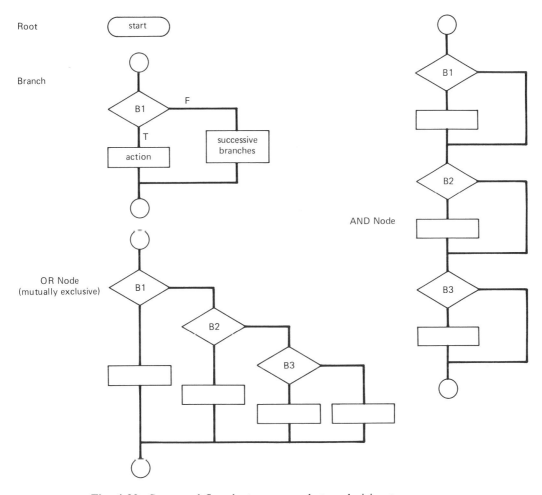

Fig. 4.20. Structured flowchart corresponds to a decision tree.

This language (or interpreter) format allows for the easy construction of decision trees which are frequently used in generative process planning systems. Similar language formats using FORTRAN, Pascal, PL/I, and so on, have been developed for general-purpose algorithms. APPAS [Wysk 1977] is a typical example of decision tree logic used for process planning. Although the approach is easy to implement, system expansion work can be difficult, especially for a programmer other than the creator.

When implementing a decision tree in data form, another program (system program) is required to interpret the data and achieve the decision tree flow. This approach is more difficult to develop (for the system program). However, once the system program has been developed, the implementation and system maintenance is significantly lessened. Again, however, it can be extremely difficult to add a function that was not originally included in the system program. There are many methods that

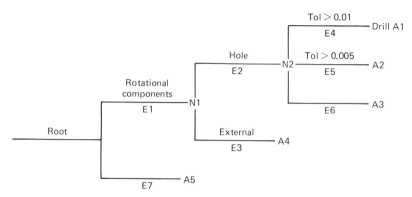

E_i represents an expression or a series of expressions

A_i represents an action

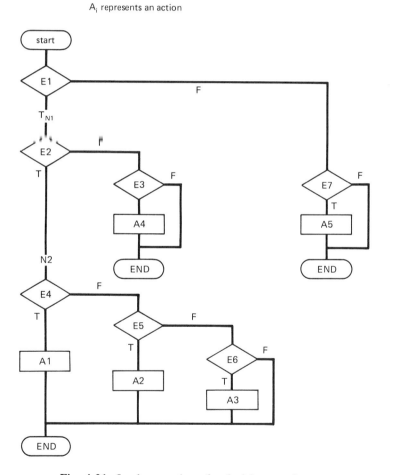

Fig. 4.21. Implementation of a decision tree in a program.

can be used to design such a system program. A simple example will be presented to demonstrate a basic structure that one can use.

We will call the example system DCTREE. DCTREE uses a query system to obtain design information and then print the final conclusions. In DCTREE, there are three major components: (1) the decision tree data, (2) a compiler, and (3) a system run-time module. Part one is supplied by a user who translates a decision tree from graph form into DCTREE input language format. The DCTREE compiler compiles the input and saves it in a computer-usable format. Finally, the system run-time module uses the compiled decision tree to generate questions, make decisions, and printout conclusions.

We will first look at the input language. There are two parts of each input: (1) expression definition, and (2) tree structure definition (Figure 4.22). In the expression definition, each expression is followed by an expression identifier (id). Each id must be unique. An expression with an id initial of Q or A (query or action) is simply stored in a buffer. Other expressions will be compiled as condition expressions. A condition expression (such as $\&1 \leq .002$) uses postfix notation and stack operations. A variable ($\&1$) will cause the run-time module to input a real number and store it on a stack. Therefore, these expressions can be compiled as a simple code instead of using a simple constant or a variable datum.

The tree structure is represented by expression ids and pointers. For instance, an arrow ($\rightarrow$) represents "point to." The syntax is

$$E_{n_0} \rightarrow \begin{bmatrix} AND \\ OR \end{bmatrix} (E_{n_1}, E_{n_2}, \ldots, E_{n_m}) \mid A_i$$

where E_{n_0} = root branch (source)
$\quad E_{n_i}$ = expression number (destination action)
$\quad A_i$ = execution action
$\quad \mid$ = either E's or A's but not both

During compiling each E_n is assigned an address in the tree structure file. E_{n_i}'s in parentheses are substituted by pointers. A_i's are marked with negative values to indicate their actions. Figure 4.22 shows how a decision tree can be represented by DCTREE.

The system run-time module performs the I/O and decision making. In Figure 4.23 a run-time module algorithm is shown. Where $E_{n_i} \rightarrow$ represents the expression pointed to by the root branch, each time $E_{n_i} \rightarrow$ is called in a procedure, it increments forward to the next branch (i.e., $E_{n_0} \rightarrow$ yields AND or OR, $E_{n_0} \rightarrow$ again yields E_{n_1}, $E_{n_0} \rightarrow$ yields E_{n_2}, . . .). A(K) and Q(K) are obtained from expression definitions. E(K) signal the system to evaluate expression definition E_{n_k}. The recursive algorithm can evaluate the entire tree structure and return conclusions.

4.3.4.2 *Decision Tables*. Decision tables have long been a popular method of presenting complex engineering data. Decision tables can also be easily implemented on a computer. Using decision tables for process planning, however, normally re-

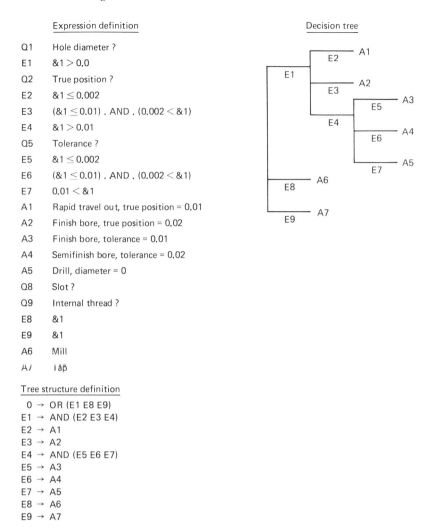

Expression definition

Q1	Hole diameter ?
E1	&1 > 0.0
Q2	True position ?
E2	&1 ≤ 0.002
E3	(&1 ≤ 0.01) . AND . (0.002 < &1)
E4	&1 > 0.01
Q5	Tolerance ?
E5	&1 ≤ 0.002
E6	(&1 ≤ 0.01) . AND . (0.002 < &1)
E7	0.01 < &1
A1	Rapid travel out, true position = 0.01
A2	Finish bore, true position = 0.02
A3	Finish bore, tolerance = 0.01
A4	Semifinish bore, tolerance = 0.02
A5	Drill, diameter = 0
Q8	Slot ?
Q9	Internal thread ?
E8	&1
E9	&1
A6	Mill
A7	Tap

Decision tree

Tree structure definition

```
 0 → OR (E1 E8 E9)
E1 → AND (E2 E3 E4)
E2 → A1
E3 → A2
E4 → AND (E5 E6 E7)
E5 → A3
E6 → A4
E7 → A5
E8 → A6
E9 → A7
```

Fig. 4.22. Input to DCTREE.

quires a special preprocessor program or computer language to implement the table and control the operation of the table. Such software is generally called a decision table language. A decision table language consists of:

1. A base language
2. A decision table
3. An outer language

A base language is the foundation of a decision table language. For example, FOR-TAB of the RAND Corporation and S/360 DLT of the IBM Corporation use FOR-TRAN as their base language [McDaniel 1970]. DETAB/65 [Silberg 1971] of SIG-

```
Procedure DCTREE

Do tree (0 , J) enddo
    (:0: root)

stop
;
procedure tree (Eᵢ,J)

set J := 'F'     (: J = 'T' search successful)

set iflag := 'T'  (:iflag = 'T' or node)

set K := Eᵢ → (:K pointer to first object)

while K ≠ 0 do

    if K < 0 then write A(−K) and set J := 'T'

    (: reach the terminal)

    else if K = 'and' then set iflag := 'F'

            (: define and node)

            else write Q(K) and

            if E(K) then do tree (K, J) and

                if J·iflag then set K := 0

                else K := Eᵢ → endif enddo

            endif endif endif

        endif endif endif

enddo return
```

Fig. 4.23. Run-time module algorithm.

PLAN of ACM (Association of Computing Machinery) uscs COBOL as its base language. A base language is extended to include statements that can describe a decision table in a more easily implemented manner. A preprocessor is occasionally written to translate the decision table language program into its base language program.

The decision table is the most essential part of a decision table language program. It is represented in its original table format. For example, the decision tree in Figure 4.21 can be represented by the decision table in Figure 4.24. Using a pseudolanguage, this decision table can be written as shown in Figure 4.25. Decision table techniques (discussed in Chapter 3) can be used to simplify and/or parse complex tables.

The third element (the outer language) is used to control the decision table. Figure 4.25 illustrates that a decision table does not contain any input/output or control statements, therefore, it is not a complete program. An outer language can eliminate this void. Again, we can use the example to show how this can be done, and DCTABLE will be the name given the decision table language. The table program in Figure 4.25 is written in DCTABLE. A procedure, TAB(N), will evaluate a table N. All variables in DCTABLE are global variables; therefore, no parameters are passed. When table parsing is required, a TAB(N1) can be added to the stub of a table N;

Hole	X	X	X	X	X		
Diameter = 0.0	X	X	X	X	X		
Slot						X	
Internal thread							X
T.P. ≤ 0.002	X						
0.002 < T.P. ≤ 0.01		X					
0.01 < T.P.			X	X	X		
Tol ≤ 0.002			X				
0.002 < Tol ≤ 0.01				X			
0.01 < Tol				X			
Rapid travel out	X						
Finish bore		X	X				
Semifinish bore				X			
Drill				X			
Mill						X	
Tap							X
T.P. = 0.01	X						
T.P. = 0.02		Y					
Tol = 0.01			X				
Tol = 0.02				X			
Diameter = 0					X		

Fig. 4.24. Decision table.

therefore, several tables can be connected. The following program demonstrates the control of a decision table.

```
(: Decision table program for the process selection)
read shape, dia., TP, TOL
Set IFIND := 1
set P:= ƀ
while IFIND = 1 DO TAB(100) and
write 'Process selected' , P and
If P:= ƀ then set IFIND := 0
else set IFIND := 1 endif and
set P:= ƀ enddo
stop
(: ƀ is an empty entry)
```

In the program above, shape, diameter, true position, and tolerance data are input. A process array P which stores a selected process name is set empty (ƀ). Flag IFIND is set as 1. When none of the rules in the table are true, IFIND becomes zero. A procedure, while . . . do . . . enddo, is executed until no rule is true.

```
$ 100 table
```

C							
Shape = hole	.T.	.T.	.T.	.T.	.T.		
Dia > 0.0	.T.	.T.	.T.	.T.	.T.	.T.	.T.
Shape = slot						.T.	
Shape = I thread							.T.
TP ≤ 0.002	.T.						
(0.002 < TP) .and. (TP ≤ 0.01)		.T.					
0.01 < TP			.T.	.T.	.T.		
Tol ≤ 0.002			.T.				
(0.002 < TOL) .and. (TOL ≤ 0.01)				.T.			
0.01 < TOL					.T.		
C							
P := Rapid travel out	X						
P := Finish bore		X	X				
P := Semi-finish bore				X			
P := Drill					X		
P := Mill						X	
P := Tap							X
TP := 0.01	X						
TP := 0.02		X					
TOL := 0.01			X				
TOL := 0.02				X			
DIA := 0					X	X	X

```
C
$ ENDT
```

Fig. 4.25. Decision table program.

A simple algorithm for TAB(N) can be shown as follows. Let

C_i be the condition stub expressions $i = 1, 2, \ldots, n$.

A_j be the action stub expressions $j = 1, 2, \ldots, m$.

$R_{k\ell}$ be the rule entries $k = 1, 2, \ldots, n + m$; $\ell = 1, 2, \ldots, M$.

Step 1. Set $\ell := 0$; while $\ell < M$, do steps 2 through 5 enddo.

Step 2. Set $k := 0$; set LOGIC:= .T.; set $\ell := \ell + 1$.

Step 3. Set $k := k + 1$ while $R_{k\ell} \neq \not b$; do set 4 enddo.

Step 4. If $C_k \neq R_{k\ell}$, then set $k := n + 1$; else LOGIC := .F. endif.

Step 5. If LOGIC = .T., then set $\ell := M + 1$ and do step 6; else, endif.

Step 6. For $j = 1$ to m, do step 7 enddo.

Step 7. If $R_{j+n,1} \neq \not b$, then do A_j enddo; else, endif.

```
LOGIC FUNCTION C(k)

Common ISHAPE, TP, TOL, DIA, P

INTEGER DATA HOLE/'HOLE'/,SLOT/'SLOT'/,THREAD/'THREAD'/


       Go To (10, 20, 30, 40, 50, 60, 70, 80, 90, 100) ,k

10     C = ISHAPE .EQ.Hole
       RETURN

20     C = DIA .GT. 0.0
       RETURN

30     C = ISHAPE .EQ. SLOT
       RETURN

40     C = ISHAPE .EQ. THREAD
       RETURN

50     C = TP .LE. 0.002
       RETURN

60     C = TP.GT. 0.002 .AND. TP .LE. 0.01
       RETURN

70     C = TP .GT. 0.01
       RETURN

nn     n  Tnl  ı r n.nnʔ
       HEıUHIv

90     C = 0.002 .LT. TOL .AND. TOL .LE. 0.01
       RETURN

100    C = 0.001 .LT. TOL
       RETURN

       END
```

Fig. 4.26. Condition stub implemented in a function subprogram.

In the example on p. 151, we assume that a decision table language is used. However, one may not find a formal decision table language appropriate for the programming of an entire process planning system. One can always implement decision table logic using a procedure-oriented language, such as FORTRAN, PL/I, or Pascal. Although the implementation is not as easy as using a decision table language, it is not so difficult as to prohibit the use of decision table logic. The algorithm for TAB can be used with minor modification. C can be a procedure (subprogram) which consists of n expressions, and A another procedure which consists of m expressions (Figure 4.26). The variables used are global variables stored in common blocks. Each time C is called, a parameter, k, is required to index the expression. The logic returns a Boolean value, .T. or .F.. A is similar to C except that it does not return any value. Figures 4.26 and 4.27 show an implementation using FORTRAN. Entries in the table can be assigned as either data statements or input as data.

```
C    ACTION STUB

     SUBROUTINE A(k)

     COMMON ISHAPE, TP, TOL, DIA, P

     INTEGER DATA   RTO/'RTO '/ ,FB/'F-B '/ ,SFB/'SFB '/ ,
                    DRL/'DRL '/ ,MILL/'MILL'/ ,TAP/'TAP '/

     GO TO (10, 20, 30, 40, 50, 60, 70, 80, 90, 100, 110) ,k

10   P = RTO
     RETURN

20   P = FB
     RETURN

30   P = SFB
     RETURN

40   P = DRL
     RETURN

50   P = MILL
     RETURN

60   P = TAP
     RETURN

70   TP = 0.01
     RETURN

80   TP = 0.02
     RETURN

90   TOL = 0.01
     RETURN

100  TOL = 0.02
     RETURN

110  DIA = 0
     RETURN
     END
```

Fig. 4.27. Action stub implemented in a subroutine.

4.3.5 Artificial Intelligence

Artificial intelligence (AI) has become one of the major topics of discussion in computer science. AI can be defined as the ability of a device to perform functions that are normally associated with human intelligence. These functions include reasoning, planning, and problem solving. Applications for AI have been in natural language processing, intelligent data base retrieval, expert consulting systems, theorem proving, robotics, scheduling, and perception problems [Nilsson 1980]. Process planning applications have been considered as part of an expert consulting system.

In an expert system, the knowledge of human experts is represented in an appropriate format. The most common approach is to represent knowledge by using rules. Rule-based deduction is frequently used to find an action. Since AI is too large a subject to discuss in this text, potential applications in process planning will be illustrated.

There are two types of knowledge involved in process planning systems: component knowledge and process knowledge. The component knowledge defines the current state of the problem to be solved (it is also called declarative knowledge). On the other hand, the knowledge of processes defines how the component can be changed by processes (it is also called procedural knowledge). Applying the process knowledge to a component in a logical manner is called control knowledge.

There are several methods available to represent declarative knowledge. First-order predicate calculus (FOPC), frames, and semantic networks [Nau 1981] are two popular methods. Since FOPC is used more often, we will only consider it. FOPC is a formal language in which a wide variety of statements can be expressed. In a predicate calculus language, a statement is expressed by predicate symbols, variable symbols, function symbols, and constant symbols. For example.

$$\text{Depth (Hole(X), 2.5)}$$

represents the depth of hole(X) as 2.5 units. Such a representation is called an atomic formula. In the atomic formula, depth is a predicate symbol. Hole is a function symbol, X is a variable symbol, and 2.5 is a constant. A legitimate atomic formula is called the well-formed formula (wff). The above atomic formula is a wff. A wff can be either T or F. For example, the depth of hole (1) is 2.0, therefore, depth (HOLE(1),2.5) is false. When we use FOPC to describe a component, all wff must be true. The example shown in Figure 4.19 can also be considered descriptive knowledge for the hole design.

Procedural knowledge can be represented by

IF (condition) THEN (action)

statements which are similar to decision trees or decision tables. In AI, such statements can be called production rules. A system using production rules to describe its procedural knowledge is called a production system. In a production rule, a condition can be a conjunction of predicates (wff). For example,

$$(= (\text{shape \&x}) \text{ hole})$$
$$(> (\text{DIA \&x}) 0.0)$$
$$(\leq (\text{TP \&x}) 0.002)$$
$$== >$$
$$(\text{rapid-travel-out \&x})$$
$$(:= (\text{TP \&x}) 0.01) 0.8)$$

where (= (shape &x) hole), (> (Dia &x) 0.0), and (≤ (TP &x) 0.002) are wffs using prefix notation. They form the condition of a production rule. The symbol "==>" represents "THEN." Actions of the rule are assigned rapid-travel-out to surface &x and change TP (true position) to be 0.01. The 0.8 in the action implies a weighting factor or preference of accepting these actions. It is useful when several rules can be applied for a certain state (e.g., several processes or sequences can be used). The AI process planning system GARI and the medical consulting system MYCIN [Davis et al. 1977] use a similar representation for their procedural knowledge.

Even after the descriptive and procedural knowledge have been represented, conclusions (process plans) still cannot be obtained, because we do not have a mechanism to apply the appropriate rule(s) to the problem domain (descriptive knowledge). Control knowledge is similar to human knowledge in reasoning, which deduces certain facts from the knowledge base concerning a problem. This can be very difficult to program on a computer.

Nilsson [1980] listed three control strategy approaches. First, a control strategy problem can be solved by another AI production system. The system for the control strategy problem is called a meta-level AI system. A meta-level AI system has declarative and procedural knowledge relevant to the control of the original problem.

A second approach uses AND/OR solution graphs. In an AND/OR graph, either a goal or a fact can be decomposed and later combined by production rules to reach the opposite state (i.e., from the goal to the fact—backward planning, or from the fact to the goal—forward planning). An AND/OR graph is shown in Figure 4.28. In the graph, the goal is to find A. Rule 1 is (B AND C => A), rule 2 is (D OR E => B), and rule 3 is (F AND G => C). D, E, F, and G are facts in the original state. Using rules 1, 2, and 3, we can find the goal A.

A third method embeds the control knowledge in the rules. The rule also acts like a program. For example, a GOAL statement will search for a goal from the knowledge base (i.e., run a rule program): an ASSERT statement adds a new fact (predicate expression) a RETURN statement returns the control of the program to the program from which it was invoked; and an IF statement evaluates the predicate expression, "If it is T then terminate the current program and return." In the system we have three facts and two rules; prefix notation is adopted.

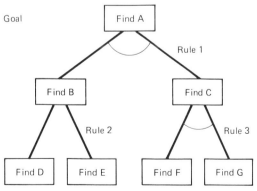

Fig. 4.28. AND/OR graph.

The top-level control program can be written

```
BEGIN
READ "surface id" ?x
GOAL (make-hole ?x)
END
F1:   hole-1 (dia, 2)
F2:   hole-1 (Tol, 0.001)
F3:   hole-1 (TP, 0.001)
      (descriptive knowledge about hole-1)
      R1   (DRILL ?X)
           GOAL (?X dia ?y)
           IF (LESS ?y 0.0) Fail
           GOAL (?X Tol ?y)
           IF (LESS ?y 0.005) Fail
           GOAL (?X TP ?y)
           IF (LESS ?y 0.005) Fail
           ASSERT (?X dia 0)
           PRINT "DRILL"
           RETURN
      R2   (BORE ?X)
           GOAL (?X dia ?y)
           IF (LESS ?y 0.0) Fail
           GOAL (?X Tol ?y)
           IF (LESS ?y 0.001) Fail
           ASSERT (?X Tol 0.01)
           ASSERT (?X TP 0.01)
           PRINT "BORE"
           RETURN
      R3   (Make-hole ?X)
           GOAL (BORE ?X)
           GOAL (DRILL ?X)
           RETURN
      (procedural knowledge for a process)
```

When this program is running, the first input will be for hole-1, the first surface to be planned. The GOAL (make-hole hole-1) will run R3. The first expression in R3, GOAL (bore hole-1), runs R2. In R2, the first expression, GOAL (hole-1 dia 1), returns ?y=2. Since ?y > 0.0, control passes to the next expression. The ASSERT expression changes Tol and TP in hole-1 to 0.01, and BORE is printed. Using the same logic, DRILL can be found and printed. The example above shows only a very simple application. More complicated control knowledge can also be represented.

AI is a comparably new field in computer science (CS). Although there are numerous research programs in CS, few applications for process planning have evolved. Because of the fast deduction capability, AI systems have potential to plan a component in a global sense (consider interrelationships of surfaces) compared with the local planning (surface-by-surface planning) of most other approaches. However, a significant amount of effort is required before it can become a practical tool for process planning.

4.3.6 Closing Remarks

In this chapter the information discussed in previous chapters was integrated into a unified application approach to process planning. A computer-aided process planning system is a system that reads in design specifications, then uses the built-in knowledge to determine the required manufacturing processes. As discussed, there are two approaches: variant and generative. The concept, structure, and complexity of systems using these two approaches are very different. These two approaches have been distinguished. A simplified variant system (VP) was discussed in detail to illustrate how to build variant systems. Since most variant process planning systems are "similar," the VP system represents a typical variant process planning system.

There are many methods (decision logic) that have been and can be used in generative planning. Three major decision procedures were discussed (decision tables, decision trees, and artificial intelligence). The majority of existing systems use one of these three methods. However, the detailed structure is limited only by one's imagination.

Thus far, the complete concept of computer-aided process planning has been presented. In the next chapter, some existing systems are reviewed to show how they are constructed.

REVIEW PROBLEMS

4.1. A small job shop currently operates 12 machines and bids on the manufacture of items for larger industries. They have been awarded 17 major parts contracts for the next 3 months. These contracted items, it turns out, have severe penalties accessed if they are delivered after the contracted due date.

The owner-manager of the shop informs you (his production control manager) that he has overextended his facilities and does not believe that there is enough capacity or time to manufacture these items the way they have been manufactured in the past. The owner also hands you the form shown in Table P4.1, which he has had prepared by one of his specialists. (It simply shows the machining required for each item.)

Knowing what you know about production flow analysis, what suggestions could you make? (Do the actual hand operations involved in grouping into families.) Use the rank order cluster algorithm.

4.2. Develop a FORTRAN or BASIC program that will automatically cluster the parts in Problem 4.1.

4.3. Code the family search procedure described in Section 4.2.3 in FORTRAN or BASIC.

Table P4.1.

Machine	1	2	3	4	5	6	7	8	9	10	11	12	13	14	15	16	17
Press 1		×				×	×							×			
Press 2		×				×	×			×				×			
Bender		×								×				×			
Drill 1						×	×			×				×			
Drill 2	×			×				×									
Saw	×		×	×	×			×			×	×					
Lathe	×		×		×			×			×	×					
Mill 1					×			×									×
Mill 2								×	×		×		×				×
Screw machine			×						×		×		×	×	×	×	
Grinder									×		×		×	×	×	×	
Plating tank			×						×				×		×	×	

Part Number

4.4. Discuss the advantages and disadvantages of the two basic types of standard plan editors used in variant process planning systems.

4.5. Describe the differences between forward and backward planning. From a computation/software standpoint, what advantages accrue from using both systems?

4.6. What are the advantages and disadvantages of using code or graphics input for generative process planning? What other possibilities are there?

4.7. Create a simple decision tree to use for investment purposes. Code the tree into a FORTRAN or BASIC program.

4.8. Artificial intelligence has been advertised as being the answer to resolving automated process planning. Comment on its use and appropriateness.

COMPUTER-AIDED PROCESS
PLANNING SYSTEMS

5.1 IMPLEMENTATION CONSIDERATIONS

From the discussion in previous chapters, we can conclude that the process planning function is manufacturing system dependent. This implies that no one single process planning system can satisfy all of the different manufacturing systems' needs. The same process planning system can be used for two different manufacturing systems with little modification of the process knowledge data base if these two manufacturing systems are similar (equipment and products). However, this is not true when manufacturing systems are significantly different (equipment and products).

There are several factors that must be considered when one attempts to implement a process planning system. These include:

1. Manufacturing system components
2. Production volume/batch size
3. Number of different production families

5.1.1 Manufacturing System Components

The planning function is affected directly by the capability of the manufacturing system that will be used to produce the component. A manufacturing system that has

162

5

precision machining centers can produce most of its products on a single machining center. However, in other systems, several machines may be required to achieve the same precision. This is true for both process and machine selection, and even more true for machine parameter selection or optimization. The process knowledge data base depends on the manufacturing system.

A variant process planning system contains no process knowledge per se. Process plans are retrieved from a data base. The standard process plans in the data base are prepared manually by human process planners. The capability of the manufacturing system was embedded in the process plans by the process planners when they prepared the system. Consequently, the standard plans must be changed when major factory renovation takes place. Variant process planning structures have been adopted by different manufacturing systems; however, the data base must be rebuilt for each system. The lengthy preparation stage is unavoidable. Implementation of a variant planning system requires that a unique data base of component families and standard plans be constructed.

On the other hand, a generative process planning system has its own knowledge base, which stores manufacturing data. The user modifies the knowledge base in order to suit the particular system. A generative process planning system provides the user with a method to describe the capabilities of the manufacturing system. The process knowledge representation as described in Chapter 3 can be created and stored using several methods. It is essential, however, that the user interact with the system so that he or she can easily change the process knowledge base. This must be considered when purchasing or creating a generative process planning system.

5.1.2 Production Volume/Batch Size

Production volume is a major consideration in the selection of production equipment. As a basic rule of thumb, special-purpose machines and tooling are used for mass production, and general-purpose equipment is used for small-batch production. The economics of production determines this decision. These same "economies of scale" must also be applied to process planning.

Different process plans should be used for the same component design when the production volume is significantly different. For example, it is appropriate to turn a thread on an engine lathe if we only need one screw. However, when 10,000 screws are required, a threading die should be considered. Similarly, machining a casting is also more desirable than complete part fabrication for large production volume.

In a variant process planning system, the production volume can be included as a code digit. However, standard plans must be prepared for different levels of production. Preparing standard plans for each production level may not be feasible, since components in the same family may need quite different processes when the production volume increases. When the batch size is not included in the family formation, manual modification of the standard plan for different production than necessary.

In a generative process planning system, the production volume can be considered a variable in the decision model. Ideally, the knowledge base of a system includes this variable. Processes, as well as machines and tool selection, are based not only on shape, tolerance, and surface finish but also on the production volume.

5.1.3 Number of Production Families

The number of different production families used is a function of the number and difference in the components being planned. A variant process planning system is of little value if there are many families and few similar components (family members), because the majority of effort will be spent adding new families and standard plans. A generative process planning system is more desirable for this type of manufacturing environment.

Certain manufacturing systems specialize in making similar or identical components for different assemblies. These components can usually be designated by their features (we typically call them composite components). Since each feature can be machined by one or a series of processes, a model can be developed for each family. In the model, processes corresponding to each feature are stored. A process plan can be generated by retrieving processes that correspond to the features on a new component. This type of generative process planning system utilizes the major benefit of group technology. It is easier to build this type of system than a general generative

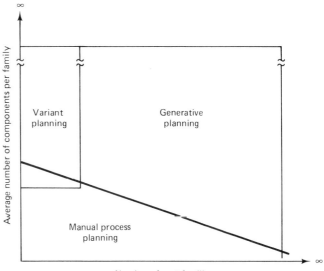

Fig. 5.1. Economic regions for different process planning systems.

process planning system; yet it can provide very detailed plans (depending on the part families being produced).

For a moderate number of component families and many similar components in each family, a variant process planning system is usually the most economic automated planning alternative. Although a long variant preparation stage is still necessary, a variant process planning system is much easier to develop. Such a system can be used very effectively when there are many similar components. On the other hand, significant product variation usually dictates generative process planning as the most economic alternative. Figure 5.1 illustrates the economic regions for the different planning alternatives.

5.2 A SURVEY OF PROCESS PLANNING SYSTEMS

The majority of existing process planning systems are of a variant nature (e.g., CAPP, MIPLAN, MITURN, MIAPP, ACUDATA/UNIVATION, CINTURN, COMCAPP V, etc.). However, there are some generative systems, such as CPPP, AUTAP, and APPAS. Table 5.1 contains a list of some process planning systems and their characteristics. A check in the various columns of the table indicates that the corresponding planning function, shape, or other characteristic is part of a planning system.

1. *Input*

   Input in Table 5.1 refers directly to the information required for selecting processes. A code implies that a part or GT code is used as input for describing

Table 5.1. SUMMARY TABLE

System name	CAP	ACUDATA/ UNIVATION	AUTAP	AUTOPLAN
Part shapes				
Rotational		✓	✓	✓
Prismatic		✓		
Sheet metal	✓		✓	
Input				
Code				✓
Special language			✓	
CAD data base				✓
Others	Part number	Part number		
Planning approach				
Variant				
Code based				
User				✓
Build-in				
Others	Part number	✓		
Generative				
Code based				
User				✓
Build-in				
Others			Decision table	
Automated functions				
Process seq.			✓	✓*
Material			✓	✓*
Machine			✓	✓*
Tool			✓	✓*
Fixture				✓*
Parameters			✓	✓
Cutter path			✓	
User supplied logic	Process plan	Process plan	Decision table	Std. plan
Manual editing	✓	✓		✓
Commercial/academic			Commercial	Commercial
Designer	Lockheed	Allis-Chalmers	Aachen Tech Univ.	Metcut
Comments	• Data base report generator 1963 completed	• Retrieval system interfaced with prod. planning		• Graphical planning aids
References	[Tulkoff 1981]	[Doran 1978]	[Eversheim et al. 1980a]	[Tempelhof 1980]

*Interactive

Table 5.1. SUMMARY TABLE (CONT.)

System name	APPAS	AUTOPROS	CADCAM	CAPP
Part shapes				
Rotational				✔
Prismatic	✔		Hole making	✔
Sheet metal				✔
Input				
Code	COFORM			✔
Special language				
CAD data base			✔	
Others				
Planning approach				
Variant				
Code based				
User				✔
Build-in				
Others				
Generative				
Code based				
User				
Build-in	Decision tree			
Others			Decision table logic	
Automated functions				
Process seq.	✔	✔	✔	✔
Material				
Machine				
Tool	✔		✔	
Fixture				
Parameters	✔		✔	
Cutter path				
User supplied logic				Std. plan
Manual editing				✔
Commercial/academic	Academic	Commercial	Academic	Commercial
Designer	Wysk/Purdue	NAKK	Chang/Va Tech	McAuto/CAM-I
Comments	● Detailed surface code 1977	● Not enough information	● Graphics input ● Extension of APPAS 1980	● Retrieval system 1976
References	[Wysk 1977] [Wysk et al. 1980]	[Chisolm 1973]	[Chang and Wysk 1980, 1981]	[Link 1976] [Schilperoot 1975] [Tulkoff 1978]

*Interactive

Table 5.1. SUMMARY TABLE (CONT.)

System name	CIMS/PRO	COBAPP	COMCAPP V	CPPP	DCLASS
Part shapes					
Rotational		✔	✔	✔	✔
Prismatic	✔		✔		✔
Sheet metal					✔
Input					
Code		APPOCC	CODE	✔	DCLASS
Special language	CIMS/DEC				
CAD data base					
Others				Detailed information	
Planning approach					
Variant					
Code based					
User					
Build-in			✔		
Others					
Generative					
Code based					
User					
Build-in		✔			
Others	✔*			Decision model	Decision tree logic
Automated functions					
Process seq.	✔	✔	✔	✔	✔
Material					✔
Machine	✔			✔	✔
Tool	✔			✔	✔
Fixture					
Parameters				✔	
Cutter path	✔				
User supplied logic			Std. plan	Process model	Decision tree
Manual editing			✔	✔	✔
Commercial/academic		Academic	Commercial	Commercial	Commercial
Designer	Iwata et al (Japan)	Phillips/ Purdue	MDSI	UTRC	Allen/U. Utah
Comments	• Capable of recognizing the surface shape	1978	• Retrieval system	• Special process modelling language	
References	[Iwata 1980]	[Phillips 1978]		[Dunn and Mann 1978] [Mann et al 1977] [Kotler 1980a,b]	[Allen and Smith 1974, 1978, 1979, 1980]

*Interactive

168

Table 5.1. SUMMARY TABLE (CONT.)

System name	EXAPT	GARI	GETURN	GENPLAN	MIAPP
Part shapes					
Rotational	✔		✔	✔	✔
Prismatic	✔	✔		✔	✔
Sheet metal				✔	
Input					
Code				Lockheed/Opitz	MICLASS
Special language	✔ APT		✔		
CAD data base					
Others		✔			
Planning approach					
Variant					
Code based					
User					✔
Build-in				✔	
Others	NA		NA		
Generative					
Code based					
User					
Build-in					
Others		AI expert system			
Automated functions					
Process seq.		✔		✔*	✔*
Material					
Machine				✔	
Tool			✔	✔	
Fixture					
Parameters	✔		✔		
Cutter path	✔		✔		
User supplied logic		Production rules		Std. plan	Std. plan
Manual editing	✔			✔	✔
Commercial/academic	Commercial	Academic	Commercial	Commercial	Commercial
Designer	EXAPT	Descotte et al.	GE	Lockheed	OIR
Comments	• Part programming	• Using MACLISP language	• Part programming 1975	1979	
References	[Budde 1973]	[Descotte and Latombe 1981]		[Tulkoff 1981]	[Schaffer 1980]

*Interactive

169

Table 5.1. SUMMARY TABLE (CONT.)

System name	MIPLAN	MITURN	PI-CAPP	RPO
Part shapes				
Rotational	✔	✔	✔	✔
Prismatic	✔		✔	
Sheet metal			✔	
Input				
Code	MICLASS	MICLASS	✔	✔
Special language				
CAD data base				✔
Others	Part number			
Planning approach				
Variant				
Code based				
User				✔
Build-in	MICLASS	✔	✔	
Others				
Generative				
Code based				
User				✔
Build-in				
Others				
Automated functions				
Process seq.	✔*	✔*	✔*	✔*
Material				
Machine				
Tool				
Fixture				
Parameters				✔
Cutter path				
User supplied logic	Std. plan	Std. plan	Std. plan	
Manual editing	✔	✔	✔	✔
Commercial/academic	Commercial	Commercial	Commercial	Commercial
Designer	GE/OIR	OIR	Planning Institution	GE/Metcut
Comments			• Super CAPP • Multiple user • Graphics output allowed	• Based on AUTOPLAN
References	1980 [Schaffer 1980] [TNO 1981]	1974 [TNO 1981]	1980 [Planning Institute 1980]	[Tipnis et al. 1980] [Vogel 1980]

*Interactive

Table 5.1. SUMMARY TABLE (CONT.)

System name	XPS-1	SIB	SISPA	CAPSY
Part shapes				
Rotational	✔			✔
Prismatic	✔		✔	
Sheet metal		✔		
Input				
Code	For variant	✔	✔	
Special language				Dialogue
CAD data base				
Others	Code & description	Operation sequence		
Planning approach				
Variant				
Code based				
User	✔			
Build-in				
Others				
Generative				
Code based				
User				
Build-in		✔		
Others	Decision table logic			Decision table
Automated functions				
Process seq.	✔			✔
Material	✔			
Machine	✔	✔	✔	✔
Tool	✔	✔	✔	✔
Fixture	✔		✔	✔
Parameters	✔			✔
Cutter path				✔
User supplied logic	Decision table			
Manual editing	✔			Interactive
Commercial/academic	Commercial	Academic	Commercial	Academic
Designer	/CAM-I	IPA Stuttgart/ Siemens AG	Siemens	Tech U. of Berlin
Comments	● Both variant & generative ● Under development			● Under development
References	[CAM-I 1980]	[Weill et al. 1982]	[Weill et al. 1982]	[Weill et al. 1982]

*Interactive

parts. When a particular coding system is used, it is indicated in the entry. "Special language" implies that a part description language is used. "CAD data base" means that the input description for a part comes from a CAD model. When two entries are marked, it implies that: 1) either both types of input are required and 2) the system is capable of using either.

2. *Planning approach*
   Planning approaches are noted as either variant or generative. "Code based" implies that the process plan retrieval or generation system is based on a code (the input section). When more than one entry is marked, it implies that more than one approach can be used. "NA" indicates that it is not applicable.

3. *Output contents*
   Various types of information can be retrieved or generated by process planning systems. In the case of a pure retrieval system, detailed information can be retrieved from a standard plan. For this case only the process sequence entry is marked.

4. *User-supplied logic*
   When user-supplied decision logic is required before the system can function, a check is indicated in this entry.

5. *Commercial/academic*
   This category indicates the nature of the system development. When a system is specifically developed for a single company or when it is unclear what the nature of the system is, the entry is left blank.

6. *Designer*
   The designer refers to the individual or organization that developed the system.

7. *References*
   References are given at the end of this book.

In the following sections, we discuss some process planning systems in more detail.

5.2.1 CAM-I CAPP

The CAM-I automated process planning system (CAPP) [Link 1976, Schilperoot 1975] is perhaps the most widely used of all process planning systems. It is a variant system developed by McDonnell Douglas Automation Company (McAuto) under a contract from CAM-I. CAPP was first demonstrated and released to its sponsoring members in 1976.

CAPP (Figure 5.2) is a data base management system written in ANSI standard FORTRAN. It provides a structure for a data base, retrieval logic, and interactive editing capability. The coding scheme for part classification and the output format are added by the user. A 36-digit (maximum) alphanumeric code is allowed. A coding scheme tailored to the user application is usually appropriate. For example, Lockheed-Georgia used a modified Opitz code for their CAPP system and achieved successful results [Tulkoff 1978]. PI-CAPP, an extension of CAPP, has its own (built-in) coding

Flow diagram

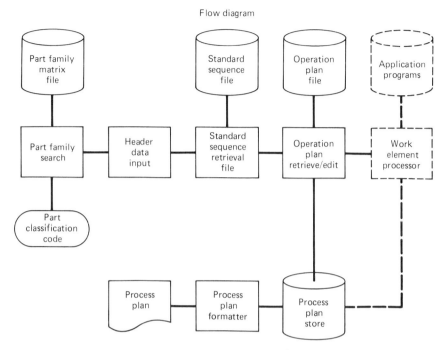

Fig. 5.2. CAPP system. [Courtesy of Computer-Aided Manufacturing International, Inc.]

and classification system. (This eliminates the requirement of a user-developed coding scheme.)

A typical process planning session using CAPP would probably look as shown in Figure 5.3. The main menu for the CAPP system contains 11 entries. A header display (HD) is used for each new plan to be created. Assuming that an arbitrary coding scheme has been implemented, Figure 5.4 shows the kind of information that would be required to create a new plan. The family number and GT code attributes (page 1 of the header menu) are used for standard plan retrieval. FS (part Family

```
      FS    MS    SA    FP    DP    HD    OS    OP    PP    GT    LO
                  ** CAPP RELEASE 2.1 **
PART FAMILY SEARCH       FS
MATRIX SEARCH            MS/CLASSIFICATION CODE
SEARCH ATTRIBUTES        SA/COL. NO., VALUE(S)
FORMAT PLAN              FP/PARTNO,PLAN TYPE,STATUS
DELETE PLAN              DP/PARTNO,PLAN TYPE,STATUS
CREATE NEW PLAN          HD
RETRIEVE OPCODE SEQ      OS/PARTNO,PLAN TYPE,STATUS
RETRIEVE OP PLAN         OP/PARTNO,PLAN TYPE,STATUS
PROCESS PLAN REVIEW      PP/PARTNO,PLAN TYPE,STATUS
GROUP TECHNOLOGY         GT
LOGOFF                   LO
```

Fig. 5.3. CAPP main menu. [Courtesy of Computer-Aided Manufacturing International, Inc.]

```
OS  SI  SC  RR  FS  DS  MM  PD  PU  FI  LO

FILL IN THE FOLLOWING FOR STORAGE AND RETRIEVAL PURPOSES

PLANNING I.D. =                              /
PLANNING REVISION NO. =                      /
PLANNING TYPE= /
FAMILY NUMBER=001/
G/T CODE=                                     /

NOW PAGE DOWN TO FILL IN THE ACTUAL HEADER DATA

              HEADER MENU (PAGE 1)


OS  SI  SC  RR  FS  DS  MM  PD  PU  FI  LO

<+> <+> <+> <+> <ASSEMBLY INSTRUCTIONS > <+> <+> <+> <+>
                                                        /
PROGRAM    =                    D/M=     PA=           /
PLAN TYPE  =               FAMILY NO.=   DATE=MM-DD-YY/
PART NO.   =                    REV=     PC=           /
PART NAME  =                                           /
PLANNER    =                            DATE=MM-DD-YY/
CHECKER    =                            DATE=MM-DD-YY/

<+> <+> <+> < ENGINEERING REFERENCE DRAWINGS > <+> <+> <+>

ENG DWG=                 REV=                          /
EO'S=                    REV=                          /
P/L=                     REV=                          /
DW'M                     DEV=                          (
W/L=                                                   /
EO'S=                                                  /
SCH=                                                   /
EO'S=                                                  /
NEXT ASSY=                                             /

              HEADER MENU (PAGE 2)
```

Fig. 5.4. New plan creation. [Courtesy of Computer-Aided Manufacturing International, Inc.]

Search), MS (Matrix Search), and SA (Search Attributes) are used to retrieve process plans.

In Figure 5.5 a part family searching session is illustrated. The upper portion of the figure represents an arbitrary part family matrix file. The code used is a five-digit code with five-values for each digit. After the search is completed, a standard plan can be retrieved. The standard plan is structured in a manner so that it also returns a standard sequence for the part. The sequence is called an OP (operation) sequence in the CAPP terminology. In the OP sequence, operations are represented by OP codes which are alphanumeric codes. For each OP code in the sequence, an operation plan consists of a description of the detailed operation steps, machine, tools, fixtures, operation time, and so on, all of which can be retrieved. The complete process plan is a plan with operation plans imbedded in the sequence.

CAPP also allows the user to use an existing GT system in the process plan search. This feature requires only minimum modification by the user during the system implementation. CAPP-like systems are easy to learn and easy to use. The range of

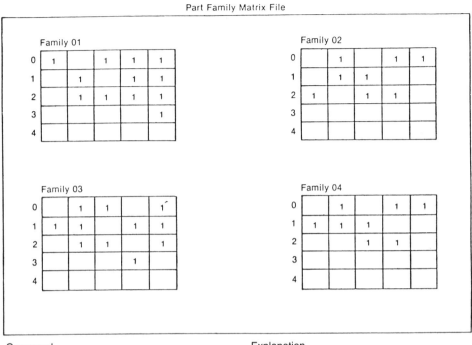

Fig. 5.5. Part family search.

components that can be planned by CAPP is dependent on the capability of the coding scheme. Approximately 400 CAPP systems (1980) have been purchased through the CAM-I library or the CASA Organization of the Society of Manufacturing Engineers.

5.2.2 MIPLAN and MULTICAPP

Both MIPLAN [Schaffer 1980, TNO 1981] and MULTICAPP were developed in conjunction with OIR (Organization for Industrial Research, Inc.). They are both variant systems that use the MICLASS coding system for part description. They are data retrieval systems (Figure 5.6) which retrieve process plans based on part code, part number, family matrix, and code range. By inputting a part code, parts with a

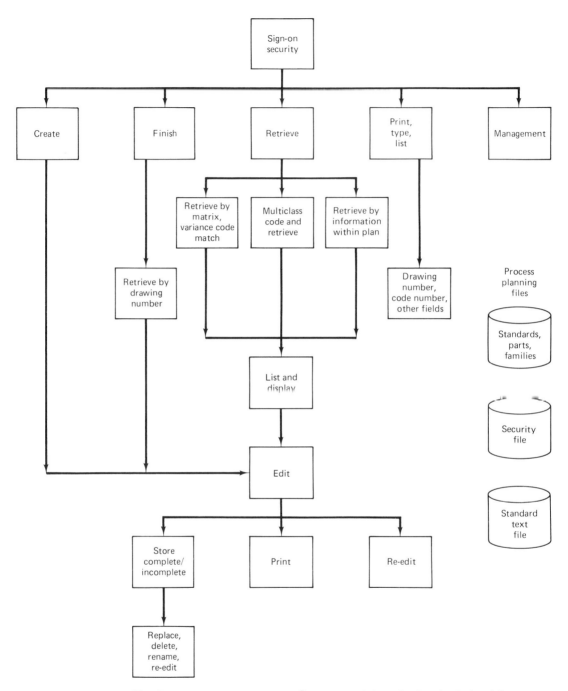

Fig. 5.6. MULTICAPP system. [Courtesy of Organization for Industrial Research, Inc.]

similar code (user-defined similarity) are retrieved. The process plan for each part is then displayed and edited by the user. They are similar to the CAM-I CAPP system with MICLASS embedded as part of the system.

5.2.3 APPAS and CADCAM

APPAS (an acronym for "Automated Process Planning And Selection") is a generative system for detailed process selection. CADCAM is an extension of AP-PAS. CADCAM operates using a CAD "front end" to interface with APPAS. It also uses decision table logic for the process selection. The major difference between APPAS and other planning systems is in the surface description. APPAS describes the detailed technological information of each machined surface by means of a special code. A single machined surface is typically described using a data string of 30 to 40 attributes, and a built-in decision tree controls the decision making for the selection of detailed processes. The selection criteria is based on the capabilities of the individual processes, which are represented in a process boundary table (Table 5.2). The system is capable of selecting multiple passes and processes for the designated machined surface (such as: twist drill → rough bore → finish bore). Multiple-diameter holes with special features such as an oil groove, slot, or thread can be planned as single machined surfaces. The details of APPAS include the selection of feed rate, cutting speed, diameter of the tool, number of milling cutter teeth, length of the tool, and length or depth of cut for each tool pass. The user can select the detail method, that is, use pure table look-up or optimize machining parameters. Time and cost estimates are also given as part of the process plans.

CADCAM provides an interactive graphics interface to APPAS. Components can be modeled graphically and edited interactively. A decision table approach also lessens the difficulty required to expand the system. An example of the CADCAM system is shown in Figures 5.7 and 5.8. Both APPAS and CADCAM are written in standard FORTRAN.

5.2.4 AUTOPLAN and RPO

AUTOPLAN [Vogel and Adlard 1981] and RPO [Tipnis et al. 1980] were both developed by Metcut Research Associates. RPO is an installation of AUTOPLAN in the GE Aircraft Engine Group for Rotating Parts Operation. AUTOPLAN is gener-

Table 5.2. PROCESS BOUNDARY TABLE

```
*********************************************
RECORD 4                      FINISH BORE
-------------------------------------------
LINKAGE ADDR:        0   0   0   0
-------------------------------------------
MINIMUM DIA :  0.375  MAXIMUM DIA : 10.000
MAXIMUM DEPTH : 10.000 X HOLE DIA
TOLERANCE :
    POSITIVE : .0002 X DIA ** 0.0 +.00010
    NEGATIVE : .0002 X DIA ** 0.0 +.00010
STRAIGHTNESS : .0 (L/DIA) ** 0.0 +.00030
PARALLELISM : .0 (L/DIA) ** 0.0 +.00050
ROUNDNESS : 0.0003
TRUE POSITION : .0001
SURFACE FINISH (BEST) : 8.
```

Process plan for hole: (0.7500, 2.0000, 2.0000)

— Hole located at center: 0.7500   2.0000   2.0000

    Process sequence:
      1: Twist drig
      2: Tap

— For hole located at center: 0.7500   2.0000   2.0000

Deep hole application   Length–diameter ratio = 3.00

Twist drill this hole

Drill diameter = 0.242000

Feed: 0.0155   Speed: 302.98   Time (HSS Tool): 0.0393

Spindle stroke: 1.1002

Cost for this step: 0.04

Ductile material, use fluteless tap

Tap size: 0.2500   Feed: 0.10000   Speed: 456.55   Time: 0.02

Cost for tapping: 0.02

Total cost for this hole: 0.06

Fig. 5.7. Process plan for hole.

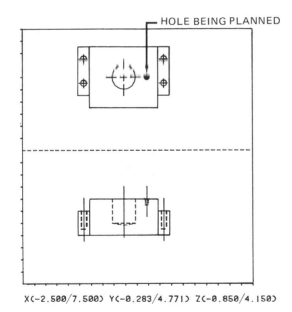

COMMAND:

HOLE BEING PLANNED

X(-2.500/7.500) Y(-0.283/4.771) Z(-0.850/4.150)

Fig. 5.8. Design model of CAD/CAM.

ative only in the detailing of the part. The process selection and process sequencing level does not differ significantly from CAPP or MIPLAN. The four major modules of the system are:

1. *GT retrieval*—process plan retrieval
2. *Graphical planning aides*—tooling layout, verification, and work instruction preparation

3. *Generative process planning*—tooling recommendations, cut recommendations, and machine tool settings
4. *Process optimization*—minimum cost or maximum production rate

The unique feature of the system is the graphics interface. This provides the user with the capability to interactively view the selection and verify the plans. A GT code with decision tree logic is used for the generative process planning. AUTOPLAN took 10 to 12 person-years to develop (Vogel and Adlard 1981) and contains some 325 subprograms and 40,000 lines of source code.

5.2.5 AUTAP

The AUTAP system is one of the most complete planning systems in use today. AUTAP is capable of material selection, process selection, process sequencing, machine tool selection, tool selection, lathe chuck selection (for turned parts), and part program generation. The feature that makes AUTAP unique is its part description

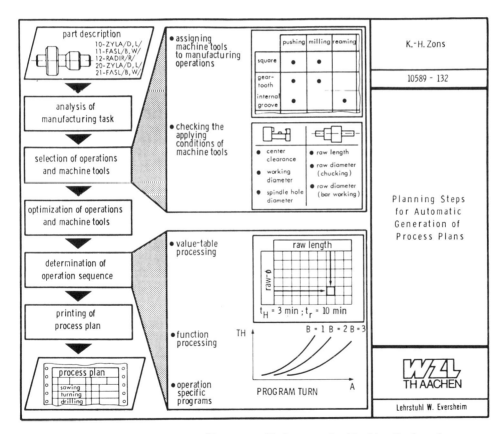

Fig. 5.9. AUTAP system. [Courtesy of Laboratory for Machine Tools and Production Engineering of Technical University of Aachen.]

		No.	1	2	3	4
	Machine Tool Selection					
Condition	300 < Length < 500	1	X	X		
Condition	Dia < 200	2	X	X		
Condition	Max Speed < 3000	3		X		
Condition	Tolerance < 0.01	4	X			X
Condition	Lot Size > 100	5		X	X	
Condition	Fixture 123 Exist	6		X	X	
Condition	Fixture 125 Exist	7			X	X
Conclusion	Machine 1001	1	X			X
Conclusion	Machine 1002	2		X		
Conclusion	Machine 1003				X	

Fig. 5.10. Decision table.

language. AUTAP uses primitives to construct a part similar to a constructive solid geometry (CSG) language. A somewhat limited modeling process is used in AUTAP, and the use of AUTAP must follow the part modeling procedures, using only union operations (as compared with the entire set of Boolean operators used in CSG).

Figure 5.9 shows a rotational component that is described using the language. The component is decomposed into three distinct entities starting from the left. The codes starting with "1" (i.e., 10, 11, 12, and 13) describe the first entity, which consists of a cylinder (10), a straight chamfer (12), and a fillet chamfer (13). A unique descriptor is assigned to each feature. Therefore, any shape and technological information (i.e., geometric tolerances, etc.) can be described. The complete input includes the part description and organizational data such as part number and lot size. Currently, AUTAP can plan rotational and sheet metal parts.

In the process planning phase of AUTAP; first, the part description is evaluated, and then the outermost contour is selected. Comparing this information with existing stock, the raw material is selected. The process selection, process sequence selection, and machine tool selection are based on decision table logic (Figure 5.10). Decision table contents (variables) are supplied by the user for the specific application.

The interface of AUTAP with AUTAP-NC can provide further planning functions, such as tool selection, fixture selection, and part program generation. AUTAP-NC is capable of planning rotational parts. The final output of AUTAP-NC is an NC part program. By coupling AUTAP with the EXAPT system [Eversheim et al. 1980], final Cutter Location DATA (CLDATA) and a verification drawing can also be obtained.

AUTAP is a system designed especially to interface with a CAD system. It can be installed as part of an integrated CAD/CAM system, and applications by several German companies have been reported.

5.2.6 CPPP

CPPP (Computerized Production Process Planning) was developed by the United Technologies Research Center, partially under U.S. Army funding. It was designed for planning cylindrical parts. CPPP is capable of generating a summary of operations and the detailed operation sheets required for production. Operation sheets include sketches of the fully dimensioned workpiece with tolerances. Machine tool, cut sequences, reference surfaces, clamping surfaces, tools, and machining parameters are also specified.

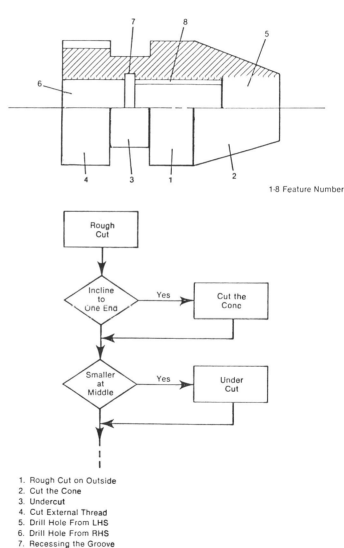

1-8 Feature Number

1. Rough Cut on Outside
2. Cut the Cone
3. Undercut
4. Cut External Thread
5. Drill Hole From LHS
6. Drill Hole From RHS
7. Recessing the Groove
8. Internal Threading
9. Part Off

Fig. 5.11. Composite component.

The principle behind CPPP is a composite-component concept. A composite component can be thought of as an imaginary component which contains all the features of components in one part family. By building a process model that contains the solution for every feature, components in the entire family can be planned (Figure 5.11). CPPP incorporates a special language, COPPL, to describe the process model. COPPL is an English-like language that can be used by manufacturing personnel with little training or computer programming experience. The following is a valid COPPL expression.

Turn outside surface on manual lathe if surface is an open diameter (and) diametral tolerance is $>= 0.002\$$.

Operations	Part Surface/Feature									Machines
	1	2	3	4	5	6	7	8	9	
Turn	X			X	X	X		X		Bar
Turn		X	X						X	Chucker
Grind	X									Surface Grinder
Grind					X	X				OD Grinder
Grind									X	ID Grinder
Nitride									X	Furnace
Drill							X			Drill Press
Grind									X	ID Grinder
Hone									X	Auto Hone
Total Operations	2	1	1	1	2	2	1	1	5	

Operation Matrix

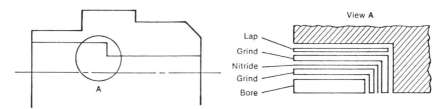

Fig. 5.12. Process steps defined by an Operation Matrix for a part surface. [Courtesy of Numerical Control Society.]

Process selection and sequencing is based on the process model discussed previously. The results of selection and sequencing are combined with the part surface and operation data (tooling, machine tool, setup, etc.) to form an operation matrix (Figure 5.12). Cut sequence (the order of surface cuts within the same process), machine tool, and tools are selected by using the information in the operation matrix. Each cut can be displayed on a CRT screen for verification. CPPP also allows an interactive mode whereby the planner can interact with the system at several fixed interaction points.

The development of a process model is necessary for every part family. An average of 4 person-months' effort is required for each model [Dunn and Mann 1978]. CPPP is most suitable for those applications in which there are few part families, but each family member contains many variations.

5.2.7 GARI

GARI is an experimental problem solver which uses artificial intelligence (AI) techniques. The unique feature of GARI is the representation of planning knowledge. GARI employs a production rule knowledge base to store process capabilities. The form of each rule is

conditions ==> pieces of advice

Each piece of advice is assigned a weighting factor to represent its importance. Since GARI is implemented in the MACLISP language, LISP notations are adapted here. A typical rule can be stated as

$$-(>== \text{(surface-quality \&x) 6.3)}$$

$$==>$$

$$(9 \text{ (roughing-cut \&x))}$$

which means:

> If the surface quality of an entity "&x" is higher (poorer) than 6.3, then one
> is advised (with a weight equal to 9) to avoid a roughing cut for &x.

The part being planned is described using a special notation. The notation includes a maximum of 20 different attributes, which represent shape, tolerance, surface finish, and so on. An example can be shown.

Let H be a hole to be described. S1, S2, and S3 are defined surfaces for H:

(H (type countersunk-hole)

(starting-from SI)

(opening-on S3)

(diameter 6)

(countersink-diameter 12)

(surface-quality 7))

(line feed space)

(distance H S2 19)

(countersink-depth H S1 3 + −80)

(perpendicularity H S3 + −50)

In a manner similar to the medical consultation counterparts (e.g., MYCIN [Shortliffe 1976]), a search is used to find the goal—plan the part. When a different solution (contradictory conclusions from different rules) is detected, the system is able to discard certain pieces of advice in order to resolve the problem. This kind of system can be developed by consulting expert planners and adding new rules to the system. This, in fact, is the major advantage of rule-based systems. Because other functions of process planning, such as machine, tool, and fixture selection, are more routine, and parameter optimization is more mathematical, AI is not an appropriate tool for those functions. GARI does not try to plan these functions; only process selection and process sequencing can be planned with this system. No practical application of GARI has been reported.

5.3 SUMMARY

In this chapter a review of some existing automated process planning systems has been presented. Several commercial and experimental systems have been developed. Industries that employ computer-aided process planning systems have reported reductions of as much as 95% time savings for new part planning activities. The use utility and payback for these systems, however, is a function of the manufacturing system that the planning systems will support. Some computer-aided process planning systems perform well in one environment, yet poorly in another. Some of these application needs have been discussed.

REVIEW QUESTIONS

5.1. A small manufacturing company involved in the manufacture of turned parts is considering an automated process planning system. The company is a job shop specializing in small production lots. Products are seldom repeated; however, there is now a large dissimilarity in most items. What advice would you give the plant manager/owner? What systems should he explore?

5.2. What are the differences between CAPP, MIPLAN, and AUTOPLAN? For what applications might each system be used?

5.3. How does AUTAP differ from the other process planning systems discussed in this chapter? What are its advantages?

5.4. Using AUTAP primitives or AUTAP-like primitives, construct a part of your choosing.

TIPPS: AN INTEGRATED PROCESS PLANNING SYSTEM

Thus far, several topics related to process planning have been discussed. The input for process planning (engineering design or CAD), process capabilities, approaches to process planning, and information decision systems have all been discussed in significant detail. Although all of these topics are closely related to process planning, an integrated approach to generative process planning has yet to be presented. Unfortunately, this has also typified much of the research on process planning both in the United States and abroad. In this chapter a unified approach to process planning is presented.

The discussion in this chapter focuses on a structured approach to process planning. A process planning system called TIPPS (Totally Integrated Process Planning System) is presented in the chapter. The organization of TIPPS along with its structure, software, and required hardware are discussed. Some examples of components that were planned using TIPPS are also presented.

6.1 TIPPS: AN OVERVIEW

TIPPS is a generative process planning system that has evolved from the APPAS [Wysk 1979] and CADCAM [Chang and Wysk 1981] systems. TIPPS is one of the few (perhaps the only) systems that integrates CAD and generative process planning into a unified system. In TIPPS, the logical divisions of process planning are broken

6

into functional modules (see Figure 6.1). The modules within the dashed lines in Figure 6. 1 have already been implemented as TIPPS software. However, even this software is small when compared to the total manufacturing planning system shown in Figure 1.11.

TIPPS input comes from a CAD data base. In TIPPS, an object (component) is represented by its boundaries (a boundary model). Faces are defined by their limiting edges, and these faces form the boundaries of the component. Dimensions can be measured from the edges, and technological information such as size, tolerance, and surface finish are also included in the data base and are linked to corresponding faces. The model of an object contains the information necessary for display as well as for process planning. The format for TIPPS input will be discussed later. Currently, TIPPS is confined to box-shaped components with holes and machined surfaces that can be approached only from the top of the part. Graphical displays can be in either of two forms: a two- or three-dimensional drawing (without hidden-line removal). Figure 6.2 illustrates these two drawing modes.

In TIPPS, surfaces that require machining are identified by a designer or process planner. [TIPPS provides a tool (a cursor) to identify (mark) surfaces interactively.] The descriptive information relevant to the marked surface is stored in a surface file that contains surface codes. Also contained in this file are the faces corresponding to each surface and the surface relationships. TIPPS also allows the user to modify the surface file. Figure 6.3 shows a graphical display of different mark surfaces.

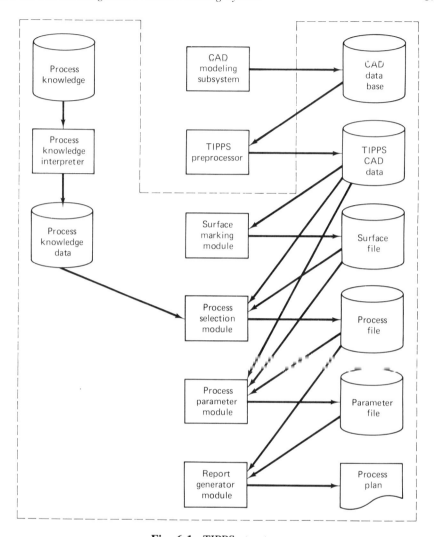

Fig. 6.1. TIPPS structure.

The process selection module uses information from the surface file and the CAD data base to select appropriate processes. The process knowledge that represents the capabilities of a process is described by using a simple description language—PKI. The description is translated into a link list data file—process knowledge data. When the process selection module is invoked, it runs as a language interpreter in which the process knowledge data becomes the program. Backward planning and recurrent calls are used in the process selection phase. A feasible sequence of processes and tools can be selected for a component (Figure 6.4). The resultant processes are saved in a process file.

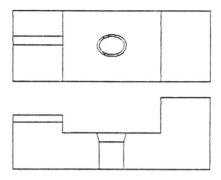

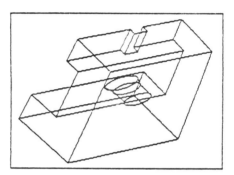

Fig. 6.2. Two- and three-dimensional display of a component using the TIPPS planning system.

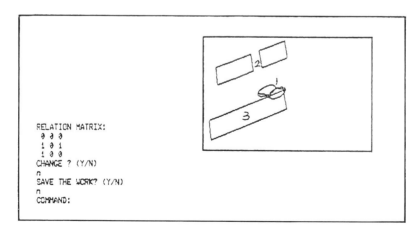

Fig. 6.3. Surface identified.

```
COMMAND:
proc

**** SURFACE : 2 ****

PROCESS:  R F MILL

**** SURFACE : 3 ****

PROCESS:  R F MILL

**** SURFACE : 1 ****

PROCESS:   TWST DRL
PROCESS:   RGH BORE
COMMAND:
```

Fig. 6.4. Process selection information from TIPPS.

Process parameters (feed and speed) are determined by the process parameter module. A table-look-up procedure is currently used in selecting appropriate parameters. Input to this module includes material type, hardness, tool material, tool diameter, surface shape, and dimension. Output from this module are feed, speed, and machining time. Although the module is capable of finding optimum parameters, a fixed tool life is usually employed.

Finally, there is a report generator which prints the final process plan in a human-readable format. Figure 6.5 shows a printout of a process plan that contains processes, tools, feeds, speeds, and machining time.

TIPPS is a research-based system which is by no means complete; however, it does demonstrate how a generative process planning system can be developed. It also provides a structure for future expansion.

6.2 TIPPS DESIGN PHILOSOPHY

The major concept used in designing TIPPS is to construct a generic framework for a modular system. The system can interface with a CAD system and can be

```
+------------------------------------------------------------------------------+
|                                                                              |
|                         P R O C E S S    P L A N                              |
|                                                                              |
| PART NAME: BRACKET TWO                     PART NUMBER: B-10002               |
| MATERIAL:        2                         PLANNER:      T. C. CHANG          |
|                          DATE :AUGUST 13, 1982                               |
|                                                                              |
+------------------------------------------------------------------------------+
| OP |   SURFACE     |  L   |   D   |      | PROCESS | TOOL  | FEED   | SPEED  | TIME  | REMARKS|
| NO | ID | TYPE     |  L   |   W   |  H   |         | DIA   | (IPR)  | (RPM)  | (MIN) |        |
|                                                                              |
| 1  | 2  | FLAT     | 4.000| 2.000 | 0.0  |R F MILL | 2.040 | 0.02091| 147.34 | 1.30  |        |
| 2  | 3  | FLAT     | 4.000| 2.000 | 0.0  |R F MILL | 2.040 | 0.02091| 147.34 | 1.30  |        |
| 3  | 1  | HOLE     | 1.000| 0.995 | 0.0  |TWST DRL | 0.995 | 0.02139| 204.25 | 0.23  |        |
| 4  |    |          |      |       |      |RGH BORE | 1.000 | 0.00412| 124.10 | 1.95  |        |
+------------------------------------------------------------------------------+
|                               TOTAL PROCESSING TIME :     4.78 MINUTES        |
+------------------------------------------------------------------------------+
```

Fig. 6.5. TIPPS process plan.

expanded easily because of the structure of its process knowledge and functional capabilities. A partial list of some important attributes of TIPPS includes the following:

1. It has a modular structure.
2. It can interfere with a CAD system.
3. It allows for interactive surface identification.
4. It contains a process/knowledge description language.

6.2.1 Modular Structure

Generative process planning is a complex task. If one were to try to solve the entire planning problem as a whole, it would be very difficult (if not impossible). The system would also be too complex to understand. Expansion or modification of the system would be extremely difficult. However, using a modular approach to decompose the tasks and construct modules for each decomposed subtask (function) makes generative planning achievable. Each module uses its input to create output and is functionally separate from the other tasks. However, through data input and output, these modules can communicate with each other and achieve total process planning.

Since each module contains a decomposed subtask, the planning tasks become more meaningful and are more easily understood. Expansion and modification of the system is possible by simply modifying modules. Interactive modules can be implemented when automatic planning modules do not exist or are difficult to develop. After a solution technique for a missing function is developed, the corresponding modules can be changed easily to interface with other modules.

The major functions (modules) of process planning can be listed as follows:

1. Material selection
2. Process selection
   Surface identification and classification
   Design information retrieval
   Candidate process selection
3. Machine selection
   Candidate machine extraction
   Machine selection
4. Tool selection
   Candidate tool extraction
   Tool selection
5. Intermediate surface determination
6. End effector selection
7. Fixture selection
   Fixture model retrieval
   Fixture verification
8. Process sequencing

9. Machining parameters selection
   Model selection
   Optimization
10. Cutter path generation
    APT program generation
    CLDATA generation
11. Cost and time estimation
12. Process plan preparation
    Resource list—tools, fixtures, machines, end effectors
13. Data file maintenance
    Process boundary file
    Machine capability file
    Tool capability file
    End effector file
14. Plan verification

Each function listed can be constructed as a software module. Information requirements for each function are shown in Table 6.1.

6.2.2 CAD Interface

An CAD becomes more efficient and less expensive in the field of engineering
design, more and more design work will be performed using a CAD system. It follows
that the input to a process planning system will be either a hard copy drawing prepared

Table 6.1. FUNCTIONAL RELATIONSHIP

A_m	Material availability	A_{mc}	Machine availability
A_t	Tool availability	A_f	Fixture availability
C_m	Cost of material	C_p	Process cost
C	Total cost	C_ℓ	Cutter path
D	Dimensions	E	End effector selected
F	Fixture selected	G	Geometrical shape
I	Intermediate surfaces	P_m	Machining parameters
M	Material selected	M_c	Machine selected
P	Process selected	S	Process sequence
S_f	Special features	T	Tool
T_m	Time	Tol	Tolerances
W	Weight		

$$M = f_1(G, A_m, C_m)$$
$$P = f_2(G, D, Tol, S_f, C_p)$$
$$M_c = f_3(P, A_{mc})$$
$$T = f_4(P, D, M, A_t)$$
$$I = f_5(G, T, C_\ell)$$
$$E = f_6(G, D, W)$$
$$F = f_7(G, P, M_c, I, A_f)$$
$$S = f_8(P, M_c, T, F, E)$$
$$P_m = f_9(G, Tol, C, P, T)$$
$$C_\ell = f_{10}(G, P, T)$$

by a CAD system or a geometric model in a CAD data base. In either case, a CAD model for the component will be resident in (or can be obtained in a straightforward manner from) the CAD system. It would be wasteful to have a process planner interpret a two- or three-dimensional display since the interpretation can be time consuming and prone to interpretation error. The effort to translate a design display to a format acceptable by the process planning system can be more time consuming than preparing the process plan. This process can be likened to a non-Japanese-speaking American foreman in a Japanese factory, where every order would require the service of an interpretor.

TIPPS links directly to data in a CAD data base. Component models in any CAD system can be postprocessed into a TIPPS (or other planning system) compatible format. The TIPPS data (an internal representation) is an acceptable CAD data representation. Furthermore, TIPPS allows the user to manipulate both two- and three-dimensional displays interactively. Another function of TIPPS is that it directly retrieves dimensions and technological information from a CAD data base. This not only reduces the time required for preparing process planning data input, but also reduces the likelihood of errors.

The CAD interface for process planning is a small step toward closure of the gap between CAD and CAM. The ultimate goal in CAD/CAM is to have an integrated system in which the same data is used throughout the system where no "out of flow" data preparation is required.

6.2.3 Interactive Surface Identification

Surfaces that require machining are normally identified on engineering designs. It is a standard practice to put surface finish symbols or machining indicators on those surfaces that need special care. It is impractical to assume that one can design a system which will determine which surface(s) need to be machined automatically. Two major reasons lead to this conclusion. The first is the technical difficulty required. The machining of a surface depends on the design as well as the workpiece selected. It is not clear how one determines the difference between a design and workpiece (initial and final geometry) automatically using a computer. Also, given the same design, machining requirements may differ significantly for the machining of a casting versus the machining of a solid rectangular workpiece. The second reason that makes automatic identification impractical is the efficiency of such a system. Even if the first issue could be resolved, it is again necessary to construct a model of the workpiece. The latter is an additional task which may require substantial effort since tolerance specifics are difficult to represent with CAD.

In TIPPS, interactive surface identification is used. A menu-driven identification subsystem with graphics capability is used to identify machined surfaces. Since a human has a well-developed pattern recognition ability, TIPPS queries the user for the surface shape and faces included as part of the surface. The latter process is accomplished by using a cross-hair cursor. At this stage, it provides a convenient way to identify machined surfaces. The user's responsibility is to select an item (shape) from a menu and locate the faces of a surface with a cursor. This reduces both the surface identification process and the programming requirement.

It is conjectured that, in the future, a pattern-recognition subsystem will be capable of identifying machined surfaces. However, the interactive approach employed in TIPPS is both feasible and sound.

6.2.4 Process Knowledge Description Language

Since process knowledge is manufacturing system dependent, it is necessary to maintain flexibility in modifying process knowledge. The modification should be easy, so that it will not prohibit changes necessary to the system. The best approach is to provide a language to describe process knowledge, because a descriptive language can provide maximum flexibility. However, such a descriptive language should be constructed so that it is easy to use and isolated from other system programs.

In TIPPS, a description language, PKI (Process Knowledge Interpreter language), is provided. It follows the general format of an IF . . . THEN . . . clause. A user can describe process boundaries using reserved system words. Each reserved word is defined in the system program. PKI either fetches a piece of data from one of the system data files, stores a piece of data, or performs some computation. A user is not required to know the system program and data file structure, yet is able to describe a process precisely.

6.3 TIPPS DATA STRUCTURE

In the following sections, implementation of the previously mentioned philosophy will be discussed. First, the data structure of the TIPPS system will be explained.

The data structure is the most fundamental element of storing information. It is most important to TIPPS, since data files interact with the modules used to produce process plans. Data files in TIPPS include:

1. CAD data
2. Surface data
3. Process data
4. Parameter data
5. Process knowledge data

6.3.1 CAD Data

In TIPPS, there are two types of CAD data: One type is external (input) data; the other is the internal data. The external data are in a format that allows data exchange with other CAD systems (an IGES-like data base). The CAD drawing data can be stored on standard 80 column cards or other sequential data medium such as card images on a disk. Each card image is called a record, and in each record, the first item is a code that specifies the record type (Table 6.2). The second item is the object

Table 6.2. INPUT DATA RECORD TYPE CODE

Code	Type
100	Material
110	Plane face
120	Cylindrical face
130	Hole
140	
.	
.	Reserved
.	
200	
210	Edge
220	Circle
230	Spline
240	
.	
.	Reserved
.	
300	
310	Vertex
320	
.	
.	Reserved
.	
490	
500	Technological information

number (i.e., face number, edge number, vertex number, etc.). It is used to identify the object in the record. The remainder of items in the record either represent a data value or identifications of objects associated with the current object.

Figure 6.6 represents the external (input) data for a tetrahedron. The first line of the data contains the leader (the part name and part number). The line beginning with 100 has a material code 20 (carbon steel) and a Brinell hardness number (BHN) 250. Column one entries containing "110" indicate faces (face one consists of edges 2, 3, and 6). The second entry indicates the base numbers. A minus sign before an edge identification indicates that the direction of the edge is reversed. The direction of edges follows a right-hand rule to point to the interior of a part. "210" records contain vertex lists (i.e., edge 1 consists of vertices one and two). Finally, the "310" records contain the coordinates of a vertex. As long as all objects are defined, the sequence of the records is not important.

It is obvious that the data structure above is not efficient for graphics; that is, it results in a lot of unused space and requires interpretation when used. However, it provides an easy way to communicate with other systems. To eliminate the inefficiency, an internal data structure is used. The internal data structure requires less storage space and is much easier to manipulate.

Figure 6.7 shows an example of the internal data structure of TIPPS. Because TIPPS uses a boundary model, there are four arrays in the example (more arrays are used for other geometries). PFACE stores pointers of the face information in the FACE array. It is necessary because face information has a variable data record length

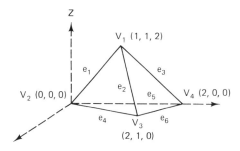

Tetrahedron				P-1000
100	20	250		
110	1	-2	3	-6
110	2	-1	2	-4
110	3	1	5	-3
110	4	4	6	-5
210	1	1	2	
210	2	1	3	
210	3	1	4	
210	4	2	3	
210	5	2	4	
210	6	3	4	
310	1	1	1	1
310	2	0	0	0
310	3	2	1	0
310	4	2	0	0
999				

Fig. 6.6. TIPPS input data format.

(i.e., three edges for triangular face, four edges for rectangular face, etc.). In the FACE array, the first item in a record is the number of edges; the remaining items are pointers to the EDGE array. The EDGE array is a two-dimensional array that stores pointers of the terminal vertex. The VERTEX array is also a two-dimensional array that stores data values for the vertex (x, y, z) coordinates.

Hole data are stored using a different format. The record length of a hole segment is fixed. In order to store multidiameter holes, a link list is used (see Figure 6.8). The HOL array is similar to PFACE in that it locates the position where the hole data are stored. The HOL array is a link list that stores the hole information. Each record in HOL has a fixed format; that is, it either stores a chamfer or a hole segment. Records are linked to accommodate any variable hole record length.

6.3.2 Surface Data

Surface marking is used to identify a machined surface. A machined surface can be a hole or a set of faces. For example, a straight slot is a machined surface, since it can be cut by a milling cutter or a shaper. Such a slot consists of a minimum of three faces—a bottom face and two side faces. Surface data records contain a code which shows the surface type and pointers that link the faces and holes together to form the

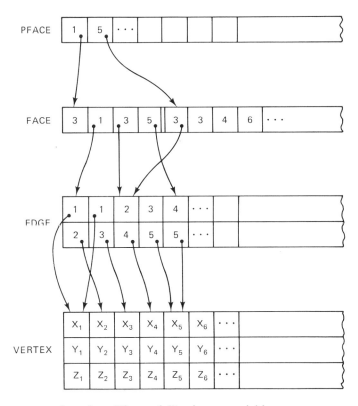

Fig. 6.7. Internal data structure.

surface. A double link list is used to store surface data (Figure 6.9), since a variable number of faces is expected for each surface. Such a data structure provides flexibility for surface identification modification.

Figure 6.9 illustrates the data structure. IRSUR is a relationship matrix. IRSUR $(I, J) = 1$ implies that surface I must be machined before surface J. This matrix is used to define the cut sequence. IPSUR is a pointer array, whose first row stores the surface type (i.e., 111—hole, 203—straight slot, and 201—flat). The second row of IPSUR stores the pointers that locate surface information in the NSUR array. Each record in the NSUR array has four items, forward and backward pointers, face type code, and pointers to the face.

6.3.3 Process Data

Process selection is automatically generated by the system software. A variable number of processes can be used to machine each surface. The data for each process has a fixed length which contains process type and tool size needed in the case of hole-making processes. A pointer array and a double linked list are used (Figure 6.10). The double link list stores process code and tool size. In the figure, FB indicates finish bore; RB, rough bore; and DRL, drill. Multiple processes can be linked together to produce a single surface.

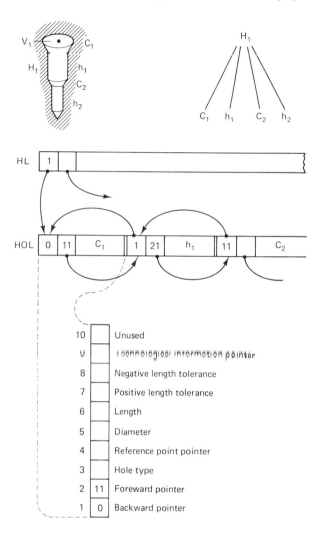

Fig. 6.8. Hole data structure.

6.3.4 Parameter Data

Parameter data include operational information for a machining process. Included in these data are feed (f), speed (V), and machining time (t_m). The data structure for parameter data is also shown in Figure 6.9.

6.3.5 Process Knowledge Data

Process knowledge in TIPPS is used as a basis for process selection via a decision table methodology. The data structure is organized so that it can be used as an interpretor language.

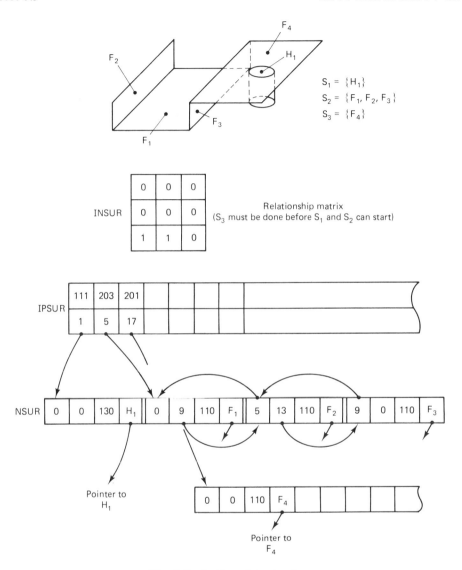

Fig. 6.9. Surface data structure.

A link list and a data array are used to store process knowledge (Figure 6.11). In Figure 6.11 a statement ((IF (SHAPE ! 111 =)) (THEN (8 PROCESS @)) is stored in the list. Each record in the list contains two elements. They can be either pointers (when they are positive), or a pointer and a variable or a data value (negative). Variables such as IF, THEN, SHAPE, and so on, are represented by a code with a negative sign, and the data value 8 is represented by a negative pointer that points to the data array. This arrangement reduces confusion between pointers in the link list and variables or data values.

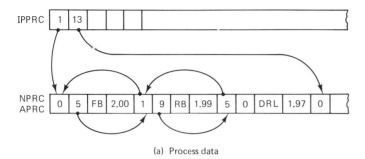

(a) Process data

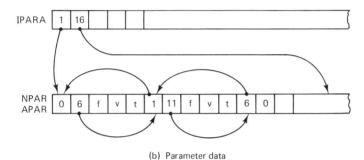

(b) Parameter data

Fig. 6.10. Process data and parameter data structure.

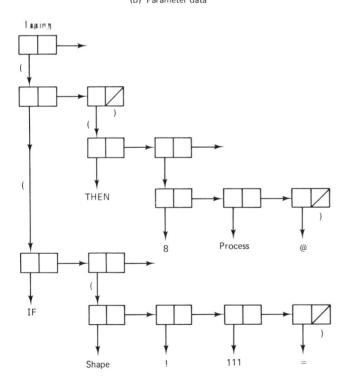

Fig. 6.11. Process Knowledge stored in a link list and a data array.

6.4 PKI: A PROCESS KNOWLEDGE INTERPRETER LANGUAGE

The heart of the process selection mechanism is the process knowledge data base. A process knowledge description language PKI (Process Knowledge Interpreter) is used to define process capabilities. Although it is used only to define process capabilities, it also has the potential to describe machine and tool capabilities. PKI uses a simple language structure in which every process is defined by a statement. A statement is written using an "IF . . . THEN . . ." form to specify the required conditions and actions. Conditions are "preconditions" of a machined surface to be planned. Actions output the process selected and change the surface conditions to reflect the result of a machining process.

Describing process capability with PKI is very simple, yet effective. PKI consists of a vocabulary of words necessary to describe each machining process. A user does not have to know anything about the interface with TIPPS. With minimum training, a user should be able to interpret and modify a process knowledge data base written in PKI. In the following sections, the syntax of PKI as well as an example will be shown.

6.4.1 PKI Syntax

The basic element in PKI is a statement. The entire data base is constructed using these statements. A PKI statement has the form

```
((IF
  (expression 1)
  (expression 2)
       .
       .
       .
  (expression n)
)
(THEN
  (expression n + 1)
  (expression n + 2)
       .
       .
       .
  (expression m)
)
)
```

where
$$\langle \text{expression} \rangle := \langle \text{atom} \rangle \; \langle \text{atom} \rangle \; --- \; \langle \text{atom} \rangle$$
$$\langle \text{atom} \rangle := \langle \text{literal atom} \rangle \; | \; \langle \text{numeral} \rangle$$
$$\langle \text{literal atom} \rangle := \langle \text{system variable} \rangle \; | \; \langle \text{operator} \rangle$$
$$\langle \text{numeral} \rangle := \text{integer or real number}$$
$$\langle \text{system variable} \rangle := \text{DIA, LENGTH, TLP, TLN, etc.}$$
$$\langle \text{operator} \rangle := \langle \text{mathematical operator} \rangle \; | \; \langle \text{stack operator} \rangle$$

⟨mathematical operator⟩ := +, −, *, /, **, =, >, <, >=, <=, ><, NEG, ABS
⟨stack operator⟩ := @, !, DUP, SWAP, ROT
(:=, equal; |, or)

Expressions 1 to n (in the IF portion) are conditional expressions that can be either true (T) or false (F). When used in a single expression, several conditions can be specified. Expressions 1 to n are then "ANDed." In the THEN portion, expressions do not take any truth value. Instead, they are actions given to a true condition. Condition expressions always have at least one condition operator (=, >, <, > =, <=, ><). However, action expressions do not.

The expressions use postfix notation (an operator follows the operands). A complete set of available literal atoms is shown in Table 6.3.

During the evaluation (execution) of a PKI statement, stack arithmetic is used. Expressions are evaluated separately. An atom is pushed onto the arithmetic stack if it is a numeral atom. The address of an atom is pushed onto the variable stack when the atom is a system variable. If it is an operator, the appropriate operation is applied.

For example, in Figure 6.12, a conditional expression (DIA ! 0.0625 >=) implies "diameter greater than or equal to 0.0625." The normal mathematical term is written DIA >= 0.0625; however, in postfix notation, the operator is put at the end

Table 6.3. PKI OPERATORS AND SYSTEM VARIABLES

Code	Reserved Word	Meaning	Code	Reserved Word	Meaning
−1	>	Greater than	−27	roundness	
−2	<	Smaller than	−28	angularity	
−3	+	Addition	−29	parallelism	
−4	−	Subtraction	−30	straightness	
−5	*	Multiply	−31	shape	
−6	/	Divide	−32	SF	Surface finish
−7	=	Equal	−33	width	
−8	>=	Great equal	−34	height	
−9	<=	Less equal	−35	then	
−10	**	Exponent	−36	IF	
−11	><	Not equal	−37	feed	
−12	@	Save	−38	speed	
−13	!	Fatch	−39	proc	Process
−14	NEG	Negation	−40	free	Terminate
−15	ABS	Absolute value	−41	DTL	Tool diameter
−16	DUP	Duplicate	−42	MACHINE	
−17	SWA	Swap	−43		
−18	ROT	Rotate	−44		
−19			−45		
−20			−46		
−21	DIA		−47		
−22	LENGTH		−48		
−23	TLP	Positive tolerance	−49		
−24	TLN	Negative tolerance	−50		
−25	FLATNESS				
−26	TRU	True position			

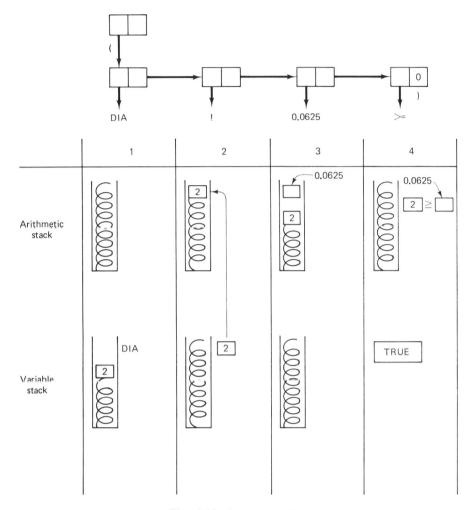

Fig. 6.12. Stack operation.

of an expression. When the expression above is evaluated, the address of DIA (position in which that value is stored) is "pushed" onto the variable stack. The symbol "!" indicates that the first item in the variable stack should be "popped out" and its address used to move the data value from the variable array to the arithmetic stack. The value in location 1 is moved to the arithmetic stack (in this case, a 2 is moved). The next atom, 0.0625, is a numeral; therefore, it is "pushed" onto the arithmetic stack directly. Finally, the $>=$ symbol "pops out" two values from the arithmetic stack and compares them. If a TRUE condition results from the comparison, the next expression will be evaluated. Conditional expressions are ANDed together. And if all conditional expressions are true, the action expressions will be evaluated.

    A few more operators are worth discussing here. All the mathematical operators are standard. However, stack operators have their own special meaning in PKI. The

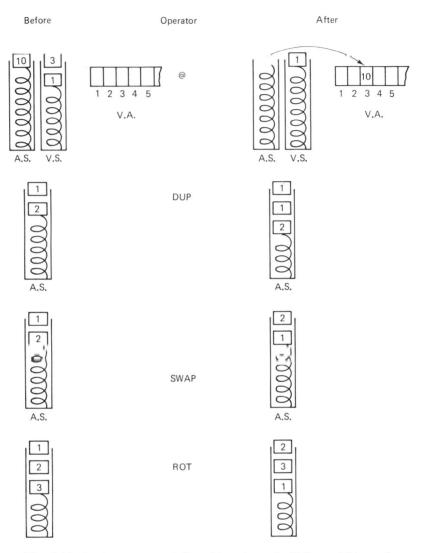

Fig. 6.13. Stack operators. A.S., arithmetic stack; V.S., variable stack; V.A., variable array.

operator "@" is very different from "!". "@" removes the first item in the arithmetic stack and then changes the part condition by placing the value in the variable array (Figure 6.13). This operation is useful for changing preconditions of a surface. DUP can duplicate the top item on the arithmetic stack. It is a handy feature when a variable is used several times in an expression. "SWAP" *swaps* the top two items on the arithmetic stack. "ROT" *rotates* three items on the arithmetic stack. By combining these operators with mathematical operators, statements describing process capabilities can be easily written. Examples using PKI will be illustrated in the next section.

6.4.2 Process Description with PKI

Process capabilities can be represented by their boundaries. For example, there are maximum and minimum hole diameters which can be drilled by twist drilling (due to tool availability). There are also boundaries on length, tolerances, and surface finish. A typical process boundary for twist drilling can be written

Length $\leq$ 12.0D (length of the hole must be less than 12 times the diameter)

$0.0625 \leq D \leq 2.000$ (tool size is restricted between 1/64 and 2.0 in. in diameter)

$t_p \geq 0.007\sqrt{D}$ (tolerance (plus) as a function of drill size)

$t_n \geq 0.007\ \sqrt{D} + 0.003$ (tolerance minus)

Straightness $\geq 0.0005(\ell/D)^3 + 0.002$

Roundness ≥ 0.004

Parallelism $\geq 0.001(\ell/D)^3 + 0.003$

True position ≥ 0.008

SF ≥ 100

Using backward planning, the process above can "change a hole to a flat surface." A machined surface is finished after a process if its condition is within the original boundaries. In order to translate these boundaries into PKI expressions, they can be written

```
(LEN ! 12.0 DIA ! * <=)
(DIA ! 0.0625 >=)
(DIA ! 2.000 <=)
(TLP ! DIA ! 0.5 ** 0.007 *  >-)
(TLN ! DIA ! 0.5 ** 0.007 * 0.003+ >=)
(STRAIGHTNESS ! LEN ! DIA ! / 3 ** 0.005 * 0.002 + >=)
(ROUNDNESS ! 0.004 >=)
(PARALLELISM ! LEN ! DIA ! / 3 ** 0.001 * 0.003  + >=)
(TRUE ! 0.008 >=)
(SF ! 100 >=)
```

Shape must also be included, since drilling only creates round holes (refer to Table 6.2 for shape code).

```
(SHAPE ! 111 =)
```

The expressions above constitute the conditional portion of a statement. Actions are then specified to include the process identification, tool diameter, and the end of the search for each process.

```
(1 PROCESS @ )
(DIA ! DTL @ )
(FREE)
```

```
;
;   TWIST DRILLING (CODE 1)
;
( ( IF
      ( SHAPE ! 111 = )
      ( LEN ! 12.0 DIA ! * <= )
      ( DIA ! 0.0625 >= )
      ( DIA ! 2.000 <= )
      ( TLP ! DIA ! 0.5 ** 0.007 * >= )
      ( TLN ! DIA ! 0.5 ** 0.007 * 0.003 + >= )
      ( STRAIGHTNESS ! LEN ! DIA ! / 3. ** 0.0005 * 0.002 + >= )
      ( ROUNDNESS ! 0.004 >= )
      ( PARALLELISM ! LEN ! DIA ! / 3. ** 0.001 * 0.003 + >= )
      ( TRUE ! 0.008 >= )
      ( SF ! 100 >= )
  )
  ( THEN
      ( 1 PROCESS @ )
      ( DIA ! DTL @ )
      ( FREE )
  )
)
```

Fig. 6.14. Twist drilling input using PKI.

The first expression moves the process identification (1) into a process data file. "DIA ! DTL @" retrieves the current hole diameter and saves it on the process data file as the desired tool diameter. FREE terminates the search.

Because the evaluation of expressions is sequential, conditional expressions should be arranged so that the more important an expression is, the earlier it is stated. Although there is no difference in the search results, the efficiency of search is affected. Figure 6.14 shows a complete set of statements for twist drilling input using PKI.

A finishing process normally does not start until a roughing process has been completed. In order to describe this, actions are required that include expressions to change the surface conditions between processes and while not signaling a FREE expression. For example, a finish boring process can be expressed as shown in Figure 6.15. (DIA ! 0.002 − DIA @) implies that finish boring can remove a 0.002 layer of material. Other expressions, such as (0.002 TLP @), (1 TRUE @), and so on,

```
;
;   FINISH BORING ( CODE 4 )
;
( ( IF
      ( SHAPE ! 111 = )
      ( DIA ! .3750 >= )
      ( DIA ! 10 <= )
      ( TLP ! .0003 >= )
      ( TLN ! .0003 >= )
      ( STRAIGHTNESS ! .0002 >= )
      ( ROUNDNESS ! .0003 >= )
      ( PARALLELISM ! .0005 >= )
      ( LENGTH ! 10 DIA ! * <= )
      ( TRUE ! .0001 >= )
      ( SF ! 8 >= )
  )
  ( THEN
      ( 4 PROCESS @ )
      ( DIA ! DTL @ )
      ( DIA ! .002 - DIA @ )
      ( .002 TLP @ )
      ( .002 TLN @ )
      ( 1 STRAIGHTNESS @ )
      ( 1 ROUNDNESS @ )
      ( 1 PARALLELISM @ )
      ( 1 TRUE @ )
      ( 50 SF @ )
  )
)
```

Fig. 6.15. Finish boring knowledge.

change the hole conditions so that a roughing process can be selected during the next iteration. More details can be found in *The TIPPS Users Manual* (Chang 1982).

6.5 TIPPS OPERATION

The TIPPS system and its structure has been detailed in the previous sections. The logical continuation is to demonstrate how TIPPS works. One can start using TIPPS after the process knowledge base has been prepared. The hardware needed for running the TIPPS system includes 150K bytes of memory, a disk system, a graphics terminal with a cross-hair cursor, and the Tektronic's PLOT-10 library. The current version of TIPPS is divided into three parts: the TIPPS executive, PARSEL, and REPORT. The TIPPS executive contains the graphics display, surface marking, and process selection modules. All of the modules can be envoked by typing commands while in the executive mode. Both PARSEL and REPORT are independent of the executive and can be evoked under the operating system of the computer.

To generate a process plan, the following logical steps are required:

1. Input and display the CAD model.
2. Identify machined surfaces.
3. Select processes.
4. Select process parameters.
5. Generate the report.

6.5.1 Input and Display of a CAD Model

The input for the CAD model is created by typing the file name in which the model is stored while running the TIPPS executive (see Figure 6.16). A typical CAD input model is shown in Figure 6.17. After a model has been input, it can be displayed in either two or three dimensions. A plot command places the system in the graphics mode. A menu prompt from the user for the desired plot is then required. Hidden lines are not removed from either the two- or three-dimensional plots. The user can scale a two-dimensional plot to find coordinate information directly from the screen. In a three-dimensional environment, the user can view the object from any direction, but the display is always scaled to fit into the display window on the screen. Figure 6.18 shows two views of the same object. Different views help the user in the next task.

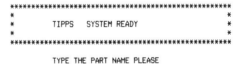

```
*******************************************************
*                                                     *
*             TIPPS    SYSTEM READY                   *
*                                                     *
*******************************************************
               TYPE THE PART NAME PLEASE


demo1
$$ COMMAND:
```

Fig. 6.16. Entering the file name.

```
TEST PART - BRACKET P-10001
100    2  200
110    1    8    1     2     3     4     5     6     7    -8
110    2    4    9    10   -11    -6     1
110    3    4   13   -12    -9    -5
110    4    4  -14   -13    -4   -15     2
110    5    8   21   -20   -19   -18   -17   -16   -15    -3
110    6    4   -2    23   -22   -21     3
110    7    4  -24    17   -26    25     3
110    8    4   18    28    27   -26
110    9    4   29   -28    19    30     4
110   10    4  -20    30   -31   -22
110   11    8   -1    33   -32   -25   -27   -29   -31   -23
110   12    8  -10    12    14    16    24    32    36   -34
110   13    4    7    35   -34   -11
110   14    4   -8    33    36   -35
210    1    1    2
210    2    2    3
210    3    3    4
210    4    4    5
210    5    5    6
210    6    6    7
210    7    7    8
210    8    1    8
210    9    6    9
210   10    9   10
210   11    7   10
210   12    9   11
210   13    5   11
210   14   11   12
210   15    4   12
210   16   12   13
210   17   13   14
210   18   14   15
210   19   15   16
210   20   16   17
210   21    3   17
210   22   17   18
210   23    2   18
210   24   13   22
210   25   21   21
210   26   20   21
210   27   20   21
210   28   15   20
210   29   19   20
210   30   16   19
210   31   18   19
210   32   22   23
210   33    1   23
210   34   10   24
210   35    8   24
210   36   23   24
310    1    0    0    0
310    2    0    0    3
310    3    2    0    3
310    4    6    0    2
310    5    6    0    2
310    6    8    0    4
310    7    8    0    0
310    8    8    0    0
310    9    6    4    4
310   10    6    4    4
310   11    6    4    2
310   12    2    4    2
310   13    2    4    3
310   14    2   25    3
310   15    2   26   26
310   16    2    2    3
310   17    2    2    3
310   18    0    2    3
310   19    0    2   26
310   20    0   25   26
310   21    0   25    3
310   22    0    4    3
310   23    0    4    0
310   24    8    4    0
310   25    4    2    2
130    1    2   25   12     5    10    10     5
130    0    1   25   10     1    10    10     6
500    1    5    5   50     5     5   100     5
500    2    5    5   50     5     5   100     5
500    3    5    5   50     5     5   100     5
500    4    5    5    5     5     5   100     5
500    5    5    5  120     5     5    10     5
500    6    5    5  120    10     1    10     5
999
```

Fig. 6.17. CAD input model.

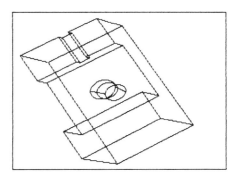

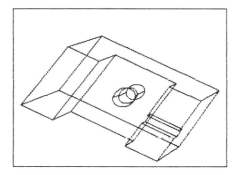

Fig. 6.18. View of an object from a different direction.

6.5.2 Surface Identification

There are two steps required to identify a machined surface. One first needs to tell the computer what the shape of a machined surface is and which faces are included in that surface. Both of these steps can be done interactively in TIPPS. The shape is identified by choosing items from a menu. The user need not know the code for different surfaces. The menu, in table format, is shown in Figure 6.19.

The linking of faces to form a machined surface is done interactively with a cross-hair cursor. The cursor is controlled by either thumb wheels or joysticks, depending on the hardware. The reference point (the center of a face) is first plotted on the display. By locating the cursor on the reference point of a face and typing a "Y", the face will be linked and saved in the surface file. A relationship matrix will be created to show the relationships of surfaces. A surface is said to cover another surface if it needs to be machined before the other surface. The rule used to determine surface relationships for process sequencing is based on the bottom face height. Because this does not always provide the correct surface relationships, an interactive modification routine is available to change the surface identifications and relationships. A surface editor is also available to add and delete surfaces as well as faces of a surface. The editing is performed directly on a CRT display,

1st Digit		2nd Digit		3rd Digit	
1	Cylindrical	1	External	1	Simple
				2	Groove
				3	Spline
		2	Internal	4	Keyway
				5	Thread
				6	Straight chamfer
				7	Inner fillet
				8	Outer fillet
2	Noncylindrical	0		1	Flat
				2	Step
				3	Straight slot
				4	Dovetail
				5	V bottom
				6	T or Y slot
				7	Pocket
				8	Square hole
				9	Curved surface

Fig. 6.19. Surface-type code table.

6.5.3 Select Processes

Process selection in TIPPS requires only a single command. The command "PROC" will initiate the process selection module. The selected processes will be stored in the process file and later displayed on the CRT screen in sequence. Figure 6.4 shows an example of this display.

6.5.4 Select Process Parameter

The process parameter selection module is a separate program. Appropriate parameters are selected from built-in tables. The parameter selection module is evoked by typing the module name "PARSEL" and then the part name. Process parameters as well as machining time are saved in the parameter file and displayed on the CRT screen.

6.5.5 Report Generation

The function of a report generator is to print a human-readable report of the results. The report includes part name, part number, material code, planner, planning data, and so on. The contents include surface identification, dimensions, processes, tool diameter, feed, speed, and machining time. Figure 6.20 shows the report generation procedure (lowercase words are typed by the user and uppercase words by the system). A process plan for the part in Figure 6.17 is shown in Figure 6.21 (see Figure 6.22 for surface identification information).

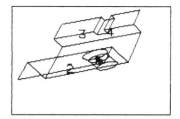

```
RELATION MATRIX:
0 0 0 0 0
1 0 1 1 1
1 0 0 1 1
0 0 0 0 1
1 0 0 0 0
CHANGE ? (Y/N)
n
```

Fig. 6.20. Identified surface.

```
CMS

report

****************************************************
*                                                  *
*          PROCESS PLAN REPORT GENERATOR           *
*                                                  *
****************************************************

              TYPE THE PART NAME PLEASE


t3d
YOUR NAME PLEASE :
t. c. chang
PLANNING DATE :
august 13, 1982
R;
```

Fig. 6.21. Report generation.

```
+------------------------------------------------------------------------------------+
|                                                                                    |
|                          P R O C E S S    P L A N                                  |
|                                                                                    |
| PART NAME: TEST PART - BRACKET                    PART NUMBER: P-10001              |
| MATERIAL:        2                                PLANNER:     T. C. CHANG          |
|                              DATE :AUGUST 13, 1982                                  |
+------------------------------------------------------------------------------------+
```

OP NO	SURFACE ID	TYPE	L (L)	D (W)	H	PROCESS	TOOL DIA	FEED (IPR)	SPEED (RPM)	TIME (MIN)	REMARKS
1	2	FLAT	4.000	2.000	0.0	R F MILL	2.040	0.02091	117.87	1.62	
2						F F MILL	2.040	0.02362	254.42	0.67	
3	3	FLAT	4.000	2.000	0.0	R F MILL	2.040	0.02091	117.87	1.62	
4						F F MILL	2.040	0.02362	254.42	0.67	
5	4	S SLO	2.000	0.500	0.400	R F MILL	0.500	0.00886	375.04	0.60	
6						F F MILL	0.500	0.01181	840.65	0.20	
7	5	STEP	4.000	4.000	2.000	R P MILL	4.000	0.00472	168.54	25.12	
8	1	HOLE	1.200	0.840	0.0	TWST DRL	0.840	0.01931	323.00	0.08	
9						CHAMF B	1.200	0.00546	161.68	0.57	
10	1	HOLE	1.200	0.993	0.0	TWST DRL	0.993	0.02139	272.99	0.17	
11						RGH BORE	0.998	0.00506	164.79	1.20	
12						F. BORE	1.000	0.00506	227.36	0.87	

```
+------------------------------------------------------------------------------------+
|                                 TOTAL PROCESSING TIME :        33.38 MINUTES       |
+------------------------------------------------------------------------------------+
```

Fig. 6.22. Process plan.

There are several aspects of the process plan shown in Figure 6.21 that are worth mentioning. First, the plan, as shown, was generated automatically. Second, the plan can be improved on, significantly, with a bit of "massaging." For instance, because of the way TIPPS generates the process sequence, the sequencing of operations does not take tool changes or fixturing changes into account. By simply inspecting the process plan, one can see that if operations 9 and 10 are interchanged, a tool change (setup) can be eliminated. The processing time reflected in the plan does not include setup or tool-change time. These times (tool change and setup), however, are system dependent. If the part were being machined on a CNC machining center, only one setup would be required; and depending on the machine, the tool-change time might be negligible. On the other hand, in a manual system, setup and tool change may contribute the largest portion of the processing time.

6.5.6 Testing Results

For any machined surface, the processes required depend on the workpiece shape and surface conditions. Using TIPPS, immediate feedback can be obtained when surface condition specification changes. When used in conjunction with a CAD system, the design specification for a surface condition can be checked before issuing the design to production. A designer can avoid specifying unnecessarily tight tolerances and surface finishes.

Table 6.4 shows the effects of surface finish to process selection and machining time. The example part (Figure 6.17) was used for illustrative purposes. Five test runs were performed with different surface-finish specifications being given to the various surfaces. The processes required for each surface are listed in the table. Since surfaces 2, 3, 4, and 5 require the same processes, only one set of processes is included in the table. From the table, a total of 29.87 min of machining time is required when all five surfaces have a 125 μin. surface finish. The total time increased to 48.02 min when the surface finish became 20 μin. This represents a 60% increase in processing time. Table 6.5 shows how a change in tolerance affects a process plan. Such information can be provided to the designer for possible modification of the design. After the modification, a process plan can be generated with no additional effort.

6.6 CONCLUSIONS AND CLOSING REMARKS

In this text, process planning system design guidelines as well as background information for process planning are provided. A process planning system is the interface between design and manufacturing. In the past two decades, much attention has been given to both design and manufacturing automation, individually. Computer-aided design (CAD) and computer-aided manufacturing (CAM) systems have evolved separately. Our current inability to communicate between CAD and CAM was realized, and CAD and CAM integration work has started. So-called "integrated

Table 6.4. PROCESSES AND TOTAL MACHINING TIME UNDER DIFFERENT SURFACE FINISH

		Surface					
	Number	Type			*Tests*[a]		
Surface Finish	1	Hole	125	60	30	30	20
	2	Flat	125	125	30	20	20
	3	Flat	125	125	30	20	20
	4	S. slot	125	125	30	20	20
	5	Step	125	125	30	20	20
Processes	1	Hole	T.D.	T.D.	T.D.	T.D.	T.D.
		Chamfer	C.B.	C.B.	C.B.	C.B.	C.B.
		Body	T.D.	T.D.	T.D.	T.D.	T.D.
				R.B.	R.B.	R.B.	R.B.
					F.B.	F.B.	F.B.
							G.
	2	Flat	R.F.M.	R.F.M.	R.F.M.	R.F.M.	R.F.M.
	3	Flat			F.F.M.	F.F.M.	F.F.M.
	4	S. slot				G.	G.
	5	Step					
Total time (min)			29.87	29.87	30.98	34.85	46.72	48.02

[a]T.D., twist drill; C.B., counter bore; R.B., rough bore; F.B., finish bore; R.F.M., rough face mill; F.F.M., finish face mill; G., grind.

Table 6.5. PROCESSES UNDER DIFFERENT TOLERANCES: HOLE BODY

Tolerance ±:	0.01	0.005	0.0005
Processes	Twist drill	Twist drill	Twist drill
		Rough bore	Rough bore
			Finish bore

CAD/CAM systems" have become available on the commercial market during the past decade. However, these systems are little more than CAD/APT systems, which save the geometry definition during past processing. This is simply a lower-level integration. A higher-level integration, CAD/process planning, is still not available.

Automated process planning is the interface between CAD and CAM. CAD is the upstream portion in the design/production information flow process, and CAM is the downstream portion. Process planning determines how to execute the operations necessary to fabricate a design in a manufacturing system. Part programming can be started only after process planning has been completed. Problems and potential solutions associated with CAD/process planning integration issues have also been addressed in this text. After reading this book, the reader should have a reasonably complete picture of process planning systems, approaches and structures. The authors would like to conclude with some discussions concerning the past and the future of process planning systems.

6.6.1 The Past

When the concept of computer-aided process planning was first conceived in the 1960s, group technology spawned as process planning's first offspring. Because of the complexity required to develop automatic planning systems, researchers were unable to develop intelligent computer software to generate process plans automatically. Assisting a process planner and saving planning time and effort was the main focus. Retrieving process plans for a similar component, the approach used was to make appropriate modifications manually. The term "variant planning" describes such an approach. In Chapter 4, the detailed steps in developing a variant process planning system were discussed. In Chapter 5 a review of several commercially available variant process planning systems was provided. Although the variant approach cannot generate process plans automatically, the ease of developing and using these systems makes them attractive. Most process planning systems in use at the present time are still variant in nature.

Based on the experience of practitioners, a variant process planning system can save up to 90% of the process planning time. The plans generated are always consistent with those of similar components. However, many problems and deficiencies also exist. The most significant problem is the inability of these systems to provide plans for new components (where no similar component has been planned before). The process plan may not be consistent when compared with components in a different family. The success of the final process plan depends on the ability of the planners who developed and modified the plan that has been retrieved. An alternative approach that can avoid these problems is more desirable.

The generative process planning concept arose at the inception of variant process planning. However, difficulties in quantifying process capabilities are probably the major reason for the delay in generative process planning system development. Most generative process planning systems use "canned process plan" segments to construct process plans. Either a detailed GT code or a descriptive language is used to describe the component to be planned. A process plan is constructed using canned process plan segments which are recalled from the data base during the planning cycle. Although this type of process planning synthesis is not the most desirable, it is feasible and drastically reduces process planning decision making requirements.

Over the years some variant process planning systems have evolved into generative systems. Several commercial systems are in this category. They are by nature variant; however, some of the auxiliary functions of process planning, such as parameter selection, tool selection, and so on, can be generated automatically. Such systems are normally called (by their designers) generative process planning systems. Although not completely generative, they are one step closer to this goal.

Only in recent years has some effort in integrating CAD with process planning systems begun. Without integration, a process planning system is part of the CAM function and is independent of the CAD system. Process planning input is prepared by interpreting an engineering drawing or output from a CAD system. Several process planning systems use CAD for cutter-path verification and tool fixture layout only. Most "CAD/process planning systems" use CAD as a display tool. None of the commercial systems use the data in a CAD data base to generate process plans. Manual interpretation of a drawing is still necessary. However, the TIPPS system is the first system that uses CAD data directly.

In the past, the main emphasis has been on developing working process planning systems. A temporary solution—variant process planning—has proven successful. However, generic deficiencies associated with this approach make it less than ideal. Therefore, the generative approach is being explored. Although a true generative system is yet to come, a satisfactory system can be expected in the near future.

6.6.2 Future Development

As is always the dream, people prefer to build more automated systems than exist today. In the past, we envisioned an unmanned factory working today. Currently, several such subsystems exist and our goal for tomorrow is to integrate the entire industry (automation from design to final manufacturing). Process planning is a bridge between design and manufacturing. A process planning system that minimizes human decision making and data preparation is therefore desirable.

In Chapter 4, difficulties associated with the development of a generative process planning system were discussed. The goal for the future is to overcome those difficulties and develop something better than exists today. To achieve this goal, it is believed that the research direction in process planning will be toward the following:

1. Develop a unified data base for both CAD and process planning.
2. Study process, machine, and tool behavior, building better mathematical (or descriptive) models which can be used in process planning systems.
3. Use artificial intelligence techniques in process planning.
4. Build a process capability knowledge base.
5. Develop techniques for marking machined surfaces automatically.

Ultimately, a generative process planning system can be a substitute for a process planner/manufacturing engineer in the design/manufacturing process. Knowledge concerning shop operations must be captured and saved in a unified design/ manufacturing data base in order to be used for both design and planning. Such information can not only assist in manufacturing planning, but can also provide feedback to the designer. The concept of design for manufacturing can be realized by using such feedback.

During the building of the data base, there are two important considerations that need to be included: process knowledge and facility information. Facility information simply describes what the system has, such as machine and tool inventory data. The process knowledge, discussed in Chapter 3, includes process capabilities. At this moment, adequate quantitative models and data for different processes are still not available. The most fundamental knowledge concerning a process is the tool-life equation. Very few sound tool-life equations have been identified. Other information concerning process capability is equally scarce. It is necessary to have complete process capability information before a true generative process planning system can be developed.

An efficient way to store and use process knowledge can determine the success of a system. The major advantage of artificial intelligence, versus the conventional approach, is the elegance of representing data and deducing conclusions from the data. It is most effective when qualitative decision making is involved. In process planning, a significant portion of the planning is not quantifiable. The AI approach can greatly improve this representation and the decision-making process. A "self-learning" AI system, in the future, would be most interesting.

The AI approach discussed above is used in process, machine, and so on, selection decision making. Another important approach is in machined surface marking. This is the determination of which surfaces need to be machined in order to change a raw material to a designed shape. Only after such a marking process has been automated can a true automated process planning system be constructed.

REVIEW QUESTIONS

6.1. What are the advantages of a modular (as opposed to a unified) planning system?

6.2. What are the advantages and disadvantages of using a CAD data base for input to a process planning system? If you do not feel that there are any major disadvantages, why are CAD data not used in more process planning systems?

6.3. Choose a part with which you are familiar. Describe how the machined surfaces were identified from the drawing. How might this process be made automatic?

6.4. The CAD data shown in Figure 6.6 look very similar to the IGES graphics standards. Use the format to describe a 2-in. cube.

6.5. Show how either shaping or deburring could be coded using PKI.

6.6 How might a system such as TIPPS be used by a designer to create an "optimum" design? Is an optimum design ever possible?

REFERENCES

ALLEN, D. K., "Implications for Manufacturing Process Taxonomy in Process Selection," International CAM Congress, McMaster University, Hamilton, Ontario, May 14–16, 1974.

ALLEN, D. K., "Computer Aided Process Planning Opcodes and Work Elements for Machined Parts," Final Report for CAM-I, Inc., Arlington, Tex., December 2, 1978.

ALLEN, D. K., "Generative Process Planning Using the DCLASS Information System," Monograph 4, Computer-Aided Manufacturing Laboratory, Brigham Young University, Provo, Utah, 1979.

ALLEN, D. K., Classification and Coding—Theory and Application, Monograph No. 2, Computer-Aided Manufacturing Laboratory, Brigham Young University, Provo, Utah, 1981.

ALLEN, D. K., and P. R. SMITH, "Computer Aided Process Planning," Computer-Aided Manufacturing Laboratory, Brigham Young University, Provo, Utah, October 15, 1980.

ARMOREGO, E. J., and R. H. BROWN, *The Machining of Metals*, Prentice-Hall, Englewood Cliffs, N.J., 1968.

BAER, A., C. EASTMAN, and M. HENRION, "Geometric Modelling: A Survey," *CAD*, Vol. 11, No. 5, September 1979.

BARASH, M. M., E. BARTLETT, I. I. FINFTER, and W. C. LEWIS, "Process Planning Automation—A Recursive Approach," in *The Optimal Planning of Computerized Manufacturing Systems*, Report 17, School of Industrial Engineering, Purdue University, West Lafayette, Ind., 1980.

BARNES, R. D., "Group Technology Concepts Relative to the CAM-I Automated Process Planning (CAPP) System," presented to the Executive Seminar on Coding, Classification and Group Technology for Automated Planning, St. Louis, Mo., p. 136, 21 Jan. 1976.

BELYAKOV, I. T., et al., "Identification Systems for Selecting an Optimum Technological Process," *Machines and Tooling*, Vol. 43, No. 7, 1972.

BERRA, P. B., "Investigation of Automated Planning and Optimization of Metal Working Process Processes," Ph.D. thesis, Purdue University, West Lafayette, Ind., 1968.

BERRA, P. B., and M. M. BARASH, "Investigation of Automated Planning and Optimization of Metal Working Processes," Report 14, Purdue Laboratory for Applied Industrial Control, West Lafayette, Ind., July 1968.

BEZIER, P. "Numerical Control: Mathematics and Applications," Translated by A. R. Forrest and A. F. Pankhurst, John Wiley, New York, 1972.

BOOTHROYD, G., *Fundamentals of Metal Machining and Machine Tools*, McGraw-Hill, New York, 1975.

BRUYEVICH, N. G., and B. YE. CHELISHCHEV, "Problems of Automation of Technological Planning: 1. Formal Description of Technological Planning," *Engineering Cybernetics*, Vol. 12, No. 5, September/October 1974, pp. 154–162.

BUDDE, W., "EXAPT in NC Operation Planning," Proc. 10th Numerical Control Society Annual Meeting and Technical Conference, 1973.

BURBIDGE, J. L., "Production Flow Analysis," *The Production Engineer*, April/May 1971.

BURBIDGE, J. L., *The Introduction of Group Technology*, Wiley, New York, 1975.

CAM-I, "Functional Specifications for an Advanced Factory Management System," Computer Aided Manufacturing–International, Inc., Arlington, Tex., March 1979.

CAM-I, "Functional Specification for an Experimental Planning System XPS-1," Computer Aided Manufacturing–International, Inc., Arlington, Tex., October 1980.

CARTER, W. A., "Computer Aided Process Planning," Conference on Computer-Aided Manufacturing, National Engineering Laboratory (NEL), East Kilbride, Glasgow, Scotland, June 20–22, 1978.

CHALLA, K., and P. BERRA, "Automated Planning and Optimization of Machining Procedures—A Systems Approach," *Computers and Industrial Engineering*, Vol. 1, 1976, pp. 35–46.

CHANG, T. C., "Advances in Computer-Aided Process Planning," NBS-GCR-83-441, National Bureau of Standards, U.S. Department of Commerce, 1983.

CHANG, T. C., "Interfacing CAD and CAM—A Study of Hole Design," Unpublished M.S. thesis, Virginia Polytechnic Institute and State University, Blacksburg, Va., 1980.

CHANG, T. C., TIPPS—A Totally Integrated Process Planning System, Ph.D. thesis, Virginia Polytechnic Institute and State University, Blacksburg, Va., 1982.

CHANG, T. C., and R. A. WYSK, "Interfacing CAD/Automated Process Planning," *AIIE Transactions*, September 1981.

CHANG, T. C., R. A. WYSK, R. P. DAVIS, and B. CHOI, "Milling Parameter Optimization through a Discrete Variable Transformation," *International Journal of Production Research,* June 1982.

CHISOLM, A. W. J., "Design for Economic Manufacture," *CIRP Annals,* Vol. 22, 1973.

CLAYTOR, R. N., "CAM-I's CAPP System," SME Technical Paper, Series MS-1976, 1976.

COELHO, P.L.F., "The Machining Economics Problem in a Probabilistic Manufacturing Environment," Unpublished M.S. thesis, Virginia Polytechnic Institute and State University, Blacksburg, Va., 1980.

COLLINS, D., "Computer Aided Process Standardization," Paper published by TNO, Waltham, Mass., 1977.

COOK, N. H., and K. L. CHANDERAMANI, "Investigation on the Nature of Surface Finish and Its Variation with Cutting Speed," *Journal of Engineering for Industry,* Vol. 86, No. 134, 1964.

DAVIS, R., B. BUCHANAN, and E. SHORTLIFFE, "Production Rules as a Representation for a Knowledge-Based Consultation Program," *Artificial Intelligence,* Vol. 8, No. 1, 1977.

DE GARMO, E. P., *Materials and Processes in Manufacturing,* 5th Edition, MacMillan, Inc., NewYork, 1975.

DESCOTTE, Y., and J.-C. LATOMBE, "GARI: A Problem Solver That Plans How to Machine Mechanical Parts," IJCAI 7, Vancouver, August 1981, pp. 766–772.

DEVOR, R. E., W. J. ZDEBLICK, V. A. TIPNIS, and S. BUESCHER, "Development of Mathematical Models for Process Planning of Machining Operations NAMRC—VII," Proc. 6th North American Metalworking Research Conference, Society of Manufacturing Engineers, 1978.

DUNN, I. M., and N. W. GERMAN, "Computer-Aided Process Planning and Work Measurement," Proc. 15th Numerical Control Society Annual Meeting and Technical Conference, Chicago, April 1978.

DUNN, M. S., and W. S. MANN, "Computerized Production Process Planning," Proc. 15th Numerical Control Society Annual Meeting and Technical Conference, Chicago, April 1978.

EARY, D. F., and G. E. JOHNSON, *Process Engineering for Manufacturing,* Prentice-Hall, Englewood Cliffs, N.J., 1962.

EL GOMAYEL, J., and M. R. ABOU-ZEID, "Piece Part Coding and the Optimization of Process Planning," North American Metalworking Research Conference, May 1975.

EVERSHEIM, W., and H. FUCHS, "Integrated Generation of Drawings, Process-Plans and NC-Tapes," SME Technical Paper, Series MS79-178, 1979; also in *Advanced Manufacturing Technology* (Proc. 4th Int. IFIP/IFAC Conf., PROLOMAT 79, 1979), P. Blake, Ed., Elsevier North-Holland, New York, 1980.

EVERSHEIM, W., H. FUCHS, and K. H. ZONS, "Automatic Process Planning with Regard to Production by Application of the System AUTAP for Control Problems," *Computer Graphics in Manufacturing Systems,* 12th CIRP International Seminar on Manufacturing Systems, Belgrade, 1980a.

EVERSHEIM, W., B. HOLZ, and K. H. ZONS, "Application of Automatic Process Planning and NC-Programming," Proc. AUTOFACT WEST, Society of Manufacturing Engineers, Anaheim, Calif., November 1980b, pp. 779–800.

FIACCO, A. V., and G. P. McCORMICK, *Nonlinear Programming,* Wiley, New York, 1968.

GE, *Operation Manual for the Carboloy Machinability Computer,* Manual MC-101-B, General Electric Company, Metallurgical Products Department, Detroit, 1957.

GILBERT, W. W., *"Economics of Machining," in Machining: Theory and Practice,* American Society for Metals, Metals Park, Ohio, 1950.

GILBERT, W. W., and W. C. TRUCKENMILLER, "Nomograph for Determining Tool Life and Power When Turning with Single-Point Tools," *Mechanical Engineering*, Vol. 65, 1943, pp. 893–898.

GORDON, W. J., and R. F. RIESENFELD, "B-Spline Curves and Surfaces," in R. E. Barnhill and R. F. Riesenfeld, Eds., *Computer-Aided Geometric Design*, Academic, New York, 1974, pp. 95–126.

GRAYS, J. C., "Compound Data Structures for Computer Aided Design: A Survey," in *Proceedings of the ACM National Conference*, Thompson Books, Washington, D.C., 1967.

GROOVER, M. P., "A Survey on the Machinability of Metals," SME Technical Paper, Series MR76-269, 1976.

GROOVER, M. P., A. M. GUNDA, and R. J. JOHNSON, "Determination of Machining Conditions by a Self-Adaptive Procedure," Proc. 4th North American Metalworking Research Conference, 1976.

HAAN, R. A., "Group Technology Coding and Classification Applied to NC Part Programming," Proc. 14th Numerical Control Society Annual Meeting and Technical Conference, Pittsburgh, Pa., March 1977.

HALEVI, G., *The Role of Computers in Manufacturing Processes*, Wiley, New York, 1980a.

HALEVI, G., "Production Planning Module of All Embracing Technology," Proc. AUTOFACT WEST, Society of Manufacturing Engineers, Anaheim, Calif., November 1980b, pp. 45–465.

HALEVI, G., and R. WEILL, "Development of Flexible Optimum Process Planning Procedure," *CIRP Annals 1980*; also in *Manufacturing Technology*, January 29, 1980, pp. 313–317.

HASSELT, R. V., and W. T. OUDOLF, "Computer Aided Work Planning for Simple Sheet Components," *CIRP Annals*, Vol. 22, 1973.

HATI, S., and S. RAO, "Determination of the Optimum Machining Conditions—Deterministic and Probabilistic Approaches," *Journal of Engineering for Industry*, Vol. 98, February 1976.

HAYES, G. M., JR., R. P. DAVIS, and R. A. WYSK, "A Dynamic Programming Approach to Machine Requirements Planning," *AIIE Transactions*, Vol. 13, No. 2, June 1981.

HEWGLEY, R. E., JR., and H. P. PREWETT, JR., "Computer Aided Process Planning at the Oak Ridge Y-12 Plant: A Pilot Project," Third Annual TNO User's Meeting, Arlington, Tex., May 1979.

HORVATH, M., "Semi-generative Process Planning for Part Manufacturing," SME Technical Paper, Series MS79–153, 1979.

HOUTZEEL, A., "Computer Assisted Process Planning—A First Step Towards Integration," Proc. AUTOFACT WEST, Society of Manufacturing Engineers, Anaheim, Calif., November 1980, pp. 801–808.

HOUTZEEL, A., "Integrating CAD/CAM through Group Technology," Proc. 18th Numerical Control Society Annual Meeting and Technical Conference, Dallas, Tex., May 1981, pp. 430–444.

HOUTZEEL, A., and B. SCHILPEROORT, "A Chain-Structured Part Classification System (MICLASS) and Group Technology," Proc. 13th Annual Meeting and Technical Conference, Cincinnati, Ohio, March 1976, pp. 383–400.

ISO, *Tool Life Testing with Single-Point Turning Tools*, International Organization for Standardization, 5th Draft Proposal, ISP.TC 29/WG22 (Secretariat 37) 91, March 1972.

IWATA, K., et al., "Optimization of Cutting Conditions for Multi-pass Operations Considering Probabilistic Nature in Machining Processes," *Journal of Engineering for Industry*, Vol. 99, February 1977.

IWATA, K., Y. KAKINO, F. OBA, and N. SUGIMURA, "Development of Non-part Family Type Computer Aided Production Planning System CIMS/PRO," in *Advanced Manufacturing Technology* (Proc. 4th Int. IFIP/IFAC Conf., PROLOMAT 79, 1979), P. Blake, Ed., Elsevier North-Holland, New York, 1980.

JACKSON, R. H., "Automated Process Planning—Key to Automating Manufacturing Support," Proc. 16th Numerical Control Society Annual Meeting and Technical Conference, Los Angeles, March 1979.

Japan Society for the Promotion of Machine Industry, "Group Technology," March 1980.

KACZMAREK, J., *Principles of Machining by Cutting, Abrasion and Erosion,* A. Voellnagel and E. Lepa, Trans., Peter Peregrinus, Stevenage, England, 1976.

KAKINO, Y., F. OBA, T. MERIWAKI, and K. IWATA, "A New Method of Parts Description for Computer-Aided Production Planning," in *Advances in Computer-Aided Manufacturing,* Elsevier North-Holland, New York, 1977.

KERRY, T. M., "Integrating NC Programming with Machining and Group Technology," Proc. 12th Numerical Control Society Annual Meeting and Technical Conference, 1975, pp. 149–162.

KING, J. R., "Machine-Component Group Formation in Group Technology," 5th International Conference on Production Research, Amsterdam, August 1979.

KING, J. R., and V. NAKORNCHAI, "Machine-Component Group Formation in Group Technology: Review and Extension," *International Journal of Production Research,* 1982, Vol. 20, No. 2, 117–133.

KOTLER, R. A., "Computerized Process Planning—Part 1," *Army Man Tech Journal,* Vol. 4, No. 4, 1980a, pp. 28–36.

KOTLER, R. A., "Computerized Process Planning—Part 2," *Army Man Tech Journal,* Vol. 4, No. 5, 1980b, pp. 20–29.

KRAG, W. B., "Toward Generative Manufacturing Technology," Proc. 15th Numerical Control Society Annual Meeting and Technical Conference, Chicago, April 9–12 1978.

KYTTNER, R., N. SHTCHEGLOV, and A. KIMMEL, "A Complex Computer-Aided Process Planning and Optimization for Machine Production," SME Technical Paper, Series MS79-158 1979; also in *Advanced Manufacturing Technology,* (Proc. 4th Int. IFIP/IFAC Conf., PROLOMAT 79, 1979), P. Blake, Ed., Elsevier North-Holland, New York, 1980.

LACOSTE, J. P., and R. ROTHENBERG, "Communication in Computer Aided Design and Computer Aided Manufacturing," in *Computer Languages for Numerical Control,* J. Havatny, Ed. (Proc. 2nd Int. IFIP/IFAC Conf., PROLOMAT 73), Elsevier North-Holland, New York, 1973, pp. 163–171.

LINK, C. H., "CAPP—CAM-I Automated Process Planning System," Proc. 13th Numerical Control Society Annual Meeting and Technical Conference, Cincinnati, Ohio, March 1976.

MACHOVER, C., and R. E. BLANTH, Eds., *The CAD/CAM Handbook,* Computervision Corp., Bedford, Mass., 1980.

MANN, W. S., M. S. DUNN, JR., and S. J. PFLEDERER, *Computerized Production Process Planning,* United Technologies Research Corp. Report R77-942625-14, November 1977.

MCDANIEL, H., *Decision Table Software—A Handbook,* Brandon/Systems Press, Princeton, N.J., 1970.

MERRIHEW, H. W., "Computerizing Process Planning for Machine Tools," *Automation* (Cleveland), Vol. 17, No. 6, June 1970, pp. 56–59.

METCUT, Research Associates, Inc., *Machining Data Handbook,* Machinability Data Center, Cincinnati, Ohio, 1980.

METZNER, J. R., and B. H. BARNES, *Decision Table Language and Systems,* Academic Press, New York, 1977.

MONTALBANO, M., *Decision Tables,* Science Research Associates, Chicago, 1974.

MYOLOPOULOS, J., "An Overview of Knowledge Representation," Proc. Workshop on Data Abstraction, Databases, and Conceptual Modeling, June 1980.

NAGEL, R. N., W. W. BRAITHWAITE, and P. R. KENNICOTT, *Initial Graphics Exchange Specification IGES Version 1.0,* National Bureau of Standards, Washington, D.C., March 1980.

NAU, D. S., "Expert Computer Systems, and Their Applicability to Automated Manufacturing," Technical Report, Industrial Systems Division, National Bureau of Standards, Washington, D.C., 1981.

NEWMAN, W. M., and R. F. SPROULL, *Principles of Interactive Computer Graphics,* 2nd ed., McGraw-Hill, New York, 1979.

NIEBEL, B. W., "Mechanized Process Selection for Planning New Designs," *ASTME Paper 737,* 1965.

NILSSON, N. J., *Principles of Artificial Intelligence,* Tioga Publishing Company, Palo Alto, Calif., 1980.

OPITZ, H., *A Classification System to Describe Workpieces,* Pergamon Press, Elmsford, N.Y., 1970.

PARSONS, N. R., Ed., *N/C Machinability Data Systems,* Society of Manufacturing Engineers, Dearborn, Mich., 1971.

PEDERSEN, J. T., B. HAUGRUD, and O. BJORKE, "General Approach to Technological Planning," Proc. 9th Numerical Control Society Annual Meeting and Technical Conference, Chicago, April 1972, pp. 92–103.

PFLEDERER, S. J., and W. S. MANN, "Principles of Computer Process Planning," SME Prepr. 760914 for Meeting, November 29 December 2, 1976.

PHILIPSON, R. H., and A. RAVINDRON, "Application of Goal Programming to Machinability Data Optimization," *Journal of Mechanical Design,* Vol. 100, April 1978.

PHILLIPS, R. H., *A Computerized Process Planning System Based on Component Classification and Coding,* Ph.D. thesis, Purdue University, West Lafayette, Ind., 1978.

PLANNING INSTITUTE, INC., "PII Press release—4-15-80," PII, Arlington, Tex., 1980a.

PLANNING INSTITUTE, INC., "PICAPP," PII, Arlington, Tex., 1980b.

PLANNING INSTITUTE, INC., "CAM-I's CAPP System: A General Interface for Interactive/ Generative Process Planning," PII, Arlington, Tex., 1980c.

PORAZYNSKI, R. J., "Using Group Technology Concepts in Manufacturing," Proc. AIIE System Engineering Conference, Kansas City, Mo., November 1977.

REQUICHA, A. A. G., "Representations of Rigid Solid Objects," in *Computer Aided Design Modelling, Systems Engineering, CAD Systems,* CREST Advanced Course, Darmstadt, September 1980, J. Encarnacao, Ed., Springer-Verlag, Berlin.

REQUICHA, A. A. G., and H. B. VOELCKER, "Geometric Modelling of Mechanical Parts and Machining Processes," *COMPCONTROL '79,* Aopron, Hungary, November 1979.

ROLT, L. T. C., *A Short History of Machine Tools,* MIT Press, Cambridge, Mass., 1967.

ROSE, D. W., Coding for Manufacturing COFORM, Unpublished M.S. thesis, Purdue University, West Lafayette, Ind., 1977.

SCARR, A. J. T., *Metrology and Precision Engineering,* McGraw-Hill, London, 1967.

SCHAFFER, G., "GT via Automated Process Planning," *American Machinist,* May 1980, pp. 119–122.

SCHECK, D. E., "Feasibility of Automated Process Planning," Ph.D. thesis, Purdue University, West Lafayette, Ind., 1966.

SCHECK, D. E., "New Directions in Process Planning," SME Technical Paper, Series MM75-908, for Meeting, Ft. Lauderdale, Fla., February 1975.

SCHILPEROOT, B. A., "Classification, Coding and Automated Process Planning," CAM-I Proceedings P-76-MM-01, November 1975.

SCOTT, R. B., "Regenerative Shop Planning," *American Machinist,* Vol. 109, March 28, 1966.

SHORTLIFFE, E. H., *Computer-Based Medical Consultations: MYCIN,* American Elsevier, New York, 1976.

SILBERG, B., "DETAB/65 in Third-Generation COBOL," *GIGPLAN Notices,* Vol. 6, No. 8, September 1971.

SMART, H. G., "Group Technology and the Least Cost Method," Proc. AUTOFACT WEST, Society of Manufacturing Engineers, Anaheim, Calif., November 1980, pp. 743–778.

SMITH, B., J. ALBUS, and A. BARBERA, "Glossary of Terms for Robotics," Automation Technology Program, National Bureau of Standards, Washington, D.C., July 1981.

SOLAJA, V. B., and S. M. UROSEVIC, "The Method of Hypothetical Group Technology Production Lines," *CIRP Annals,* Vol. 22, No. 1, 1973.

SPUR, G., "Automation of Manufacturing Planning," CIRP Conference, Chicago, 1974.

STOUT, K. J., and G. HALEVI, "A Computerized Planning Procedure for Machined Components," *Production Engineer,* Vol. 56, No. 4, April 1977, pp. 37–42.

SUBBARAO, P., and C. JACOBS, "Application of Nonlinear Goal Programming to Machine Variable Optimization," *6th NAMRC Proceedings,* May 1978.

TAYLOR, F. W., "On the Art of Cutting Metals," *Trans. ASME,* Vol. 28, 1907.

TEMPELHOF, K. H., "A System of Computer-Aided Process Planning for Machine Parts," SME Technical Paper, Series MS79-154, 1979; also in *Advanced Manufacturing Technology* (Proc. 4th Int. IFIP/IFAC Conf., PROLOMAT 79, 1979), P. Blake, Ed., Elsevier North Holland, New York, 1980.

THROOP, J. W., "Computer Assisted Speed and Feed Selection for Automated Process Planning," CAM-I Standards Committee Report R-76-SC-02.

TIPNIS, V. A., M. Field, and M. Y. Friedman, "Development and Use of Machinability Data for Process Planning Optimization," SME Technical Paper, Series MD75-517, Chicago, February, 1975.

TIPNIS, V. A., S. A. Vogel, and C. E. Lamb, "Computer-Aided Process Planning System for Aircraft Engine Rotating Parts," SME Technical Paper, Series MS79-155, 1979; also in *Advanced Manufacturing Technology* (Proc. 4th Int. IFIP/IFAC Conf., PROLOMAT 79, 1979), P. Blake, Ed., Elsevier North-Holland, New York, 1980.

TIPNIS, V. A., S. A. Vogel, and H. L. Gegel, "Economic Model for Process Planning," NAMRC-IV, University of Florida, Gainesville, April 16–19, 1978. *In Proc. 6th North American Metalworking Research Conference,* Society of Manufacturing Engineers, 1978, pp. 379–387.

TNO, "The Miturn Programming System for Lathes," *Metaalinstituut TNO,* (The Netherlands), December 1974, J. A. Jochems, Ed.

TNO, "Introduction to MIPLAN," Organization for Industrial Research, Inc., Waltham, Mass., 1981.

TRUCKS, H. E., *Designing for Economical Production,* Society of Manufacturing Engineers, Dearborn, Mich., 1974.

TULKOFF, J., "CAM-I Automated Process Planning (CAPP) System," Proc. 15th Numerical Control Society Annual Meeting and Technical Conference, Chicago, April 1978.

TULKOFF, J., "Lockheed's GENPLAN," Proc. 18th Numerical Control Society Annual Meeting and Technical Conference, Dallas, Tex., May 1981, pp. 417–421.

VAN DYCK, F., M. M. TSENG, and O. D. LASCOE, "Study of Computerized Process Planning with Continuous and Discrete Data Base," *AIIE Transactions,* Vol. 8, No. 3, September 1976, pp. 320–327.

VOELCKER, H. B., and A. A. G. REQUICHA, "Geometric Modeling of Mechanical Parts and Processes," *Computer,* Vol. 10, No. 12, December 1977.

VOGEL, S. A., "Metcut Machinability Process for NC," First Annual Conference on Computer Graphics in CAD/CAM Systems, Massachusetts Institute of Technology, Cambridge, Mass., April 1979, pp. 5–15.

VOGEL, S. A., "Integrated Process Planning at General Electric's Aircraft Engine Group," Proc. AUTOFACT WEST, Society of Manufacturing Engineers, Anaheim, Calif., November 1980, pp. 729–742.

VOGEL, S. A., and E. J., ADLARD, "The AUTOPLAN Process Planning System," Proc. 18th Numerical Control Society Annual Meeting and Technical Conference, Dallas, Tex., May 1981, pp. 422–429.

VOGEL, S. A., and E. J. ADLARD, "The AUTOPLAN Process Planning System," Metcut Research Associates, Inc., Cincinnati, Ohio.

VOGEL, S., and V. A. TIPNIS, "The Concepts and Applications of the Metcut Machinability Processor for NC Machining," Proc. 14th Numerical Control Society Annual Meeting and Technical Conference, Pittsburgh, Pa., March 1977, pp. 365–377.

WANDMACHER, R. R., "Group Technology Concepts and Computer Aided Process Planning," *SME Prepr. 750944,* 1975.

WARNER and SWASEY, *CUTS,* A brochure on Computer Utilized Turning System, 1973.

WILLIAMS, R., "A Survey of Data Structures for Computer Graphics Systems," *Computer Survey,* Vol. 3, No. 1, March 1971.

WYSK, R. A., "An Automated Process Planning and Selection Program: APPAS," Ph.D. thesis, Purdue University, West Lafayette, Ind., 1977.

WYSK, R. A., "Process Planning Systems," *MAPEC Module,* compiled by School of Industrial Engineering, Purdue University, West Lafayette, Ind., 1979.

WYSK, R. A., D. M. MILLER, and R. P. DAVIS, "The Integration of Process Selection and Machine Requirements Planning," Proc. AIIE 1977 Systems Engineering Conference, 1977.

WYSK, R. A., T. C. CHANG, and R. P. DAVIS, "Analytical Techniques in Automated Process Planning," *MAPEC module,* compiled by School of Industrial Engineering, Purdue University, West Lafayette, Ind., 1980.

INDEX